2

Therapeutic Dimensions of
Autobiography in Creative Writing

of related interest

The Self on the Page
Theory and Practice of Creative Writing in Personal Development
Edited by Celia Hunt and Fiona Sampson
ISBN 1 85302 470 8 pb
ISBN 1 85302 469 4 hb

The Therapeutic Potential of Creative Writing
Writing Myself
Gillie Bolton
ISBN 1 85302 599 2

Writing Well
Creative Writing and Mental Health
Deborah Philips, Debra Penman and Liz Linnington
ISBN 1 85302 650 6

Narrative Approaches to Working with Adult Male Survivors of Child Sexual Abuse
Kim Etherington
ISBN 1 85302 818 5

Storymaking and Creative Groupwork with Older People
Paula Crimmens
ISBN 1 85302 440 6

Storymaking in Education and Therapy
Alida Gersie and Nancy King
ISBN 1 85302 520 8 pb
ISBN 1 85302 519 4 hb

Reflections on Therapeutic Storymaking
The Use of Stories in Groups
Alida Gersie
ISBN 1 85302 272 1

Healing Arts
The History of Art Therapy
Susan Hogan
ISBN 1 85302 799 5

Therapeutic Dimensions of Autobiography in Creative Writing

Celia Hunt

Jessica Kingsley Publishers
London and Philadelphia

The right of Celia Hunt to be identified as author of this work has been asserted by her in accordance with the Copyright, Designs and Patents Act 1988.

First published in the United Kingdom in 2000 by
Jessica Kingsley Publishers Ltd,
116 Pentonville Road,
London N1 9JB, England
and
325 Chestnut Street,
Philadelphia PA 19106, USA.

www.jkp.com

Library of Congress Cataloging in Publication Data
Hunt, Celia.
Therapeutic dimensions of autobiography in creative writing/Celia Hunt.
    p.   cm.
Includes bibliographical references and index.
ISBN 1 85302 747 2 (pbk. : alk. paper)
1. Creative writing--Therapeutic use. 2. Autobiography--Therapeutic use. 3. Psychotherapy. I. Title.
RC489.W75 H85 2000
616.89'165--dc21   00-030150

British Library Cataloguing in Publication Data

ISBN 1 85302 747 2

Printed and Bound in Great Britain by
Athenaeum Press, Gateshead, Tyne and Wear

Contents

For Randolph
with love and thanks

Acknowledgements

Excerpts from, 'A Guest at the Spa' from *Autobiographical Writings* by Hermann Hesse, Picador, 3rd printing, 1978. Reprinted by kind permission of Suhrkamp Verlag, Frankfurt am Main. Excerpts from 'Digging' and 'Toome' from *Opened Ground: Selected Poems 1966–1996* by Seamus Heaney. Copyright © 1998 Seamus Heaney. Reprinted by kind permission of Faber and Faber, London, and Farrar, Straus and Giroux, LLC, New York. Excerpt from 'St. Botolph's' from *Birthday Letters* by Ted Hughes. Copyright © 1998 Ted Hughes. Reprinted by kind permission of Faber and Faber, London, and Farrar, Straus and Giroux, LLC, New York. Excerpt from 'One off the Short List' from *A Man and Two Women* by Doris Lessing. Copyright © 1963 Doris Lessing. Reprinted by kind permission of Jonathan Clowes Ltd., London, and Alfred A. Knopf, New York, a Division of Random House Inc., on behalf of Doris Lessing.

I am also grateful to the Editorial Board of *Auto/Biography*, for permission to reproduce material first published under the title 'Finding a Voice – Exploring the Self: Autobiography and the Imagination in a Writing Apprenticeship' in *Auto/Biography* Volume VI (1 and 2), 1998, pp.93–98; to Messrs. Taylor and Francis, London, for permission to reproduce material first published in my paper 'Creative Writing and Problems of Identity' in Janet Campbell and Janet Harbord (eds), *Psycho-politics and Cultural Desires,* 1998; to Messrs. Rebus Press, London, for permission to include material first published in my paper 'Psychological Problems of Writer Identity' in Duncan Barford (ed.), *Psychoanalysis and Theories of Learning,* 2000.

Some material contained in Chapters 1 and 4 was previously published in my chapters 'Writing with the Voice of the Child' and 'Autobiography and the Psychotherapeutic Process' in Celia Hunt & Fiona Sampson (eds), *The Self on the Page: Theory and Practice of Creative Writing in Personal Development,* Jessica Kingsley, London, 1998.

Introduction

In 1982 I started to write a novel. I hadn't written fiction before and knew very little about novel writing, and the only thing I had to write about was myself and what I thought of as 'my predicament'. At that time I was locked into a deeply dependent marriage and being a life support system for someone else meant that I was not in a position to go out and develop myself professionally. And in some ways I guess this must have suited me because, in spite of having been a bright child, I had been unable, for reasons I did not understand, to develop my talents and abilities to the point where I could make use of them in some satisfying way. As a result, I suffered from a serious lack of confidence in myself. The idea that I might make a novel out of my life seemed to offer a way of transcending these difficulties. Not only was this something I could do without going out into the world, as my subject matter was myself and I knew myself better than anything else, it seemed a fairly straightforward undertaking.

Writing the novel proved to be anything but straightforward. The main problem, as I soon discovered when I attended a creative writing course, lay in the 'voice' that I was trying to use to tell my story. I just couldn't get it right; sometimes I seemed to be speaking in the voice of the person I used to be and sometimes in the voice of the person I had become. There was no consistency. Like many projects I had embarked on in the past, this one too seemed doomed to be abandoned in its early stages. Yet somehow I managed to persist with it, and at the end of a long and painful five years, I had completed a 500-page novel. The fact that it was ultimately unpublishable (it was taken on by a London literary agent but not placed with a publisher) was not a total disaster. Completing it taught me that I could write a long and tolerably workable piece of fiction, and this gave me confidence to embark on a second novel. But even more important, in the process of struggling to find a voice for the story of my past I discovered that I had learned a few things about the person I was *in the present*, and these insights helped me to understand myself better.

Soon after the novel was finished, I went into psychotherapy and, to my surprise, found myself involved in a process that was in many ways very similar to the process of writing my autobiographical novel. Here, too, I was struggling to make sense of myself and my story, and the means I and my therapist used to do that seemed to have more to do with fictions than facts. Progressively, the two activities came even closer together when I started writing poems and short stories around images that arose in therapy and took them into the sessions to discuss with my therapist. Somehow, these two apparently very different activities, the writing and the therapy, were helping me to find the truth about myself, or rather not *the* truth but *my* truth, my own *personal truth*, which turned out to be a mixture of fiction and reality.

In 1991 I started teaching a creative writing course at the University of Sussex Centre for Continuing Education. I had already observed from my time as a student on such a course that, like me, most apprentice writers tended to use themselves as a starting point for fiction. So this seemed the logical place to get my own students to start, bearing in mind the difficulties of doing this, as well as the advantages. I called the course 'Autobiography and Fiction'. Several years further down the line, my course, now called 'Autobiography and the Imagination', was incorporated into a three-term, undergraduate level Certificate in Creative Writing, as the introductory course. As I continued to teach it I began to see that, as had been the case for me, some of the students, apart from developing their writing skills, were unexpectedly discovering things about themselves that were enlightening. Others seemed to be attending the course not only because they wanted to become writers, but because they were already aware that it had a potential for clarifying who they were and therefore of helping them to make sense of their lives. I was far from being the only one who found autobiographical creative writing powerfully therapeutic.

In 1994 I had the opportunity of undertaking a D.Phil research project. Having already explored, for an MA, the similarities, in my own experience, between writing fictional autobiography and engaging in psychotherapy, it seemed a logical next step to broaden my explorations and to look in detail at the therapeutic benefits that some of my students were experiencing. This book contains the results of that research. It focuses on apprentice writers who have derived therapeutic benefit by chance rather than by design as a result of writing fictional autobiography, as well as on those who consciously set out to use their writing as a means of gaining insight into themselves. It then moves on to consider the possibility of using fictional autobiography as a means of self-therapy or self-analysis, or as a tool in psychotherapy or psychoanalysis.

To gather the necessary information, I issued questionnaires covering a range of issues around creative writing and its relation to self to all the students who had taken my course over a period of five years. In spite of the fact that some of my questions were quite personal and involved a considerable degree of self-exposure, well over half of the students completed the questionnaire. A selection of their responses is incorporated into relevant chapters below. I also conducted interviews with four students with whom I wished to work in greater depth. These students, by default rather than by design, were all women, as there were no suitable male candidates. Each of the case studies revealed quite different but related effects of the writing, but in discussing them I have grouped them under two separate headings: therapeutic dimensions of fictionalising ourselves, and therapeutic dimensions of fictionalising significant people in our lives.

The book is arranged as follows. Chapter 1 looks in detail at my creative writing course, and examines the idea of a 'writing voice' or 'writing identity', both in terms of its role in a writing apprenticeship and of its therapeutic dimensions. I draw attention to the drawbacks and difficulties of using autobiography in creative writing teaching and assess the implications for the creative writing teacher who may find herself in the role of counsellor or therapist without the appropriate skills. Chapters 2 and 3 present the case studies arising out of the interviews. The stories of 'Sarah' and 'Jane'[1] are examples of the role of fictional autobiography in clarifying personal identity and alleviating problems that inhibit or block the writing process; they fall into the category of writing that provokes a confrontation with self and has a therapeutic effect by chance rather than by design. The stories of 'Jennifer' and 'Jessica' are examples of the conscious use of fictional autobiography as a means of self-exploration: in Jennifer's case the re-writing of an oppressive personal narrative 'written' in the psyche by family and society, in such a way that it becomes more comfortable; in Jessica's, the quest to find a form for a personal narrative which gives shape to her fragmented sense of identity.

1   These are pseudonyms.

Chapter 4 takes the idea of therapeutic benefit arising from the writing of fictional autobiography out of the creative writing sphere and into the therapeutic field proper. Here I explore the similarities and differences between writing autobiography and engaging in psychotherapy, and discuss the notion of 'personal truth'. I consider the possibilities for using autobiographical writing as a method of self-therapy or self-analysis, explore the notion of transference in relation to writing the self, and examine the difference between writing and speaking in a therapeutic context. I look briefly at existing therapies that employ creative writing and suggest ways in which fictional autobiography might be used as part of a formal psychotherapy or psychoanalysis. I conclude with some thoughts on the possible tensions between 'writing as art' and 'writing as therapy'.

After much prevarication, I have settled on the term 'fictional autobiography' to describe the sort of writing I am discussing, although sometimes I use the term 'autobiographical creative writing' by way of clarification. Both these terms indicate a type of writing that draws on personal memories and experiences, but does not necessarily attempt to portray the 'facts' of the past or of the present; rather it seeks to convey the essence of these memories and experiences through the feelings and emotions associated with them, using the techniques of fiction and with a literary end product in view. I follow Paul John Eakin (1985), Liz Stanley (1992) and others in believing that autobiography already contains a fair degree of fiction. Where 'fictional autobiography' differs from 'autobiography' is in the relationship between the writer and her words on the page. Whilst in writing autobiography a writer may not be aware of the extent to which she is fictionalising, in fictional autobiography she has given herself permission to fictionalise herself and her experience, but this does not mean that she has abandoned the quest for truth[2]. I agree with Liz Stanley that 'fictions often enable more of "truth" about a life to be written than a strictly "factual" account' (Stanley 1992, p.67), but that this 'truth' is more in the nature of a 'personal truth', a felt authenticity, rather than objective truth.

Again, I have experimented at different times with various terms, such as 'personal development' or 'therapeutic benefit', to describe the positive effects of engaging in autobiographical creative writing, but for the present work have settled on the latter. The word 'therapeutic' here denotes benefi-

---

2   Suzanne Nalbatian's term 'aesthetic autobiography' in which writers 'reclothe personal facts in poetic relations' contains a similar idea (Nalbatian 1994, pp.44-45).

cial psychological change, which might include increased inner freedom, greater psychic flexibility, a clearer or stronger sense of personal identity, and an increased freedom to engage with other people as well as in creative pursuits. Such change might be effected through favourable life circumstances, such as the availability of an empathic listener, or through psychotherapy or counselling, or through artistic practices such as creative writing, where the process of writing about oneself or reflecting on the work produced may elicit insight into the inner life or into relationships in the outside world. It is a rather more focused term than 'personal development', which not only embraces 'therapeutic benefit' as defined above, but also the development of life skills through education and professional training, and is therefore not as appropriate here.

In trying to understand the material arising out of the interviews, I have used a combination of literary, narrative and psychodynamic theory, so that the resulting analysis is in the nature of a psychoanalytic literary criticism of students' writings and spoken words. I realise this is a somewhat unusual approach and that some people may regard it as inappropriate. Shelley Day Sclater, for example, who also uses a combination of a narrative approach and psychodynamic theory, says: 'It may well be unethical to attempt a psychoanalytically-based reading of our subjects' stories of their lives' (Day Sclater 1998, p.90). This would clearly be the case if the reading were done without the subjects' knowledge, but I do not agree that such an approach is unethical in principle although, as I say in the Appendix, where I include a retrospective on the research, it is not without its problems. In adopting this approach I have sought the collaboration of the students themselves at every stage, and I am satisfied that there have been benefits for them arising out of this collaboration. I believe a psychoanalytic approach is important because it allows the exploration of unconscious processes and intrapsychic mechanisms not taken into account by a narrative approach, which focuses primarily on social and cultural factors.

Shelley Day Sclater also suggests that a psychoanalytic reading of subjects' lives 'is rendered problematic by the recognition that the interviewer herself is instrumental in the production of the account' (p.90). It is not clear to me at this point whether or to what extent a psychoanalytic reading might be more problematical than other narrative-based approaches. As Liz Stanley points out, any reading of the life story of another person is 'a contingent activity deeply rooted in our autobiographies and the tools, means and knowledges these provide' (Stanley 1992, p.84). In that sense any piece of narrative-based research will be, to a considerable extent, a subjective reading, and the present book is no exception. I hope, though, that the approach adopted here has produced a 'vital'[3] reading, if not a 'true' one.

The psychoanalytic approach I have adopted is primarily object-relations oriented, with an emphasis on the theory of Karen Horney, whose work is not generally speaking thought of as within the object-relations fold, but which is regarded as consonant with it to a considerable degree (Ingram and Lerner 1992). Apart from her feminist essays, Horney's work is little known in Britain, and my use of her theories here might be considered rather unusual, especially as she would be regarded by some people as an essentialist. It is certainly true that Horney's theory rests on the notion of a 'real self', but this real self is not a fixed and unitary entity; rather it is fluid and open-ended, partly given genetically and partly constructed by the social and cultural environment into which a child is born. I believe that Horney's theory has much to offer to current debates around subjectivity, especially as she puts the emphasis, in trying to understand psychological problems, on the *present* structure of the psyche; unlike Freud, who places the emphasis very firmly on the past. I say more about her theory in Chapter 2. Apart from Horney, I draw on the psychodynamic theories of Christopher Bollas, Donald Winnicott and Marion Milner. I have also found the literary theory of Mikhail Bakhtin highly relevant.

Any piece of research has its limitations and this one is no exception. In adopting a primarily Horneyan literary-psychoanalytic approach, I have not focused on broader cultural or sociological questions of class, gender or ethnicity, although gender in particular proved to be a major feature of the material emerging from the interviews. It would have been possible to pursue an alternative and potentially very interesting approach to understanding this material from the point of view of current feminist thinking. However, I have chosen not to do that here. Another limitation arises from the selection for the case studies of four women who are highly literate and self-reflective. My findings and conclusions are not going to apply so readily to people who do not have such skills or the environment in which to develop them. Seeing, however, that these women are typical of those people who apply for creative writing courses, at least the ones I teach, this limitation is built into the context in which I work.

---

3   This is a term used by Leitch (1983) and quoted by de Shazer (1991).

I am deeply indebted to all those students who have contributed to this work, in particular to Sarah, Jane, Jennifer and Jessica for allowing me to make extensive use of their written and spoken words and to interpret those words theoretically. I am deeply grateful to my friend and colleague Bernard Paris, whose wise guidance and keen logical eye forced me again and again to seek clarity in my writing and thinking. Others to whom thanks are due include Trevor Pateman, my D.Phil supervisor, who has been a stimulating and supportive companion on the 'long voyage'; Peter Abbs, whose work on the use of autobiography in education was the initial inspiration for my own work; Sue Roe, for her friendship and support; and Jan Campbell, for introducing me to the work of Christopher Bollas. I am indebted to the Economic and Social Research Council for providing me with a Research Studentship with which to pursue my topic, and to the University of Sussex Institute of Education for providing me with the facilities to carry out the research. I am also grateful to Dr Vivienne Griffiths and Professor Ben Knights who examined the thesis, for their stimulating and helpful comments.

Last, but certainly not least, this work would not have been done without the constant encouragement and support of my husband, Randolph Morse, who provided me with a safe and empathetic environment in which I could pursue my work in peace and comfort.

CHAPTER I

Finding a Writing Voice

The Notion of 'Writing Voice'

Over the years I have been teaching creative writing it has become clear to me that there are two main areas of learning involved: first, mastering the craft of writing and, second, finding a 'writing voice'. Mastering the craft of writing is obvious; in the case of fiction, with which I am primarily concerned, it will involve the acquisition and practice of a repertoire of narrative techniques, such as characterisation, dialogue, setting and point of view, as well as plotting and structuring. Finding a 'writing voice' is much less obvious and needs clarification.

It is useful, when thinking about the notion of 'writing voice', to distinguish between the reader's and the writer's perspective. A reader engaged with a novel will be able to identify a particular style or tone in the writing; if she is familiar with other novels by the same author, she might notice that certain themes or certain turns of phrase recur regularly. These could be said to constitute the 'voice' of the novel or the 'voice' of a particular author that recurs throughout his or her *oeuvre*.[1] From the writer's perspective the term 'voice' will have different connotations. Discussions of this term with students at the start of my course have given rise to many and varied interpretations, including finding out what it is one has to say, being able to say it completely and without fear, developing a style or way of writing of one's own, and finding one's own rhythms. All of these are important aspects of a writing voice, but they omit a central and crucial element. When a writer says that she has 'found her voice', it seems to me she is saying that she has developed a deep connection in her writing between her inner life and the words she places on the page. When the writing is working well, she is able to

---

1   I use the term 'voice' here in a similar way to Foucault's 'author-function' (Foucault 1977).

access her own rich, emotional material and to use it imaginatively on the page. The term 'writing voice', then, in this internal sense, is a metaphor for a style of writing which contains the author's sense of self[2].

Seamus Heaney succinctly captures this internal sense of 'writing voice' in his essay 'Feelings into Words': 'Finding a voice means that you can get your own feeling into your own words and that your words have the feel of you about them' (Heaney 1980a, p.43). As an example of what he means, Heaney discusses the writing of his celebrated poem 'Digging' where, at the end, he uses for the first time the 'pen/spade analogy' which was to become so important to him:

> The cold smell of potato mould, the squelch and slap
> Of soggy peat, the curt cuts of an edge
> Through living roots awaken in my head.
> But I've no spade to follow men like them.
>
> Between my finger and my thumb
> The squat pen rests
> I'll dig with it.

This, according to Heaney, was the first poem he wrote where 'I thought my *feel* had got into words':

> This was the first place where I felt I had done more than make an arrangement of words: I felt that I had let down a shaft into real life. The facts and surfaces of the thing were true, but more important, the excitement that came from naming them gave me a kind of insouciance and a kind of confidence. I didn't care who thought what about it (pp.41–42).

This was 'poetry as revelation of the self to the self' (p.41).

Whilst Heaney is talking here specifically about poetry, his definition of a 'writing voice' has, I believe, much relevance to fiction writing, for many people come to fiction writing with the idea that it is simply about the arrangement of words on the page. But words on the page, even if technically well crafted, may be lifeless if they do not contain feelings. One of the most important elements of good mimetic[3] fiction writing is that it enables the reader not only to get into the minds of the characters portrayed, but also to experience the emotions of the characters, as if they were real people, and this

---

2   Similar points could be made about finding an authentic voice for an academic paper; see Stanley (1992) and Williams (1993). Cf. Pateman (1998a).

3   Scholes and Kellogg (1966) divide characters into 'mimetic', 'illustrative' and 'aesthetic'.

implies that the author, when creating the work, was able to do so as well. There are novels, of course, in which emotional involvement with the characters is not the most important feature. For example, in the writings of Alain Robbe-Grillet the minute physical description of people and objects is paramount and anything even faintly resembling emotional or psychological content is rigidly excluded for the sake of the overall effect. Those novels, however, which strive wholly or in part for a mimetic effect, a representation of, or approximation to, real life, derive their strength from the way they involve the reader in a felt emotional world.

Creating a felt emotional world in fiction – or getting one's feelings into one's own words – is not, however, something that happens automatically when one starts to write, and this is particularly noticeable in the creation of autobiographical narrators and characters. Apprentice fiction writers often create narrators, based on themselves, who are shadowy figures lacking substance; or they create characters, based on people they know, who do not have a felt emotional life on the page. Instead of *getting inside* the feelings and emotions of their characters and letting them *show* us how *they* feel, the authors stand on the sidelines and *tell* us how we should think and feel about their fictional creations. As authors, they have not taken the important step of entering into the writing and imbuing it with authentic feelings and emotions. This is the celebrated difference between 'showing' and 'telling' (Booth 1991, pp.3–9) about which people new to writing will hear in any creative writing class.

The ability of writers to engage emotionally with their fictional characters and narrators seems to imply an ability to engage with emotions generally, whether their own or other people's, and this skill is not one which is normally discussed in books on the art of writing fiction[4]. The extent to which writers are able to engage with their emotions will, of course, depend on their upbringing and experience, and on whether or not they have suffered psychological damage of a gross or subtle kind. By gross damage I mean, for example, physical or sexual abuse by adults in childhood; by subtle damage I am thinking of developmental problems which may or may not have involved other people. It would probably be safe to assume that most people, at some stage in their life, experience emotional problems of a more or less serious kind and that, therefore, many of those who set out to write

4   Brande (1934) and Goldberg (1986) are particularly helpful in encouraging a 'felt' involvement in creative writing. Peter Abbs' work (1974), (1989) and (1994) on autobiography in the training of teachers is also relevant here.

fiction will have to confront difficult psychological issues in the course of their writing, if they are to develop the work. Some writers are able to use their emotional problems to fuel their writing, but for many others the problems inherent in getting in touch with and using their own emotional material interfere with their attempts to write, and often lead to the abandoning of the whole enterprise.

My course 'Autobiography and the Imagination' was specifically devised to help apprentice writers learn how to find their writing voice in the internal sense I have outlined above and to provide a working environment in which the problems of doing so can be discussed and hopefully overcome. Over the ten weeks of the course, they engage in freewriting, getting in touch with spontaneous imagery arising from the unconscious; they explore early memories, thinking themselves back into the experience of the past through sensory imagery and expanding those memories through imagination; they write from photographs of themselves when they were young, trying to find appropriate voices for themselves at different ages; they create characters out of people they know, focusing in particular on their felt, inner lives; they consider the ways in which places they have lived or visited have contributed to their inner landscapes; they write about themselves from different points of view, placing themselves as narrators in fantasy or historical settings, learning about the relationship between themselves as author and the roles they inhabit on the page; they dramatise moments from their lives through dialogue; they plot their lives using a time line, identifying significant moments, people and places in their lives that might be used as themes in their writing; and throughout this work they are encouraged to engage with the *feeling tone* of their writing, to move beyond the surface to the felt interior.

This approach has proved very successful in helping apprentice writers to develop a deeper relationship with their writing and to energise it with their own rich source material. Because it encourages a close engagement with the inner life, it has also proved valuable, for some people, in gaining insight into themselves and in developing a clearer or stronger sense of their own identity. In some instances, finding a writing voice has had a profoundly therapeutic effect on students' relationship with themselves and with significant people in their lives. I discuss all of these benefits, and the attendant difficulties, in the chapters that follow.

Coursework from 'Autobiography and the Imagination'

The following writing exercises I have either devised myself or adapted from ideas put forward by others. They have given rise to fascinating and sometimes outstanding pieces of prose fiction, as well as to students' discovery of key themes and preoccupations that have subsequently played an important role in their personal development or the development of their writing. In adopting this approach, I encourage students to use their autobiographical material as a *trigger* for the imagination, rather than trying to encapsulate the 'truth' of the past. This involves a willingness to blur the edges of their experience, to let it go slightly out of focus, so that the end product becomes something quite other than the original, yet still retains the essence of it.

Overcoming the Block: Freewriting

Most students of creative writing will encounter a technique that utilises a free association method. It is advocated primarily as a means of getting in touch with ideas for writing which are pre-conscious or unconscious and was the preferred writing method of surrealist writers such as André Breton, and Allan Ginsburg and the Beat poets. Whilst the idea has been around for a long time, it does not seem to have been systematised as a workshop technique until the American educationist Peter Elbow published his book *Writing Without Teachers* in 1973[5].

Elbow espoused the idea that writing is facilitated if the writer is taught to separate the two parts of the writing process: the creating and the editing. Many people, he says, come to writing with the idea that they have to know what they are going to write about before they put pen to paper. According to Elbow, this can create a block to the writing process: it provides an opportunity for the internal censor to exert its influence, which may include convincing us that we have nothing to say, or that if we do, then it is not worth committing to the page anyway. Elbow rightly believes that writing is a developing process: *we find out what we have to say in the actual engagement with the medium.* On this model, writing becomes a process of, first, 'throwing' words onto the page and, second, shaping them; we are encouraged to let go of the conscious control we are accustomed to exerting over the things we do, to allow the

---

5   Peter Wason maintains that he came up with the idea in 1970, independently of Elbow, and called it 'the exteriorisation method of writing' (Green and Wason 1982).

chaos of our unconscious to express itself and, only when this has happened, to apply the critical faculty.

To facilitate this process, Elbow devised an exercise in two parts. The first consists of two or three writing periods of, say, five minutes. During each of these periods you write continuously. For the first period there is no given starting point; you simply begin writing whatever is in your head. You do not stop to reflect on what is emerging; you do not go back and correct spelling or grammar, indeed you are discouraged from paying attention to all aspects of grammar, including full stops, initial capitals and paragraphs. If you get stuck, then you simply repeat the previous word or phrase until the flow starts again. In this preliminary stage, it is not the words as such that are important as much as the experience of keeping the flow going, outwitting the tendency to impose a critical eye prematurely. As Elbow puts it: 'Producing writing...is not so much like filling a basin or pool once, but rather getting water to keep flowing *through* till finally it runs clear' (Elbow 1973, p.28).

When the five minutes are up, the next stage is to read through the text and to underline anything that seems in any way interesting or significant. At first attempt there may not be anything interesting there at all; the result may be a rather stilted or antagonistic reaction to the imposition of 'this stupid exercise' or dismay at producing 'rubbish' when you really want to write beautiful prose. This stage can be overcome with a little practice. Once the idea of creating a flow has taken hold, you may find in the resulting text interesting words or phrases, or an image or theme which repeats itself. These should be underlined and one of them selected as a starting point for the next stage of the exercise.

The next stage is to write the selected word, phrase, image or theme at the top of a new sheet of paper and then to engage in a further five minutes of freewriting, using the heading as the trigger. It is not necessary to focus uninterruptedly on this heading; if digressions occur, they can be followed for as long as they seem fruitful; if they peter out, you can return to the main heading or pursue other ideas that may have arisen in the meantime. Again, the emphasis is on keeping the flow going, without stopping to reflect or correct. This stage of the exercise can be repeated several times, if desired, using the same focus each time or changing it as new ideas or images arise. Having thus engaged in two or more freewriting periods, you should have sufficient material for the final stage of the exercise.

You then proceed to the editing stage. At least twenty minutes should be allocated to this, and you are now free to reflect on your words, to correct grammar and syntax, to introduce changes and add new material; in sum, to create, in a much more leisurely and reflective way, a pleasing shape out of what has emerged.

Some two thirds of the students who completed the questionnaire found this exercise useful. Many of them were struck by its power to open up unexpected areas of thought. Here are some reactions: 'Freewriting loosened up my mind, made me less self-conscious and as a result allowed me to explore areas I would not have done otherwise'; 'The freewriting exercise loosened my inhibitions and made me realise that I had something to write…'; 'It really freed up my mind to take off into imagination and sensation'. One student found that it helped her to get in touch with material which went even deeper than the personal: '…the piece I wrote out of this method felt imbued with a kind of mythological/archetype-ridden subtext'. Some of those who found it a difficult and challenging exercise nevertheless found it beneficial: 'I find freewriting quite threatening, but feel it's good for me even so!'.

To those students who do find freewriting useful, I suggest (following Elbow) that they use it as a diary, to reflect on the day's activities. They might use it when they are looking for new starting points, or to explore ideas that have already emerged, or to brainstorm a block in their current writing project. Alternatively, it can be combined with an approach advocated by Dorothea Brande in *Becoming a Writer* (1934). Brande's book, although dated in some respects, is still one of the best on writing and the creative process. Brande also advocates separating the two stages of the writing process and has some very useful suggestions for eliciting the state of mind in which the free flow of ideas, uninhibited by the internal censor, can occur. Her main suggestion is to wake up half an hour earlier than usual and, before doing anything else, to write down whatever comes into your mind. This may be the remains of a dream, something you did yesterday, something you will do today, or any extraneous thoughts. At this early stage of waking, Brande argues, the internal censor is not as strong as when you are fully awake, so there is more opportunity here of slipping into the trancelike state she believes is necessary for writing.

Whilst Brande does not suggest the freewriting method as such, it could easily be used in this context to considerable effect. The main difference between Brande's and Elbow's approach is that Brande does not advocate reading through the results of the morning exercise for at least a week, in case the internal censor dismisses these scribblings prematurely. After a delay, when you are sufficiently distanced from the material, she says, you may return to the text and see if there is anything there which could be used for further development.

Writing with the Voice of the Child: Exploring Early Memories

I begin this exercise by asking students to think about their early memories and to say something about their nature. A few say that they have long tracts of memory from their early lives in linear form. Some claim to have very little early memory or even none at all. The majority report that they have strong memories of individual events or a series of linked events, or that they have fragments of memories of which the full memory is lost. For the purposes of this exercise the fragmentary or episodic nature of early memory is helpful rather than not. The point of the exercise is not to find the 'objective truth' of the past. After all, from research on memory we know that, whilst autobiographical memories contain a high degree of self-reference, they are never true in the sense of being literal representations of past events. As Martin Conway says: '...they may be accurate without being literal and may represent the personal meaning of an event at the expense of accuracy' (Conway 1990, p.9). This means that autobiographical memories are interpretations of past events from the point of view of the present. They will therefore include information about current thoughts, wishes and motivations, as well as the beliefs and understanding of the rememberer (p.11).

To get students thinking about their early memories, I ask them to note down images or incidents from early childhood which come to mind and to discuss them with a partner[6]. They select one of these fragments of memory to work on and I ask them to concentrate on the visual image, to 'walk into it' and to ask themselves: 'What do I see?', 'What do I hear?', 'What do I smell?', 'What do I taste?', 'What do things feel like under my fingers when I touch them?'[7]. I encourage them to spend some time with their eyes closed, immersing themselves in the memory and experiencing what it feels like, and expanding it through imagination.

The next step is to start writing about the memory, using what I call the 'strong words and phrases method'. This involves writing down individual

6   Photographs can be used as an alternative, along the lines suggested below (pp.26–28).
7   This is a development of an idea suggested in Fairfax and Moat (1981).

words and phrases which come readily to mind when associating with the memory. Nouns, adjectives and adverbs that encapsulate the sights, sounds, smells, tastes and tactile sensations are important, as are verbs of motion, particularly present participles, which help to introduce movement into the memory. These associations can be written down randomly on a sheet of paper or linked together in a spider diagram of the kind suggested by Gabriele Rico's 'clustering' technique (Rico 1983). When students have accumulated a sufficient amount of material, they are ready to develop a more connected piece of writing, whether prose or poetry.

As examples of different forms that can be used for early memories, we discuss extracts from Virginia Woolf's 'Sketch of the Past' (1989b), which recreates the sense impressions of the child's world in the voice of the adult, and Nathalie Sarraute's *Childhood* (1984), in which she re-inhabits the emotions of her child-self and speaks them with the voice of the child.

'Writing with the voice of the child' is a very popular and productive exercise which helps writers both to capture authentic voices of the past in fictional form and to use objectified parts of the self as fictional characters or narrators. It can also help writers to restore contact with aspects of themselves with which they have lost touch. Here are some typical responses from students: 'Exploring fragments of early memory through imagination…helped me regain the feeling of myself as a child'; 'I found it surprising how much visual material I could recall to expand on and how much easier I could conjure up emotional feelings'; 'Finding the feeling of another world and substantiating the shadows of people long gone out of my life was an absorbing exercise. The dead made quick. The little girl trying to make sense out of life'.

People on the Page: Transposing Real People into Fictional Characters

Where the previous exercise encourages students to immerse themselves in earlier versions of themselves, 'People on the Page' encourages them to immerse themselves in versions of significant people in their lives, such as parents or siblings. The main purpose is to enable students to create characters who are not only visible on the surface, but authentic emotional beings. This means that the writers have to get inside the characters and *to become them* whilst they are in the making, and this can have a significant effect on writers' perspectives on the people they are transposing into fiction, as well as on their perspective on themselves.

I start the session by initiating a discussion about the different aspects of people we know and the different ways these aspects can be used in creating fictional characters. As an example, we examine Blake Morrison's portrayal of his father in *And When Did You Last See Your Father?* (1994). Morrison's father is a larger-than-life character who is successfully brought to life in a number of different ways: through dialogue, action and physical description. The book is a painful and disturbing exploration of the parent-child relationship. It portrays Morrison's quest to find a lasting image of his father to take away from a lifetime's close contact, and he manages, through clever selection of physical and psychological characteristics, to bring him powerfully alive on the page, even in his death throes. Whilst this is an autobiography, by using the techniques of fiction Morrison enables the reader to get inside the man, to feel what he feels like, and to feel too what it felt like to be the child of such a parent.

For students' practical work on characterisation, I make a number of suggestions for transposing a real person into a fictional character. First, I ask them to identify the main physical characteristics of the person they want to fictionalise. Does he or she have a particular way of walking, eating or talking, or particular gestures or idiosyncrasies, such as the movement of hands or eyes? They are asked to describe this character using third-person point of view.

Second, I ask students to identify the predominant 'feeling-tone' of the person they are fictionalising. Is he or she, for example, predominantly angry, sad, joyful, withdrawn, hyperactive, dull or self-analytical? They write a piece in third-person point of view showing how this 'feeling-tone' manifests itself in the character's everyday life. Creating a feeling-tone for characters involves stepping inside them and, to facilitate this, I suggest that students play-act their characters. They spend a little time preparing for the role-play, noting down key words and phrases that this person uses, practising typical gestures, posture, ways of walking. Then they divide up into small groups of three or four and take it in turns to interview each other in role for about ten minutes. I usually ask them to start by asking the interviewee's name and age. Questions can then be about any aspect of the character's life, their interests, for example, their likes and dislikes, their opinions.

Having established their characters more fully through role-play, students return to their writing, this time placing their characters in a setting other than their usual ones, in such a way that their particular idiosyncrasies and characteristics are displayed. They might, for example, bring these fictionalised people into contact with other characters they have created or characters from well-known novels, and write about the encounter from the point of view of the latter.

Students find these suggestions useful for creating authentic characters. For example, one says: 'I had always used "real people" in writing before, but it always felt "wrong". I liked the idea of separating considerations of appearance from that of "feeling tone", of using "aspects" of characters rather than trying to shoe-horn a real person into a piece of fiction.' Students also find the exercises helpful in enabling them to stand outside of themselves and see themselves in a different light: 'My character as written by my son was most revealing.' As I show in detail in Chapter 3, inhabiting significant people from one's life can also be of considerable therapeutic value in re-writing family or personal narratives which have become uncomfortable or oppressive.

Pictures in the Mind: Writing from Photographs

I call this session 'Pictures in the Mind' for two reasons: first, because old photos are often the only remnant of a memory that we have – the memory itself consists primarily of the memorised photo; and, second, because memories are themselves often like photos in the mind, even when there is no actual photograph to record the event. The first visual image of someone who will later become significant for us is often permanently imprinted on the lens of memory. Ted Hughes' poem 'St. Botolph's' contains a perfect example of this in his first meeting with Sylvia Plath: '…suddenly you./ First sight. First snapshot isolated/ Unalterable, stilled in the camera's glare./ Taller/ Than ever you were again…' (Hughes 1998, p.15).

Working with photos can give rise to a useful discussion about the 'truth' of memories and the sort of 'truth' that is captured by the camera. Georges Perec's *W or the Memory of Childhood* (1996) is an appropriate text for sparking off a discussion, as his rich, multi-layered autobiography draws attention to the subjectivity of photos and our different responses to them at different times in our lives[8].

Students are asked to bring some old photographs to this session, including one of themselves as a child – preferably somewhere around the age of 8 or 10, when character is already well established. I ask them to find a partner and to spend about twenty minutes discussing these photos, allocating

8   Spence and Holland (1991) is also useful for the therapeutic angle.

the time between them. They might like to talk to their partners about the photos; alternatively, they might like to give the photos to their partners and to ask them what they see there, comparing their partners' perceptions with their own. After the discussion, students choose one photo to write from.

There are a variety of ways in which photos can be used as a starting point for fiction. If students have chosen a photo of themselves as a child, they might, for example, let the child speak in his or her own voice. Or they might engage in a dialogue with the child. If they have chosen a family group, they might explore the occasion from the points of view of different members of the family, or they might adopt the position of an objective narrator who is not connected with the family and try to imagine what the photo does not say, what important pieces of information it leaves out of account. Another possibility is to put the photos aside and to focus on what remains in the imagination from the discussion with the partner, to try to identify what memories it has sparked off, what feelings evoked, and to write about these. They might use the freewriting method or the 'strong words and phrases' approach to brainstorm their response. When they have a sufficient amount of raw material, they are encouraged to develop it into a finished product.

Working from old photographs of oneself and family members can be very rich and rewarding, and often gives rise to a wide variety of written material. As one student commented:

> This [exercise] produced such varied results from each individual. In one small group we had: (a) The view of the hinterland *behind* the child in the photo [which was not visible in the photo itself]; (b) The close-up perception of the character of the person photographed; (c) The characteristic habits [of] the subjects photographed and the photographer; (d) a group photo telling an entire story within its one frame.

Many people find photographs particularly helpful in evoking the feelings of the past. One says: 'Staring into old snapshots set off a lot of memories; using the photos it was quite easy to climb back into the feelings and sensations of the time and write about them.' Another says: 'I was astonished at the way in which looking at photographs of myself and my mother opened up lines of thought and feeling that I had not experienced before.' Another found working from photographs 'very difficult and painful' because she 'became hooked into examining every detail of the photograph and found myself feeling very sad at the loss of the little girl in the photograph'. She goes on to say, however, that this was also beneficial, because 'it helped me to confront some of these feelings'. For another, it was 'a traumatic experience to go through so early in the course when trust had not yet built up'. Whilst this was an isolated response, it raises important questions about the therapeutic dimension of using autobiography in the creative writing class, a topic to which I return below.

Country of the Mind: Exploring the Relationship between Self and Place

In his essay 'A Sense of Place' Seamus Heaney refers to the 'country of the mind', a 'midworld'[9] between ourselves and the places we have lived in or visited that constitutes our own inner landscapes. His view is that these inner landscapes live in the imagination and, when recalled to mind, evoke emotional as well as visual responses.

> It is this feeling, assenting, equable marriage between the geographical country and the country of the mind, whether that country of the mind takes its tone unconsciously from a shared oral inherited culture, or from a consciously savoured literary culture, or from both, it is this marriage that constitutes the sense of place in its richest possible manifestation (Heaney 1980b; p.132).

Heaney's own poetry is, of course, a prime example of what he is talking about here. Poems such as 'Anahorish' and 'Toome' in *Wintering Out* (1972) powerfully bring together personal, historical, linguistic and mythological dimensions of place. In 'Toome' in particular, the feel of the title place name on the tongue pushes the writer back through the detritus of battles and communities long gone, 'loam, flints, musket-balls, /fragmented ware...', down into the 'alluvial mud' of Ireland's past and, one senses too, into the deep, unruly recesses of his own more personal history (p.16). It is an archaeological dig, the driving of a shaft into the self, which reveals the many different layers that constitute our personal identity. Amongst novels, Amit Chaudhuri's autobiographical *Afternoon Raag* (1994) provides a different but no less fruitful perspective on the relationship between self and place, here focusing on two contrasting geographical locations, Bombay and Oxford.

This idea of the country of the mind is a fertile ground both for material for writing and for self-exploration. I give students a number of different options for writing exercises arising out of our discussion of the above texts. For example, they might write, in first or third person, through the eyes of a character (which may or may not be themselves) focusing on a particular

---

9   This is a term used by Miller (1982) and quoted by Bollas (1993, pp.18–19).

location, whether a landscape or an interior, which reflects in some way the person through whom it is seen. Or they might write on the theme of 'windows', as if they were looking out of a window at a well-known view, asking themselves: What is the particular feeling associated with this view? Or they might write an autofictional piece that links together a number of significant places from their life, via a common feature, such as windows, houses, landscapes or flowers. As with most of these exercises, freewriting or clustering is a good starting point, to brainstorm ideas.

Students find this exercise very useful for finding locations within which to set fictional or autofictional characters: 'My home town, lost forever, is vivid in my memory. I placed my characters in their surroundings and they developed from there.' But it has also proved equally useful for deriving deeper insight into personality, whether one's own or the characters one is creating: 'The linking of character with place proved to be a valuable way into revealing aspects of personality.' 'By doing this you have to think more deeply about the character and it allows you to describe the character or his/her feelings via a description of the place.'

The Words to Say it: Dramatising Real Events using Dialogue

Dialogue is one of the most important elements in fiction writing and, at the same time, the one that new writers find most difficult. The way we *imagine* dialogue, and the way it is actually spoken, are two quite different things. Dialogue is not a neat, logical exchange between two people, each speech answering or complementing the other. Two people in dialogue are often talking *at* each other, not taking a great deal of notice of what the other is saying, just waiting for the gap to occur so that they can fill it with what *they* want to say. Or their attention may be divided between the conversation and something else going on around them, elements of which might also stray into the dialogue. Again, a great deal of what is said in a dialogue belies what is not said. Placing dialogue on the page – making it *written* rather than *spoken* – changes it yet again, because we do not have the benefit of the tone of voice or inflection of the speaker, which means that certain words or phrases present in spoken dialogue may be unnecessary or awkward on the page.

In terms of exploring our memories and personal experience, dialogue can be an important technique for taking us back into the present of the experience and re-experiencing it from the inside; or, conversely, of drawing the past or our version of the past into the present, and giving us the opportunity of exploring it more thoroughly, bringing it alive in a more vivid way, even of re-writing the past to make it more *our* version, which might be more comfortable or empowering. For dialogue places us inside the heads of the people who speak and – like the exercise transposing real people into fictional characters – potentially inside their *felt* worlds as well. It demands that the writer take on, in her imagination, the characteristics of the speaker, letting go of her usual identity and, temporarily, becoming the other. In other words, dialogue is another important device for *showing* rather than *telling*, as one student discovered: 'Using dialogue opened new vistas. I could find the voices and it helped showing rather than telling. It was a challenge to find the right voice, which I enjoyed. Remembering and writing what people said is one thing, how they said it is another. I'm still developing dialogue in this way.' Thus, she was compelled not just to find the words, but to find the right *tone* of voice for her speakers, to enter more fully into their worlds and to feel what their language would sound like. Another student comments on this shift from the cognitive to the affective: 'The dialogue exercise and writing about real people both enabled me to break through from writing in a way which I *thought* was right to one which I *felt* was right.' Another found that writing dialogue '…necessitated digging deep into memory and brought to the surface incidents that previously would have been glossed over'.

There are many excellent examples of the use of dialogue in any number of novels and short stories. Amongst autobiographical novels, I have found Jeanette Winterson's *Oranges are Not the Only Fruit* (1985) particularly useful. The narrator's mother is wonderfully characterised, largely through her manner of speaking. In addition to Winterson's novel, we sometimes look at the short story by Ernest Hemingway 'Hills Like White Elephants' (1928), in which a man and a woman are waiting for a train on a hot, remote railway station in the Spanish interior. This story is almost entirely in dialogue, with an objective narrator setting the scene. Whilst a great deal is apparently being said by both parties, one gets a strong impression that much of their discourse belies deeper and unspoken intentions, of only part of which they are themselves aware.

Using the Hemingway story as a model, I ask students to write a short piece, primarily using dialogue, under the title 'The Misunderstanding'. This is a particularly fruitful theme, as it provides scope for dialogue in which the characters are not hearing each other properly, and where the meaning of what is being said is hidden or obscure. Not only is this exercise valuable for exploring the power of dialogue to portray complex relating, it also provides an opportunity for exploring difficult real-life relationships.

Melody for Two Voices: Creating a Fictional First-person Narrator

This exercise is useful for apprentice writers, who often use themselves as narrator in their fiction *without having a clear sense of who that narrator is*, and this can result in the narrator lacking identity. It derives from Hermann Hesse's notion of a 'melody for two voices' in his autobiographical essay 'A Guest at the Spa' (1924).

Hesse was one of the most autobiographical writers of his time. He was well aware of the presence of different 'selves' within the personality, as a result of his Jungian analysis, and he makes good use of this in his fiction. 'A Guest at the Spa' is an excellent example. This essay is a distillation of his many experiences of 'taking the cure' at resorts such as Baden Baden. It is an amusing and self-mocking portrait of the writer immersed in his own hypochondria.

When Hesse arrives at the spa he prides himself on his sprightliness and good humour by comparison with the other guests who, already worn down by the rigours of their treatment, struggle along the pathways on sticks or crutches. When he reaches the hotel, however, this vision of himself as the aloof and superior outsider is quickly dispelled. He soon becomes immersed in his usual neurotic preoccupations, such as the problem of finding a room free of neighbour noise. The debilitating treatments wear him down; he creeps up and down the stairs of the hotel, totters along the flower-lined paths of the gardens, leaning heavily on his stick. He has become the chronically hypersensitive guest at the spa, absorbed into the institutionalised neurosis of the place.

Then, one day, 'creeping down to the dining room, peevish and without appetite', he suddenly becomes aware of himself: 'I was suddenly no longer simply the guest at the spa who with heavy limbs and joyless face was creeping down the hotel staircase, but I was at the same time a witness of myself' (p.130). He observes himself sitting down painfully at his 'lonesome little round table', how slowly and indecisively he takes his napkin out of the ring (p.130), how similar he is to the other guests who sit 'in front of their solitary plates with disciplined but deeply bored expressions' (p.131). He identifies the observing 'I' as the 'anti-social hermit and lone wolf Hesse', his customary persona with which he has lost touch since coming to the spa but which has now returned as a 'secret observer'. As he watches himself, he suddenly finds his double 'unbearably laughable, unbearably idiotic' (p.132):

> The spa guest Hesse was just lifting his glass, simply out of boredom …when the union of the two I's took place, the eating I and the observing I, and all at once I had to put the glass down, for I was shaken from inside by the sudden explosion of an immense desire to laugh, a quite childlike merriment, a sudden insight into the infinite absurdity of this whole situation (p.132).

He manages to contain his desire to laugh, but then he catches the eye of an elderly woman who is sitting at a nearby table:

> …and while we stared at each other for an instant the laughter rose to my face and I could not help myself, I grinned at the women in the most friendly fashion, and all the accumulated laughter within me forced my mouth open and ran out of my eyes (p.134).

His laughter is infectious. Soon the woman is also laughing and then, gradually, everyone else in the room. And this laughter breaks the spell of his immersion in a single version of himself and releases him into multiplicity, of which he makes playful use in the remainder of the essay. In the closing section he hankers after a way of writing the self which would enable him 'to find expression for duality', where the different aspects of himself would be 'simultaneously present', thus creating a 'melody for two voices' (p.145). Whilst he manages to do this only briefly here, it is in his subsequent novel, *Steppenwolf* (1927), that this way of writing the self finds its more successful form[10].

Using Hesse's notion of 'melody for two voices', I have developed a writing exercise that splits the 'I' of the writer into the self that acts and the self that observes. The purpose of this exercise is to create a first-person narrator based on oneself but with an identity which draws on one particular aspect of the personality. It consists of two stages. In the first stage I ask the writer to:

> Write a piece in which you step outside yourself and observe what you are like and the things you do. Write this in the third person. Choose a familiar situation, such as walking down the High Street on a busy Saturday morning or engaging with a group of people amongst whom

---

10   I am indebted to Stelzig (1988) for his helpful discussion of 'Guest at the Spa'.

you may feel an outsider or ill at ease. Try in particular to observe yourself in relation to other people.

This is a fairly straightforward piece of writing, reflecting on oneself in the third person. The second stage is rather more complicated:

> Using the first person, place the self-character from your first piece in a fantasy or historical setting. Your character's role now is to narrate a story in which he/she is one of the players but not necessarily the main player – there should be another character (a fictional character or someone you know transformed into a fictional character) who is the main focus of the piece.

When writing the second piece, students are asked to think of the person in the first piece of writing as a character, even though the character is themselves. There is therefore a triple distancing from self: first person has become third person, who has then become first person again, in a different guise, but that first person is, in a sense, subsidiary within the final piece, a first-person narrator who narrates someone else's story whilst being a part of that story (like Nick, the narrator of Scott Fitzgerald's *The Great Gatsby*). This distancing process enables writers to explore being themselves in a very different guise and to identify an aspect of self that is appropriate to the telling of this particular story. It is hoped that this provides the experience of what it feels like to narrate a story as oneself, but with a focused identity.

Students' reactions to this exercise are mixed. Those who find it useful often produce startlingly original pieces of writing. This technique has also proved useful in a few cases for identifying and clarifying aspects of self which were causing problems for the writing process (see 'Sarah's Story' in Chapter 2).

Autobiography as Fiction: Creating a Life Map

In this session we discuss in depth a writer who has drawn extensively on autobiographical material to create a novel. I find it particularly useful here to use a fiction writer who has also published autobiographical documents, such as diaries or letters, that record the events portrayed in the fiction, thus allowing the reader to see the 'before and after' effect of transposing life into fiction. I have successfully used Jean Rhys's novel *Voyage in the Dark* (1934), together with selected essays from her autobiography *Smile Please* (1981), particularly the piece entitled 'World's End and a Beginning', which contains the origins of *Voyage in the Dark* in a real-life incident. Sylvia Plath's *The Bell*

Jar (1963), in conjunction with extracts from *Letters Home* (1975) edited after her death by her mother, also provide a very interesting juxtaposition of autobiography and fictional autobiography.

During this session students also create their own 'life maps', which can be useful for identifying topics and themes arising out of their own experience. Using my own life map as an example, I suggest that they draw a horizontal line across an A4 sheet to indicate their lifespan from year zero to the present. Their task is to divide this line up into time segments according to moments of significant change in their lives, such as starting school, starting work, getting married or divorced. I ask them to identify for each time segment (a) significant places, (b) significant events, and (c) significant people, and also (d) to characterise in a word or phrase their relationship with the outside world during that period. My own time segment for ages 18–23, for example, reads '(a) London/Australia, (b) travelling/multitude of odd jobs, (c) F, and (d) confusion/searching for meaning'. This material is to be written underneath the line.

Once students have completed to their satisfaction the bottom half of the map, their next task is to take an imaginary step back from the personal material they have accumulated and to identify topics and themes of a more general nature which characterise the different time segments of their lives. These are written above the line. My own themes for the period 18–23 are 'on the road', 'taking on other people's identities' and 'viewing one's own culture from the perspective of another culture', and all three themes play a significant role in the first novel I completed, *Stages*. Having thus completed the life map, students choose one of the topics or themes they have identified and, using this as a trigger, write a short story or the first chapter of a novel.

Apart from providing a rich and often unexpected source of material for writing ('Absolutely fascinating how your boring little life can actually amount to something worth writing about!' was one student's response to this exercise), the life map can also be useful for discussing form and point of view in fiction writing. For example, the writer might wish, as Jean Rhys does in *Voyage in the Dark*, to set a novel in one segment of her life, such as young adulthood, but to use an earlier period, such as childhood, as a backdrop or counterpoint; or, as I attempted to do in *Stages*, to tell the story of an earlier period of my life from the perspective of a later period. Thinking about who one was during each of the different time segments and immersing oneself in how that time felt can also be valuable for creating authentic narrators for one's story and for deciding from whose point of view it would be most effective to tell it.

The life map exercise continues the work of 'objectifying the self', which is an important part of the 'melody for two voices' exercise and, as I have said earlier, an essential part of the process of finding a writing voice. Some people find the life map helpful as a preliminary 'sketchpad' stage in the planning of a novel; as in the case of the clustering exercise outlined above, it is a way of making thoughts visible and therefore more manageable. As one student put it: 'I found the life map approach very worthwhile for identifying a framework, and my research now is to identify sufficient "facts" and "feel for time and place" to be able to create the life map plus characters for my intended novel.' Another was struck by the way this exercise helped her to bring to the surface and give shape to '...the theme I'd already had at the back of my mind [which] became very obvious to me after I'd mapped out my life'.

Hearsay: Using Tape-recordings of Interviews with Family Members

A further step in 'objectifying the self' can be taken with an exercise which draws inspiration from Ronald Fraser's fascinating but difficult autobiography *In Search of a Past* (1984). Fraser is an oral historian, well known for his book *Blood of Spain* (1979), which draws together first-hand accounts of the Spanish Civil War. In his autobiography, *In Search of a Past*, he turns the tables on himself and uses his oral history methods to explore his own past. Returning to the minor stately home, the Manor House, Amnersfield, in the home counties where he was born and brought up, he tape-records interviews with former staff of the house – his nanny, the gardener, the groom, the maid – in an attempt to collect information about his family and home environment, and particularly about himself as a boy. Extracts from these interviews are woven together in the book with his own memories and observations on his past, his feelings in the present as he goes about the interviews and re-visits old haunts, and glimpses of his present encounters with his father who, now old and demented, inhabits a nursing home.

In addition to this material, Fraser incorporates into the book reported extracts from psychoanalytic sessions that he also undergoes during the ten years of the book's preparation, in which he discusses his relationships with key figures in his early life, particularly his mother and nanny. The rich and multi-layered text that results provides Fraser with both an inside and an outside perspective on his past. As the story unfolds, we see how the process of exploring his life in this way enables him to move from a third- or second-person relationship with himself, characterised by reference to himself as 'he' or 'you', towards a first person, an 'I' identity.

There are a number of useful devices in Fraser's approach that can be adapted for our purpose. Hearing about ourselves and our lives from others who shared with us significant past events is a particularly effective way of 'objectifying the self', and of loosening our hold on the 'truth' of our experience and therefore of being able to use it freely and imaginatively in our fiction writing. Relating to ourselves in the third- or second-person singular can also help us to give freer rein to aspects of ourselves over which we tend to exercise control, so that they might develop a life of their own on the page.

There are several possible options for this exercise which I suggest to students. The first is to tape-record or take notes from an interview or interviews with one or more members of their family (parent, sibling, spouse, relation) about an event in the past. These interviews are then transcribed verbatim and used to build up a picture of the event from the different points of view, including the writer's own memories of it. Students are often surprised to discover how different their own memories of an event are by comparison with those of other members of their families.

Another option is to interview your parents about yourself as a child, trying to elicit information about what you were like, or how they saw you. The material can be transcribed as before, and extracts included in a piece of prose fiction, with your own version added to it. I remember clearly a piece of writing by one student that simply juxtaposed her mother's and father's view of her as a child, in a dead-pan tone and without authorial comment. It was both funny and alarming.

A further option is to interview a member of your family about his or her own past. Again, the material can be transcribed and developed into a piece of fiction, bringing the writing alive with dialogue, characterisation and other techniques of showing. Of course, for all these exercises the writer will have to gain the permission of the interviewees before using the material, and hopefully there will also be an opportunity for letting them see the finished piece of writing and discussing it with them.

These exercises obviously rely on students having access to family who are willing or able to be interviewed. Parents or siblings may not be alive or may live at a considerable distance, or the relationship with them may not be such that interviews are an appropriate form of communication. However, interviews with current friends or acquaintances about perceptions of oneself, or about recent or not so recent events, can sometimes be as effective.

Comments on these exercises were mostly positive. One student found that: 'Interviewing a relative was extremely useful, as there were incidents I did not remember, until reminded of them.' Another found that: '...when I tape-recorded my family about an incident, we all viewed it in different ways and remembered little details that triggered off more and more memories.' One student who did not manage to do the exercise during the course felt sure that she would undertake it at some stage: '...because I'm wholly aware that some people don't see "me" at all', the implication being that finding out what their version of her actually is would be therapeutically helpful. Indeed, over the years of using this exercise I have come to feel that it may have more of a role in a therapeutic rather than a straightforward creative writing context. This is particularly borne out by the experience of 'Jennifer' (see Chapter 3), who found tape-recording interviews with her brothers and writing up their stories in fictional form helpful in laying to rest long-term resentment against them and in formulating a clearer sense of her own identity in relation to them.

Therapeutic Dimensions of Finding a Writing Voice

The above exercises, then, focus on two different but related things that are, in my view, a necessary part of finding a writing voice: first, getting in touch with oneself and one's experience at a deep, emotionally felt level and, second, objectifying that material in such a way that it can be used freely and imaginatively in one's fiction writing. This work often brings about profound changes in students' relationship to the writing process. There are a number of responses in the questionnaires that are particularly relevant here and, interestingly, they are not only by beginner writers, but by practised writers who had been experiencing writing difficulties or blocks prior to the course. Lorna, for example, had been writing for many years and was producing writing that she described as 'technically proficient', but she 'felt there was something missing at the heart of it'. Exploring herself imaginatively for several months enabled her:

to identify that I have been too detached from my writing, writing only with my head and not my heart. The freewriting technique has helped with [this] problem. I am now using [it] regularly as a means of freeing up my imagination and can see the way my writing has progressed as a result.

Phil, who was accustomed to writing non-fiction, regarded his fiction writing as 'well-written, but uninteresting – too dry'. Writing autobiographically led to a breakthrough in which he *opened up* to the experience he was trying to write about, so that instead of writing in his former rather impersonal style – writing from a distance – he was now *inside* the writing. Andrea, who was completely new to writing, said that fictionalising herself had provided her with a solid ground from which to fictionalise *beyond* her own experience. As another student put it: '…writing from experience [gives] one a solid base and then [lets] the imagination soar.' What these students had learned was to get closer to, and have confidence in, their own (sometimes difficult) material, and to have confidence in engaging with their own inner processes for the purpose of writing. This gave them a strong sense of rootedness in themselves, which allowed them to gain the necessary distance from which to explore their own material imaginatively. In other words they had developed a 'writing voice', or 'writing identity'[11], as it might also be called, which enabled them to have a flexible, workable relationship, in their writing, between freedom and control.

Many psychoanalytic writers discuss this flexible, workable relationship between psychic freedom and control in artistic creation. For Freud it is a special gift of the artist, although the artist is also, in Freud's view, necessarily neurotic because of his need to transpose his fantasies into art (Freud 1908)[12]. Marion Milner identifies two different modes of attention in the artistic process: the beamlike concentration of the mind on external objects, which is characteristic of conscious thinking, and the broad hovering attention with the body (Milner 1989, pp.29–40). This latter mode of attention, which she likens to a dome, as opposed to the sharp-pointedness of the former, is crucial, she believes, for the contact one needs with the inner 'womb-space' where a kind of dreaming goes on (p.37). It is in this internal space – Winnicott's 'transitional space' (Winnicott 1971) – that the imagination can get to work on the raw material of the unconscious and begin the process of transforming it into art.

Engaging with this internal space involves the artist in a 'temporary giving up of the discriminating ego, which stands apart and tries to see things objectively and rationally and without emotional colouring', and merging in

---

11   Roz Ivanic (1998) identifies four elements in a writing identity: 'autobiographical self', 'discoursal self', 'self as author' and 'possibilities for self-hood'.

12   Leader (1991) contains a useful discussion of psychoanalytic views on the mechanisms of creation.

an 'aesthetic moment' with the object one is creating (Milner 1955, p.27). In learning how to engage in artistic creation, the artist has to cultivate the 'internal gesture' (Milner 1952, p.72), as Milner describes this inner 'standing apart' or shelving of the ego or critical faculty, which allows the unconscious contents to be accessed via the imagination. Only when this has occurred does the critical faculty come back into play to develop the material into its final artistic form.

Hélène Cixous refers to the process of shelving the critical faculty as 'de-egoisation'; it is 'this state of without-me, of dispossession of me, that will make the *possession* of the author by the characters possible' (Cixous 1990, p.28; quoted by Sellers 1996, p.xiv, trans. Deborah Jenson and Susan Sellers). She calls it 'writing with the body' (Cixous 1986) and regards it as specifically feminine, although it is available to both men and women[13]. Similarly, Milner refers to this state of 'without-me' as the 'imaginative body', an aspect of the mind which feels like a body, 'in that its essential quality is a sense of extension in space' (Milner 1971, p.36). She discusses this in relation to her attempts to bring her drawings of objects to life, to give them *action*, to convey on the paper what she calls their 'spiritual life'. She discovered that: 'My whole relationship with other people as well as objects, works of art, nature, music could depend upon what I did with this imaginative body rather than with my concentrated intellectual mind' (p.36). I am not sure that we need to identify the 'imaginative body' as specifically feminine, although when Milner refers to the two different modes of attention as the sharp-pointed beamlike concentration with the mind and the broad, hovering, dome-like attention with the body, one can see the origin of the feminine/masculine associations. I would prefer to say that immersion in the 'imaginative body' is one side of the twofold process of engaging in artistic activity: the intuitive, creative faculty rather than the critical faculty governed by the ego[14]. The main difficulty with shelving the critical faculty and becoming immersed in the 'imaginative body' is that it involves the artist in a 'temporary loss of the sense of self' (Milner 1955, p.17) and exposes her to the chaos of her inner world. An artist, therefore, needs to have a strong

13 Cixous calls it a 'decipherable libidinal femininity which can be read in a writing produced by a male or a female' (Conley 1984, p.129).

14 Cixous increasingly wants to do away with the critical faculty altogether, as in automatic writing, and she extols the idea of the 'imund book', the book without an author (Cixous 1993). However, if writing is to be more than purely personal, it requires form and structure, hence the working together of the critical and creative faculties.

enough sense of self, so that she can 'accept chaos as a temporary stage' (Milner 1971, p.76).

A 'writing voice' or 'writing identity', then, in the internal sense, involves the development of a strong enough sense of self to facilitate 'the internal gesture', the mechanism of shelving the critical faculty, which allows 'positive regression' into the unconscious and the holding open of the 'internal space' where the imagination sets to work on the raw material of the unconscious and transforms it into art. My experience leads me to believe that by spending a period of time, in a group setting, engaging with their feelings and emotions through writing fictional autobiography, apprentice writers develop a closer contact with their inner world, and this helps them to develop a stronger sense of themselves and their relation to the writing process. Having a stronger sense of themselves enables them, in turn, to suspend or shelve their ego-identity and to immerse themselves in the imaginative process of creation – to write with the 'imaginative body' – but also to reinstate their ego-identity when necessary, in order to shape and craft their material into its final form. This flexible relationship between the critical and creative faculties provides a firm ground from which they can then proceed to find the many different voices they will use in their fiction, to become 'polyphonic' in Bakhtin's sense (Bakhtin 1984).

For some people, engaging with their inner world in this way has a strong self-developmental or therapeutic dimension. Indeed, a number of psychoanalytical writers liken the creative process to the process of self-development: Jung, for example, likens it to individuation (Chodorow 1997) and Ernst Kris sees it as a form of catharsis (Kris 1952). The link between the creative process and self-development is also implicit in Milner's discussion of the space within which the imagination functions. When discussing what she calls the 'womb space', Milner says that it is here, in this quiet room within oneself, that the self's potential develops, and that the kind of attention which she characterises as broad, hovering and dome-like is 'a kind of thinking which seems to be making contact with the unfolding personality' (Milner 1989, p.37).

Milner's view is very close to Christopher Bollas's thinking on the way self evolves. According to Bollas, the human being is born with what he calls an *idiom* or *true self*. It is the core of the self, but not a fixed, unitary entity; rather it is a potential self, 'a genetically biased set of dispositions', which exists prior to object relating and which needs mother and father to facilitate its expression (Bollas 1989, p.9). He sees the inherited dispositions that make up the *idiom* or *true self* as 'a form of knowledge' that has not yet been thought. This he calls the *unthought known* (Bollas 1987, pp.277–283). Our lives, Bollas maintains, are in a constant state of flux, 'a kind of private dreaming', in which we enact our idiom through a process of merging with and emerging from 'subjective objects' (Bollas 1993, pp.19–20). Expanding on the Winnicottian notion that the child grows and matures through the facilitating environment, he means by subjective objects not only people (the mother, the father, significant others), but aesthetic experiences of, for example, seeing a play, reading a book or painting a picture (pp.21–22).

These experiences, in which we temporarily lose ourselves, which Bollas also refers to as the 'aesthetic moment' and which he sees as a re-evoking of the state of fusion with the mother that prevailed during early psychic life (Bollas 1987, p.16), have the effect of changing us, so that when we emerge from them, part of who we are potentially has been expanded. Janet Campbell (1996) discusses the transformative role of reading fiction from this point of view. A similar claim could be made for the writing of fictional autobiography. When we write autobiographically, we use language to give shape to knowledge of ourselves that may be felt but is not known until it is enacted symbolically or metaphorically in the text. According to the psychologist Peter Wason, any kind of serious writing necessarily involves this confrontation with self; it 'creates an object which is both a part of the self and a part of the world of ideas' (Green and Wason 1982, pp.50–51). In the writing of autobiographical fiction the object referred to would be a composite of the piece of writing and the aspect or aspects of the self out of which it emerged. The writing encapsulates a part of the self that may not have been accessible before or an image that previously existed only in the form of feelings or mental pictures.

This is not to suggest that writers can only find their 'writing voice' or 'writing identity' when they get in touch with their 'true' selves. As demonstrated by the work of Bernard Paris, which draws on the psychodynamic theory of Karen Horney, celebrated fiction writers are people who are often seriously internally conflicted and self-alienated (e.g. Paris 1997). Rather than preventing them from using their emotions in their writing, the struggle with their inner conflicts often energises their work. Occasionally, as the example of Emily Bronte's *Wuthering Heights* shows, the narrative structure of the work of fiction can be seen to resolve, on the page, the implied author's own inner conflicts (pp.240–261). It may well be that identification with what Karen Horney calls the 'idealised image' may provide a writer with as much sense of 'ego-identity' as contact with the real self; indeed, the motive force of the idealised image, with its 'search for glory' might be even greater than that of the real self[15].

For students attending my course, the writing of fictional autobiography may enable them to expand their knowledge of their 'true' or 'real' self, in the fluid sense of the term discussed above, and this will therefore be part of an on-going process of self-development. Or it may provide them with a deeper knowledge of what Karen Horney calls their 'actual self' – 'everything that a person is at a given time, healthy and neurotic' (Horney 1951, p.158) – and an increased ability, in spite of inner conflicts, to work with their own, sometimes difficult, material. Whichever it is, as this knowledge grows there is likely to be an increased confidence, leading to a more solid sense of ego-identity, and this in turn will increase the feeling of safety needed in order to hold open the space for the imagination.

Finding a 'writing voice' or 'writing identity', then, is very closely linked with the extent to which writers have access to their inner life and the way they cope with their own personal material; for it presupposes, for however fleeting or intermittent a time, the ability to hold open the space for the imagination, to give the imagination free rein in order to get in touch with the spontaneously emerging material, as well as the ability to rein-in the imagination, in order to shape and structure that material. In other words it implies a *flexibility within the psyche* that allows the critical and the creative faculties to operate in harmony with each other. Bakhtin calls this a 'dialogic' relationship with self (Bakhtin 1984), and the idea of the dialogic nature of fiction and selves is centrally important to my considerations in this book.

The Dual Role of the Creative Writing Course

It follows from the above that the autobiographically based creative writing course, working as it does on the borderline between education and therapy, has a dual role: it helps some people to develop as writers and others to develop as people, although ideally one would hope that both of these might go hand in hand. Such an undertaking inevitably has its dangers as well as its advantages. Some people, for example, are not aware of the self-exploratory dimension when they enrol on the course, and sometimes find themselves having to confront difficult or painful personal or psychological issues as a

---

15   I discuss Karen Horney's theory in Chapter 2.

result of their writing, in an environment which may well be less safe or supportive than the therapeutic setting proper.

There have been comparatively few upsets amongst students I have worked with, although admittedly some did not come to my attention until after the course was over, either because they were contained among the students themselves or because those affected had their own means of support outside of the class, whether in supportive relationships or in counselling or therapy. Again, one does not always know why students drop out of a course, and one has to assume, I think, that they sometimes leave because the process of writing about themselves is too painful or disturbing.

Some people find particular exercises upsetting. Working from photographs, whilst one of the most popular exercises, elicited some negative responses. One woman felt that: 'This was a traumatic experience to go through so early in the course when trust had not yet built up. I became very anxious anticipating this session, and considered missing the class or "forgetting" the photos.' However, she did produce 'a reasonable piece of work (for private consumption only)', which she later developed into a poem. She went on to say that she 'felt this exercise was potentially dangerous and inappropriate to the stated aims of the course. It could remain as a suggestion to use at home, but should *not* be imposed in such an unsupportive setting.' Whilst this is an isolated reaction, it does point to the importance of timing in the introduction of particular exercises, as well as to the necessity of creating an appropriate supportive framework within which this work can be done safely (I say more about this in a moment). Another woman also found working from photographs very difficult and painful: 'I became hooked into examining every detail of the photograph and found myself feeling very sad at the loss of the little girl in the photograph.' However, she goes on to say that: '...it *was* also beneficial – it helped me to confront some of these feelings.'

In my experience, the majority of people who attend autobiographically based creative writing courses seem reasonably aware of the potential for self-exploration. Just over half of my respondents came to the course with events and experiences from their lives which they wanted to use as a basis for fiction. The past was overwhelmingly important by comparison with the present, with the emphasis on coming to terms with its negative aspects. Childhood was high on the list of priorities, particularly its deprivations ('...happenings from my childhood when I was conscious that I lived in extreme poverty and in buildings that were "condemned as unfit for habitation"'); adolescence, too, including school years ('Negative school experiences with left-over resentment'). Family members, particularly mother, father and grandparents, featured significantly ('I wanted to write about a family. In particular two sisters, both affected by their domineering mother and a father who "disappeared".'). Birth and motherhood were mentioned ('...post-natal depression and the effects on not only the sufferer but all those with whom she has relationships...'); death, particularly of parents; problems of sexuality and gender identity ('...the development of my lesbian sexuality in a hostile environment...'); and love affairs and marriage, current and past. Some respondents spoke of the need to express feelings, e.g. 'feelings of isolation', or 'My feeling of being a square peg, which is both positive and negative.'

A surprisingly high percentage of people were specifically geared towards the therapeutic dimension of the course. No less than one fifth of my respondents mentioned the potential for gaining therapeutic insight into themselves, and some of them saw the course as a means of extending the work they were already doing in therapy or analysis. One said: 'I have been in analysis for a period of time and welcomed the opportunity of tapping into childhood and adolescent memories, particularly as I found it almost impossible to recall some of the early periods of my life.' Another said: 'I was being pressed from within to tell about certain events in my life and I wanted to find out more about how to shape them.' One respondent had noticed a '...slight conflict in myself between my working class roots and middle class lifestyle' and felt 'that this would be something worth exploring'. Another saw the course as an opportunity of writing herself out and 'clear[ing] the jungle'. For another, the course provided an opportunity of extending the work she was doing in therapy: 'I'd reached a point in my therapy where I was dealing with the importance of my grandparents.' Some people hoped to straddle both aspects: 'I'm very interested in...the idea of "writing things out", of using the combination of personal experience and memory and imagination as some kind of catharsis at the same time as producing a readable book.'

However, there are people who want nothing to do with the self-exploratory aspect of the course ('...when the sessions threatened to become a co-counselling event I was least interested'), or had engaged in therapy or counselling and felt that this was behind them. Others felt that the circumstances of a writing course were inappropriate for self-exploration. One older woman said that the potential for therapeutic insight was there if she had wanted to write about personal episodes from her past, but that 'the group...did not lend itself to such soul searching' because it was too big, 'so we never got to know or trust each other sufficiently'. She also felt that 'the purposes of the participants were [too] different. The very young simply wanted a credit towards a degree, others wanted techniques and a small minority perhaps did it for therapy. Under the circumstances I kept painful episodes from my past well under wraps as I'm sure other older members did too.'

Whilst I would agree that there certainly is a wide and divergent range of aims and needs amongst creative writing students, it *is* possible, if the situation is handled sensitively, to cater both for those who are concerned primarily with the development of writing skills and for those who are seeking therapeutic insight. However, this does place considerable demands on the creative writing tutor, who may find herself in the role of counsellor or therapist without the appropriate skills. Perhaps this is true, to a greater or lesser extent, for all teachers, but the situation is more critical, I would argue, when one is encouraging people to write autobiographically. Whilst it would certainly be useful for the creative writing tutor to have acquired some formal counselling or therapeutic skills, it is sufficient, I believe, for her to be a good empathetic and sympathetic listener, ideally to have undergone her own therapy or counselling, and therefore to be aware of people's sensitivities and the possible distress that writing fictional autobiography might cause them. What I would regard, though, as the most vital skill of the tutor is the ability to create the sort of space within which autobiographical writing can be done safely.

In his paper 'Space for the Imagination', Trevor Pateman argues, using psychoanalytic ideas of Melanie Klein and Donald Winnicott, that the ability to explore space is something which comes about in the course of healthy development:

> ...the infant's early explorations of the outside world in looking, crawling and toddling are very much *spatial* explorations. These are made possible by a primary caregiver, usually the mother, who provides the stable home base to which the infant can, at any moment, return. Without a feeling of security about the primary caregiver, and the possibility of returning to her, exploration of the world becomes fraught with anxiety and sometimes literally impossible. As time goes by, the child who is confident of the secure home base will explore farther afield and for longer periods of time. The child is then able not only to take a look, but to take

a second look – to see the world. It also becomes able to play (Pateman 1997, p.4).

Pateman then proceeds to discuss teaching techniques, in drama and the visual arts for example, which seek to create 'analogues of the safe havens and potential spaces of early childhood', relaxation exercises which free up 'not only the hand, eye and body, but the imagination too'. These practices, he says, attempt to create 'a good-enough environment for the imagination', a *holding environment*, which enables the practitioner to feel safe enough to engage with the space or the chaos within which the imagination functions (p.4).

Helping students to create a 'holding environment' for the imagination is one of the main aims of my creative writing course, so that they have a solid ground for the more rigorous study of writing technique that follows in Course 2 of the Certificate. But to make it possible for students to develop their own *internal* holding environments, there needs to be an *external* holding environment, a safe space, both contained and open, within which students will feel able to express themselves freely but also be aware of the sensitivities of others.

One of the most important elements in such a holding environment is peer group support. Students taking my course spend half of each session reading and discussing their work-in-progress in groups consisting of three or four people, the configuration of which may change only once or twice during the period of ten weeks. Students are asked to bring enough copies of their work so that all the members of the group can look at the text whilst it is being read out, or can have the option of reading it silently to themselves. Students are also free to set guidelines for the sort of feedback they want on their writing. There may be times when they will bring to the group a very personal piece which is not ready for critical feedback. They might simply want to talk about how the piece arose and what it says to them. Or, if sufficient trust has been built up in the group, they might want to ask what themes, motifs or images members of the group see in the text and how they as readers are affected by the piece. In this way, the group becomes the necessary audience which witnesses the emergence of the writers' own sometimes very personal and difficult material, and gives approval for the openness and self-revelation which is involved in delving into the inner world.

Whilst, however, the role of the group is crucially important, it is the tutor who has overall responsibility for holding the group together, helping it to gel in the first instance, encouraging the development of trust, and ensuring that it works as smoothly as possible and to the benefit of all concerned. I agree with Peter Abbs that it is the *collaborative* nature of this work which makes it effective. However, I would not agree that we can wholly rely on the group process when difficulties arise. 'I've learnt to trust *not* myself but it, the process, the collective experience itself', he says. When someone gets upset, 'there's always someone who knows exactly what to do' (Abbs 1996, p.115). One hopes that this will be the case, but I believe that the tutor needs to have a range of skills at her disposal which will enable *her* to know what to do in such situations. And students do need to feel that the tutor has that capacity to 'hold' the group together at difficult moments. As Ben Knights says, the group needs a 'consistent authorial viewpoint until it learns to accept the inner turbulence' (Knights 1992, p.24).

In her paper discussing James Britton's application of Winnicott's theory to the teaching of writing in schools, Anne Wyatt-Brown suggests that Winnicott's therapeutic methods of detached observation with minimal interference are as applicable in the classroom as they are in the clinic (Wyatt-Brown 1993, p.294). Britton and others have 'argued persuasively for giving children space and time to develop their individual voices and sense of urgency in writing' and that this is best done through a collaborative approach to teaching that assumes 'most [children] have the capacity to learn to express themselves provided that they are allowed to develop their own style' (pp.297–298). What children have to learn in order to be able to do this is, as Winnicott says, how to be alone with their inner worlds, and they will learn this best through 'the experience of being alone in the presence of someone' (Winnicott 1958, p.33):

> When alone in [this sense], and only when alone, the infant is able to do the equivalent of what in an adult would be called relaxing. The infant is able to become unintegrated, to flounder, to be in a state in which there is no orientation, to be able to exist for a time without being either a reactor to an external impingement or an active person with a direction of interest or movement. The stage is set for an id experience. In the course of time there arrives a sensation or an impulse. In this setting the sensation or impulse will feel real and be truly a personal experience (p.34).

As long as infants feel that someone is present, they can feel safe with t*he personal impulse*. The mother – in Winnicott's phrase the *good-enough mother* – is present without making demands. This enables infants, in the course of time, to dispense with the actual presence and to establish an internal environment of their own which provides that same sense of presence.

The effective creative writing tutor, I would suggest, needs to be a 'good enough mother' in the Winnicottian sense, to develop working methods and a relationship with students, which provides both support and guidance, and which acknowledges the difficult task they face of engaging with their inner worlds. This is not to suggest that she should distance herself emotionally from participation in the group. Again, Ben Knights suggests that she will need to be 'open to her own subjectivity' (Knights 1992, p.34) and therefore willing to expose aspects of her own story when occasion demands it. However, because she has such an important role to play as stabiliser in a labile environment, she will need to work towards a balance between openness and distance (see Berman 1994).

I cannot claim that I have always been able to provide the sort of environment I am suggesting here, as learning how to facilitate autobiographically based creative writing courses has been a long and sometimes painful apprenticeship. However, there are certain things which I regard now as crucial. For example, I have found it very helpful at the outset to establish with students the parameters of what the course aims to do, to be quite clear that it is first and foremost about *writing*, but that because the writing exercises involve an engagement with memory and personal experience there is a possibility that they might find themselves exposed to painful or difficult insights, and that if this occurs, there is support available. It is helpful to highlight in particular any work which they might be asked to do around childhood and ask them if they feel uncomfortable writing about early memories. If they do, then it is important to give these students particular support or, if they absolutely do not wish to write about childhood, to suggest other things they can do. In view of the highly personal nature of the work being done, it is also important to agree some ground rules for confidentiality.

Needless to say, I try to familiarise myself with each student's writing, and take a proportion of their work home after each session, to read and make comments on. Whilst the small reading groups are working, I endeavour to sit in on the reading and discussion of at least one piece of writing from each group. Students attending my course are also entitled to a twenty minute one-to-one tutorial with me, which provides an opportunity for finding out about problems and difficulties. If required, counselling or therapeutic back-up is available at the university's Counselling and Psychotherapy Unit.

For the tutor, too, this kind of work involves a considerable degree of openness and self-exposure, and this can sometimes be difficult to handle. I often feel that tutors of creative writing courses should of necessity have supervisory or peer group support, where they can talk through the work they are doing. At the Centre for Continuing Education we have regular tutor group meetings which go some way to providing a forum where problems and difficulties can be shared.

In spite of the difficulties and drawbacks inherent in working on the borderline of education and therapy, I do believe that it is possible to create an environment where students can feel safe to engage with their 'feeling worlds' and to develop ways of expressing them on the page. From the feedback I have had, this approach certainly seems to help students to develop their writing[16] and, in many cases, it seems also to have helped them to increase their knowledge of themselves and to develop a stronger sense of identity. From a different point of view, the course has also helped some students to identify and work through problems of identity which hamper their writing. This is the subject matter of the next chapter.

16   Some 90% of respondents to the questionnaires reported a development in their writing.

CHAPTER 2

Fictionalising Ourselves

Writing and Self-Exposure

Any kind of writing involves self-exposure; we place ourselves and our views not only on the page but 'on the line'. Creative writing, particularly autobiographically based creative writing, is arguably more exposing than, say, academic writing. Because it entails a closer relationship with our inner lives, it is much more likely to reveal unconscious material which we may not feel comfortable to let others see. Students attending my writing course often express the feeling that what has been committed to the page is *a part of themselves*; they talk about 'lying naked on the page' and are understandably sensitive to comments on, or criticisms of, their autobiographical writing. Some people find the sheer prospect of placing themselves on the page frightening and feel paralysed at the thought of the self-exposure involved. The following poem is an eloquent expression of such fears:

Pagefright[1]

Something is stopping me
from writing this poem
about myself.

It's my mother
watching the page
judging my self-indulgence
or not wanting to see

---

[1]   I am grateful to the author, who wishes to remain anonymous, for allowing me to include this unpublished poem.

sadness blotting
the smooth surface.

It's feeling that
Me and I
are such big words
to commit myself to
in proud print.

It's thinking
those words
aren't really
me.

So I'm not going out there
on the page
alone.

I'll just stay here instead.

Placing herself on the page, the author seems to be saying, means relinquish-
ing control of her identity. This is risky; it involves the possibility that the
reader will judge her adversely for her self-indulgence or see the sadness
which she prefers to keep out of sight. Here, it is the mother, as implied
reader, who threatens the self-exposure and makes the writing process anxi-
ety-laden, but it might also represent a confrontation with an antagonistic
part of the author's own psyche which stands in hostile judgement on her. It
is this potential for confrontation with oneself through writing fictional
autobiography, and the therapeutic effect it can have, which concerns me
here.

One of the questions I asked students in the questionnaire was whether
and in what way fictionalising themselves had changed the way they saw
themselves in the present or helped them to discover things about themselves
which they did not know before. Some found that transposing themselves
into fictional characters opened up new dimensions of themselves or
activated less dominant characteristics. One says: 'It…made me verbalise
some of my own characteristics normally disregarded, because I don't understand why I'm like that!' Another found that '…"speaking" through a
character [based on oneself] brings into bold relief thoughts and feelings previously undetected or not addressed'. For some people, the confrontation
with themselves on the page had a positive impact on their self-perception:

'[It] has made me like myself', one says. Another found herself 'to be more positive and resilient than I had thought…'.

For some people, the new knowledge of themselves uncovered by the writing was disturbing or shocking. One says: 'I had no idea that I was still in the process of "beating the self out of myself".' One woman who felt nervous about the prospect of reading out her work to the group, because she was afraid of revealing the 'real me', was taken aback to discover again and again that the fictional characters she created out of herself had emotional difficulties in expressing themselves. 'I was quite shocked', she said, 'that I appear to be so emotionally inept in the pieces I write. It was a vague subconscious knowledge before but this problem I seem to have of expressing how I really feel comes across as a repeated theme.' Engaging with herself in this way helped her to 'open up and engage with other people' and to feel freer to write about her gender identity and 'the many experiences of death and loss throughout my life'.

Fears about how others will see us or the desire to keep hidden aspects of ourselves of which we disapprove can, needless to say, create difficulties with creative writing which might take the form of inhibitions or blocks to the writing process, or lead to the abandoning of the whole enterprise. If, for example, a writer can only tolerate positive representations of herself, she will find it difficult to allow characters or narrators based on herself to have a life of their own, in case they behave in a way which is contrary to her dominant self-image. She will find it difficult to shelve the critical faculty and will retain an undue degree of authorial control over her fictional creations, and this is likely to interfere with the spontaneity of the writing. In Bakhtin's sense, she will be unable to allow the voices of her characters or narrators to have as much authority as the voice of the author, and this will hinder the necessary dialogue between the author and the fictional entities she creates (Bakhtin 1984). However, struggling with the problems involved in creating characters and first-person narrators out of ourselves and trying to understand them can be beneficial in identifying problems of identity and in working them through.

My own experience provides a good example. In the early 1980s I began writing an autobiographical novel called *Stages*. This was a first person account of a period in my life in the 1970s when I was travelling around Australia and the East with a young Austrian man, 'Klaus', whose nomadic way of life and 'outsider' stance towards the organised world I had adopted. I was in my early twenties, had abandoned my haphazard and unhappy attempts at learning, having passed up the opportunity to go to university, and had not found any satisfactions in the secretarial work which I had undertaken after leaving school. I wanted nothing more than to remove myself from the world of work, to lose myself and my inability to find fulfilment in my life, in the vastness of Australia's hinterland. The story was told from the point of view of a 'framework narrator', representing myself at the time of writing, some ten years after the events, when I was back in England, married to a much older man, 'Hugo', and, as I liked to think then, much more mature, self-assured and independent, and certainly free of the problems which had afflicted me in my twenties. Indeed, my conscious intention for the novel was to show how I had managed to overcome the problems of the earlier period of my life and had started doing something constructive and fulfilling.

I took extracts of the developing novel to a creative writing class and showed them to the tutor. She was quite complimentary, but noted that there were 'two voices in the narrative'. This was greatly perturbing. Whilst I thought I had one narrator telling the story of the past from the perspective of the present, in fact I had two quite different first-person narrators representing myself at different points in my life, and this made the narrative inconsistent and confusing. I worked hard to integrate the two voices on the page, but without success. After much struggle, I divided the novel into two separate narratives, so that I had a first-person past-tense narrative from the point of view of my 1970s narrator, and first-person present-tense diary entries from the point of view of my 1980s narrator. When, after a long and painful five years, the novel was completed, it was over 500 pages in length and unpublishable.

It was some time later that I realised that the problem with the novel stemmed from the fact that the 1980s narrator, i.e. myself at the time of writing, had clearly *not* moved on, in terms of her independence and ability to fulfil herself. She was still as dependent as she had been in the 1970s; in the same way that she had attached herself to Klaus and taken on his identity and his 'life solution'[2], she had now taken on Hugo's identity and was trying to live through him. Clearly, there were implications here for my own sense of identity at the time of writing which I did not want to see. I had had to keep strict control over my 'framework narrator' in order to ensure that she corre-

---

2   This is a term used by Karen Horney which I discuss below.

sponded to the way I saw myself in the present. In other words, I was imposing an identity on her which was at odds with the way she would have been if I had been able to 'shelve the critical faculty' and give her a spontaneous life of her own. Thus, there was a conflict between the rhetoric of the novel and my 'framework narrator', such that the novel proved extremely difficult to write; one could perhaps describe it as trying to drive a car with the handbrake on[3]. However, this lengthy writing apprenticeship was not without its positive side. Not only did it help me to develop my writing, but confronting myself on the page, taking serious account of the new knowledge of myself which it provided, enabled me, in conjunction with a period of psychotherapy, to make significant changes in myself and in my life, to develop a more solid sense of my own identity and to find fulfilment through my own efforts, rather than living through the achievements of a partner.

Some of the students I interviewed for my research manifested similar problems of identity which were interfering with their fiction writing, and in this chapter I discuss two such examples. Sarah's story concerns her difficulties of using herself as a first person narrator in her autobiographically based novel. Jane's story demonstrates the difficulties of drawing on her own psychological material as a basis for fictional characters. Like me, both of these women found fictionalising themselves helpful in developing their writing, as well as in their lives beyond the writing. With their permission, I discuss their stories from the point of view of the theory of Karen Horney.

Using Oneself as a First-person Narrator – Sarah's Story

Sarah is a senior social worker, single and in her early fifties. She attended the Certificate in Creative Writing with the intention of writing a novel based on a period of her past in Greece, of which she had recently been reminded after revisiting the country. She had already started thinking about the project a year before the course began and she discusses this in her essay written at the conclusion of the first term:

> I set myself the task of writing a short story which would indicate a style and possible structure to the piece. I already knew the episode I would write about, but I also wanted to show the emotions, sensations

3   Re the conflict between rhetoric and character in fiction, see pages 160–165.

and feelings of that particular moment, as well as a sense of the place as I remembered it[4].

Whilst on a painting course in Cornwall, she took time out from the required tasks and used a free-association technique to focus on the piece she wanted to write. The result was several pages of text which she called 'Epitaph'.

Soon after Sarah joined the course she gave me 'Epitaph' to read. The piece was narrated in the first person by a middle-aged woman on holiday in Greece, remembering the time she spent there many years earlier and her affair with a Greek man. The writing was visually strong but the experimental approach used, mingling past and present in a self-consciously filmic style, was only partly successful. My main criticism, however, which I conveyed to Sarah in a tutorial, was that, whilst the piece was written in the first person, it did not reveal very much at all about the narrator, either in the present or in the past, and that this made the text vague and confusing. Despite Sarah's wish to 'show the emotions, sensations and feelings of that particular moment', there was clearly a problem for her in engaging emotionally with her narrator, who was to serve as a vehicle for *her own* feelings. A comment in her essay is particularly relevant to this problem:

> When I registered for the Certificate, I had not thought whether [the subject matter] might be in any way relevant to the project I had set myself. I had not even considered that what I wanted to write was autobiography – for me it was a 'story' and I wasn't too sure where it would take me.

From the outset the autobiographical exercises brought Sarah face to face with the difficulties of putting herself into her writing. This began already with the 'early memory' exercise. Sarah found that the extract from Virginia Woolf, in which the author is recalling her earliest memories of being with her mother, evoked memories of her own mother, but she was reluctant to start writing 'because the first ideas that came were sad and held an element of pathos – the timing was close to the anniversary of my mother's death'. During the week between the sessions, however, she was 'inspired by a drive home one afternoon along a lane in the autumn dusk,' which called to mind similar walks she had taken with her mother and the intimacy between them.

4   Unless otherwise stated, quotations are from Sarah's essays written for the Certificate in Creative Writing and two interviews I conducted with her.

The piece she subsequently wrote, 'Bramble Jelly', recalls how she and her mother used to make jam together:

> My mother was a creative jam-maker. I see her standing over a bubbling, spattering, stained pressure cooker, stirring the deeply coloured sticky mass with one hand while pushing back her hair from her forehead with the other... She made many kinds of jam – strawberry which was always brown, never red; strawberry and gooseberry, chewy with their tangy skins; blackcurrant thick and pippy; redcurrant jelly glowing like a ruby; rhubarb and ginger, brown and indistinguishable from the strawberry; raspberry with the seeds showing through the glass. The one I liked best was blackberry jelly. Which she didn't make unless I made a big fuss, which usually included tears and 'You don't love me!'...

> The ritual of blackberrying... My mother in wide brown slacks and a beige rubbery waisted anorak, musty and earthy. Her gardening jacket...

> We clamber and push into the bushes. Brambles tear at my hands and face. I rub away the blood with my sleeve. Prickles snag at the stitches of the balaclava. None of this bothers me. Content with my mother, reaching and pulling and picking the fruit and seeing the baskets fill. Mouth and fingers stained red and purple (extracts from 'Bramble Jelly').

In spite of its 'prickly' connotations, this is a largely positive piece of prose and the writing of it made Sarah feel warm and close to her mother. In her essay she likens the experience of drawing on childhood memories for her writing to the experience of attempting to draw a still life for the first time, whilst on the painting course in Cornwall. Confronted by 'three crumpled and rotting apples', she was extremely nervous, feeling that she just could not draw at all. But she plucked up courage:

> I drew their outline with chalk on black paper – three misshapen interlocked balls. Clammy palmed, I sat back, looked and panicked. It took great effort not to get up and walk away. Eventually, I used the tip of one sweaty finger to smudge the edge of one of the outlines. It felt good, and so I continued to smudge and obliterate the edges. I chalked and charcoaled and smudged, using not only my fingers, but the fleshy side of my palm. I began to enjoy and like what I was creating. It was a moment of great liberation.

Similarly, from the experience of writing about her mother in 'Bramble Jelly', Sarah learned that 'autobiographical experience can be felt in many ways, all it takes is the courage to start to blur the edges'. Sarah had begun to allow her perhaps ambivalent and painful feelings about her past to express themselves in her creative writing and this process continued into the next session.

As with the 'early memory' exercise, Sarah found the exercise using photographs difficult and resolved not to take it seriously:

> Rather than rummage in boxes looking for photographs, I chose to bring to the group an album from a period of my childhood when I lived in Egypt with my parents. I had always seen these as a kind of historical record – about Egypt rather than about me.

However, when it came to choosing a photograph from which to write, Sarah chose one of her alone and 'found it a painful and emotional discovery. It was as if I had rediscovered someone I had never really known'. Sarah related this experience to the writing of 'Epitaph' and found it illuminating:

> Suddenly I realised that although I was writing about someone else [the story of the Greek man], I was also writing about ME! I began to reflect on who I was at the time I was writing about, and to realise that maybe this was as interesting as the story about M.

The experience of focusing on herself was taken a step further through the 'melody for two voices' exercise. For the first part of this exercise, Sarah wrote in the third person about leading a team meeting at work. The piece describes how the team leader reacts to each member of the team as they take their places in the circle:

> She watches as they enter and observes that they sit in more or less the same place, arrive at more or less the same time and each demands more or less the same amount of her attention. She steels herself to meet those demands, a mental and physical tightening of the shoulder-blades, a concerned smile tight across her lips. She turns from one to the other and listens as they gain her attention through the general chat.

For each of the different personalities within the team she has a different way of reacting: warm smiles for the willing and good-natured, a somewhat frozen smile for the ones whose intellect and astuteness sometimes 'impedes the game she plays of forcing through issues, of inspiring the team to heights of commitment beyond those they feel themselves'. Towards 'the one who works to another agenda, who undermines her authority and manipulates the game she plays to turn it to his own ends', she is cold, unsmiling, allowing the contempt she feels towards him to manifest itself. The power she wields over these members of her staff is channelled primarily through this eye contact: 'Her eyes move round the circle. She wonders if, when they see her observe them, they know or expect the look she gives them.' She does not need to be liked; she wants to be obeyed. And in particular by the man who tries to manipulate her. She feels the desire to crush and destroy, but not for its own sake, '…only so that she can reconstruct. Not to destroy, but to win!', to motivate the team, to nurture the client group they serve (extracts from 'Leading a Team Meeting').

For the second part of the exercise, Sarah took her self-character – the team leader – out of the team meeting and placed her in a circus environment. She was influenced in her choice of setting by a lithograph of a circus scene which hangs in the room where she was writing. In 'The Circus' the team leader becomes the mistress of ceremonies whose role is to control the performers in the ring. The manipulative man from 'Leading a Team Meeting' is here transformed into the circus ringmaster and it is significant that before the mistress of ceremonies can set the acrobats in motion, she has to disempower the ringmaster:

> 'Allez hoop!' I cry and strike the tambourine. I stamp my foot. 'Allez hoop! Allez hoop!' Shafts of light crackle from my eyes and pierce the inverted black shiny triangle of the Ringmaster's back. Unseen by him who only sees the irridescence of my eyes, I look at him through the red light of contempt. 'Allez hoop! Allez hoop!' I shake the tambourine and the metal disc fringes jangle. Jingle jangle! Jagger jangle! I watch the Ringmaster raise his arms – he turns a full circle, bowing to the south, to the west, to the north, to the east. He hesitates before he turns and looks at me. Jigger Jangle! Jagger Jangle! The fingers flutter, the arms slowly drop. His heart is penetrated by the missile lights he has let through. He folds at the point of the triangle, head curling towards the ground of silver glitter, raked into the patterns of a Japanese Zen garden. The garden of nothingness. He becomes a puppet with no strings, head swaying suspended above the shimmering floor.

Having, by means of her magic powers, the 'shafts of light' crackling from her eyes, reduced him to a puppet, the mistress of ceremonies can turn her attention to the performance and the crucial task of motivating the acrobats:

The tension releases from my shoulders cooled by the damp petals of the chrysanthemum garland, and I give birth to the two doves who flutter into the smoke, turning pink, then green. Jingle tingle tinkle go my metal fringes. A soft sirocco combines the glitter and smoke into a shimmering fog. From the coloured mists above me my acrobats descend, some argent, some gilded. I twist on my tiny feet and send up an arc of silver glitter as I turn towards each figure and curtsy. The spotlight shows each one in turn. In a second I see and send out lights. Those receiving the 21 carat gold lights raise their heads and turn and twirl in the air. The silver light I send spurs them into excesses of daring accompanied by a soft, sybbilant intake of breath from the audience. A moment of hesitation before I give a purple glance which stills all movement. The red lights I send out filter through the mist and are felt in the heart. The spotlight exposes the shudder of a hand released for protection. A moment of suspension, then I watch as they drop into a cloud of glitter or scramble upwards into the obliterating darkness. I finish my pirouette of curtseys by spinning a tornado of glitter. The audience bursts into cheers. The acrobats slither to the ground... (extracts from 'The Circus').

Again, the power is all in the eyes, which magically send out laser-like rays of silver and gold, red and purple, to spur the acrobats to 'excesses of daring'.

Whilst the performance has been underway, the defeated ringmaster has been crawling on the ground, choking in the 'sandstorm of glitter'. As the mistress of ceremonies takes her final bow, he is raised up to stand beside her, 'arms hanging lifeless', and slowly removes his tophat, from which 'one white dove flaps upwards'. Whilst defeated, he is not destroyed, the dove symbolising, perhaps, his ultimate acceptance of his role as an integral part of the whole performance rather than as its controller.

In writing 'The Circus' Sarah isolated one particular characteristic of the third-person narrator of 'Leading a Team Meeting' and transposed it into the realms of fantasy or magical realism, where physical attributes take on super-natural dimensions. The strength of the image created clearly reflects the importance, for the writer, of this part of her personality. In the first of the two recorded interviews with her some months after these pieces were written, she spoke about how she felt when writing them:

I did a freewriting exercise and I don't think I...really knew what I was going to write about, but I wrote about the staff meeting and

I…saw…myself as at the centre of a circle…I mean it's happened again today, because we had a staff meeting…I see this semi-circle of people whose attention is on me and…I am like…[Sarah points to the lithograph of the circus scene on the wall]…I mean I know I'm bossy and authoritarian, but I do *know* it, I can accept that could be okay and [means that I'm] good at organising, but it can also be oppressive and all those kinds of things as well.

Sarah clearly felt rather uncomfortable with this self knowledge, but in trying to understand it she found that it also had its positive side:

I felt quite liberated, I…laughed about it…. Because I thought, well I *am* manipulative and I know it. I don't know whether anybody else knows it, but I do play these games and…to…acknowledge it, I almost felt like celebrating it.

What the writing of these pieces seems to have done then is to bring into focus for Sarah an aspect of her personality – the bossy, authoritarian, manipulative side of herself – of which she was aware, but rather critical, even disapproving. But now, bringing it out and dramatising it in this way, acknowledging it to herself, as well as to an audience, she 'felt like celebrating it'. It was 'another way of looking at me', of finding out who she was. And, after all, this side of her personality did have a positive role in her life – it enabled her to be a good, strong organiser and leader.

These insights led Sarah to look more carefully at who she had been in the past, in particular who she was in the photograph of herself as a child:

The really interesting thing about the photograph was that I looked very strong…as if I was kind of fronting up and saying: 'here I am, you can try to beat me, but you know I'm pretty strong'. And I suppose…part of my problematic relationship with my mother was [about] control, which is why I am reasonably aware of my own tendency to do it. And I think a lot of it was me trying to exert my own personality and character as against this control.

I asked her whether it had surprised her, noticing the 'fronting up' in the picture.

Yes, it was shocking. It was a real shock… I felt very sad at first and I felt like crying, because I thought: Where did this person go? What happened to this person? How did I survive and did I survive? And is that…what I was doing then in order to exert my own identity against a strong controlling person? And then afterwards I think it…remained with me for a very long time and then I suppose it still remains with me, and I suppose then I began to feel well I did survive and here I am, the ringmaster [sic]. I'm doing it, I know I'm doing it. And there's a game in it.

What Sarah seems to be saying here is that, in order to cope as a child and to protect her vulnerable self, she had to construct a tough, unemotional front. As she grew into an adult, this front developed into a life strategy of dominance and control, in which vulnerability did not have a place. Therefore, an important part of herself, connected with the gentler emotions, became repressed and unavailable to her.

Sarah's rediscovery of this lost part of herself seems to have enabled her to be much freer in the subsequent writing of her novel about the relationship with M. Whilst, as she says, 'I am controlling the story at the moment', she has also 'tried hard to allow myself to be vulnerable'.

Looking at the new material, I feel that it is markedly different from the earlier drafts. The inclination to 'fog up' the narrative with unrealised experimental techniques has disappeared. Instead the first-person narrative voice has become clear and dominant. The piece of work submitted for assessment at the end of the second term intended as an introductory first chapter to the proposed novel, is a first-person account of the narrator's journey by train from England to Greece. It conveys, through a vivid evocation of place and encounter with fellow travellers, a strong sense of the narrator's youthful vulnerability, naïveté and anxious anticipation of the adventure before her. The piece submitted for assessment at the end of the third term is a deeply moving account of the narrator's three-week stay with M on a Greek island where he is involved in the making of a film. The intensity of the narrator's feelings for M reverberate through the text, as does the pain of the realisation that the relationship cannot last. Here the writing is certainly closer to Sarah's stated aims of 'showing the emotions, sensations and feelings of that particular moment'. This is because, as Sarah puts it, whereas before, 'I had real difficulty in forefronting myself in any kind of way in [the story]', now a sense of who '[I am] is coming through'.

Some eight months after the first interview with Sarah, I conducted a second. For most of the interview she talked about the writing and her ups and downs in the small writing group which she had joined after the course ended. In spite of some harsh criticism from members of the group of recently written sections of the novel and a consequent 'slough of despond' during which she had stopped writing, she had found her confidence again and was continuing to develop the novel. A number of further coincidences, such as reading a recent novel set in Greece during the period she was there and seeing a film by the director with whom M had worked and hearing someone refer to M by name, had given her additional impetus.

Just before the end of the interview, Sarah looked at her notes to see if there was anything she had forgotten and started talking about 'Leading a Team Meeting' and its relation to her current situation at work:

> …I was quite interested in that, because the [junior colleague] that was causing me all the grief went, and [a new person was appointed in] September, and that's been a really really painful experience. It was not easy.

This was the first time Sarah had talked specifically about the character in 'Leading a Team Meeting' for whom the narrator 'has contempt' and who is subsequently, in 'The Circus', transposed into the ringmaster who is defeated by the mistress of ceremonies. I asked her what it was that she had not found easy about the appointment of the new person:

> Initially…I got very depressed and very stressed about [the relationship] and wondered whether that was because I had had an uneasy relationship with the previous [postholder] and now was having an uneasy relationship with the present one, and the common factor was me. So I went through quite a bad time about that. But listening to the tape…things have moved forward a bit recently, and so I felt that…writing about the staff meeting and talking about it on the tape and thinking about it actually highlighted for me that I was controlling. And what the new person has done is subverted that…subverted my control and has resisted it.

Sarah went on to explain that the new colleague, who this time was a woman, had undermined Sarah's habitual strategy of controlling the work situation, which had been in effect prior to her arrival. As a result, the staff team had rearranged its whole way of working. A management group had been formed in which 'we are all beginning to share those decisions and take a part in that decision making'. This meant that Sarah had had to relinquish some of her power at work.

When talking about her new colleague, Sarah placed her in the fictional setting of 'The Circus'. Whereas her male colleague had been seen as the ringmaster:

> I thought maybe [the new female colleague] was a clown and maybe one of those clowns who can be quite cruel and…empties a bucket of frozen fish over your head or something like that. And that's been quite a painful thing for me, but I think I would perhaps not have been able to handle it or take on what was being said to me if I hadn't written that piece.

Thus, the writing had allowed Sarah to explore, using the metaphor of the circus, a difficult aspect of her working life. By changing the context, framing it in a playful way, she had found it easier to confront her own contribution to the difficulties. In this sense the writing had a dual character:

> …I allowed myself…to be placed in a position…where I…could be seen as a funny character…but it could also be seen as, you know, quite dangerous…a powerful position. And so there was this dual thing: there was the playing with the characters and making of them what I wanted and the…oppression of the ringmaster.

She also recognised that being controlling was not only damaging to others, but 'quite damaging to me as well' and that maybe 'this is [not] such a good place to be'. It affected the way she wrote fiction: '[holding] control over myself in the writing of the M piece, by not putting myself in it and then perhaps putting myself [in] in a particular way'. Whilst, in the piece about the island, she had allowed herself to be present in the text in a more vulnerable way, she had then felt threatened and had returned to 'control mode'. Perhaps this was why the writing group had reacted unfavourably to the later pieces: because she was not in them, they did not say very much to other people. But the process of change at work had made her feel 'a bit more liberated' and the writing had also loosened up again.

Sarah's main problem with her writing, then, was that she had difficulties putting herself spontaneously into the text. It is significant that, when she began the course, she did not think of the novel she wanted to write as autobiographical. It was simply a story about M. It was only at the end of the first term that she began to realise that what she was doing was writing fictional autobiography and that she was trying to formulate a more compelling picture of herself. Up to that time she had been in the habit of keeping a very tight control on the way she appeared on the page. Where her presence was necessary, she either left herself vague, as she did with the narrator of the story about M, or she put herself into the text in retrospect, when she was sure that the picture she was creating was acceptable to her: 'First I write the piece', she says, 'then I stuff myself into it.' This seems to indicate not just a fear of revealing herself to others, but of revealing herself to herself, of seeing clearly an aspect of herself of which she disapproves. Transposing herself and an aspect of her professional life into a metaphor subverted Sarah's customary control: by allowing herself to be playful in the writing of 'The Circus', she unwittingly overcame the inner restraints which normally kept out of full awareness the consequences, both for herself and for others, of her dominant way of being.

Karen Horney's Theory of Inner Conflicts

In trying to understand Sarah's problems with putting her feelings into her writing, I have found particularly helpful the psychodynamic theory of Karen Horney. As Horney's work is not well known as a whole in Britain, it will be useful to provide a summary here.

Karen Horney (1885–1952) was a second generation Freudian who left her native Germany in the early 1930s and made her career in America, first in Chicago under Franz Alexander, then as a member of the New York Psychoanalytic Institute. She subsequently set up her own institute in New York, which continues to operate. She is the author of five major books (Horney 1937, 1939a, 1942, 1946, 1951) and many separately published papers. Her views went through several significant changes during her lifetime. She is best known for her early papers on the psychology of women (Horney 1967), which were the first to take serious issue with Freud's views of female sexuality (Garrison 1981, p.673). However, she quickly moved away from her feminist concerns to focus on interpersonal factors in the formation of personality[5], and in particular on the role of social and cultural factors (Horney 1937). The late phase of her work, which Bernard Paris calls her 'mature theory' (Paris 1994), concentrates on both interpersonal and intrapsychic factors in personality disorder (Horney 1951).

Fundamental to Horney's understanding of personal development is that there is a 'real self'. She was the first psychoanalytic thinker to use this term

5   Paris (1994, pp.92–96, 232–238) discusses possible reasons for this.

(Horney 1939b, p.130), and it is this more than any other aspect of her work which makes her theory problematical in the postmodern world. 'Real self' is seen as an outmoded essentialist notion, implying a fixed unitary substance which will 'unfold in definite, innate stages towards its "natural end" or purpose (adult maturity/health)' (Flax 1993, p.99). This, however, is to misunderstand Horney's idea of the real self. Whilst there are certainly moments in Horney's writings when it does sound like an essentialist notion, she stresses that the real self is not a fixed entity but a set of 'intrinsic potentialities', the '"original" force toward individual growth and fulfilment', a 'possible self', felt rather than seen (Horney 1951, pp.17 and 158). Whilst these 'intrinsic potentialities' are the consequence of our genetic make-up, they can only be actualised through interpersonal relationships in the outside world. Thus, the way people's potentialities develop is very much dependent on the way they interact with the social and cultural environment, and the dominant narratives therein. The 'real self', then, on Horney's view, is both innate and the product of an individual's experience within a particular social world.

Horney does not discuss the notion of the 'real self' in great detail in her writings[6]; her main focus is on understanding the psychic processes which ensue when a person loses touch with the 'real self' or becomes *self-alienated* (Horney 1951, p.13). Neurosis[7], for Horney, is the consequence, in the first instance, of difficult interpersonal relations in childhood. Her view is that healthy psychological development requires an environment in which the child receives love, respect and acceptance of its own individuality, and thus develops a feeling of safety and belonging. In such conditions of good object relating, the child will be able to develop its potentialities, although, as I have said, the environment will play a significant role in determining which potentialities develop and the form they take. In the absence of such conditions, the child is likely to become anxious and feel 'isolated and helpless in a potentially hostile world' (Horney 1946, p.41). This *basic anxiety* causes the child to abandon its innate drive to develop its potential and to find 'ways to

6   Christopher Bollas's elaboration of Winnicott's notion of the 'true self' provides a
     useful extension of Horney's notion of the 'real self' (see Bollas 1987 and 1989).
7   Horney's definition of neurosis changed and developed over time, along with her
     views as a whole. The major features of neurosis which she identifies are basic anxiety
     and alienation from self, leading to disturbances in relations with self and others, in
     particular 'a certain rigidity in reaction and a discrepancy between potentialities and
     accomplishments' (Horney 1937, p.22).

cope with this menacing world' (p.42). Echoing the emergency reaction of fight, flight and submission in animal behaviour, Horney suggests that the child will move *against people* and become hostile, *away from people* and become detached, or *toward people* and become dependent (p.42). Social and cultural factors will play a significant role here in determining the choice of one defence over another, so that girls will tend to move towards people and overvalue love, whilst boys will tend to move against people and overvalue power.

Unless favourable life circumstances intervene, by the time the child has become an adult these defensive childhood strategies will develop into what Horney calls *life solutions*. She identifies three main kinds, which she regards as 'directions of development' rather than clear-cut 'types': the *expansive*, the *resigned* and the *self-effacing* solutions, with expansiveness being divided into the *narcissistic*, the *perfectionistic* and the *arrogant-vindictive* solutions (pp.187–290). Each of these solutions involves what Paris calls a 'bargain with fate' (1991a), a kind of devil's pact, according to which the solution is adhered to rigidly in exchange for certain benefits. For example, a woman who adopts the self-effacing solution will try to gain safety, love and esteem through dependency, humility and self-sacrificing 'goodness'; her 'bargain' will run: 'If I am helpful and submissive and do not seek my own gain or glory, I will be treated well by fate and other people'[8]. The adoption of a single life solution, such as self-effacement, can bring about a certain freedom from the inner conflicts resulting from alienation from self, and this can provide a sense of identity and a degree of security. However, as all three life solutions tend to be present simultaneously, this apparent stability is illusory, for the other solutions which have been repressed into the unconscious simply generate new conflicts, which in turn require further remedies.

Horney regards this *intrapsychic* development, originally set in motion by *interpersonal* difficulties in childhood, as a crucial stage in the consolidation and integration of the chosen life solution, and it forms the core of her later work. At the heart of this development lies what she calls the *search for glory* (Horney 1951, pp.17–39). Because a person has moved away from the centre

---

8   Horney's life solutions can usefully be thought of as self-concepts which contain a narrative, including a powerful narrative of 'shoulds' which determines how a person *should* behave, what she *should* be doing with her life, what sort of relationships she *should* be engaging in, etc.

of himself[9], has become self-alienated, his 'inner strength and coherence' are severely impaired and he cannot develop self-confidence (p.20). He therefore feels inferior to other people and needs a means of lifting himself above them. He does this through imagination, by creating what Horney calls an *idealised image* of himself (p.22). The elements which go to make up the idealised image are not arbitrary: they derive from 'the materials of his own special experiences, his earlier fantasies, his particular needs, and also his given faculties' (p.22), and they will be strongly influenced by his chosen solution. For example, a woman who adopts the self-effacing solution may create an idealised image of herself as the perfect wife and mother; in her behaviour she will try to please others and to be exquisitely sensitive to their needs, and will avoid expressing direct hostility.

The idealised image is a very powerful tool in the search for glory. It can, even if sporadically and unreliably, lift a person above the sense of inferiority which results from alienation from self. Therefore, the drive to realise this image in reality, to become the *idealised self*, is very strong. The idealised image generates what Horney calls the *pride system* (p.111), a series of mechanisms whose function it is to bludgeon the person to achieve the impossible demands of the idealised image. First, it gives rise to intense pride in the characteristics of the idealised image, and this *neurotic pride* (pp.86–109) justifies the need to make *neurotic claims* on others. *Neurotic claims* (pp.40–63) are wishes or needs turned outwards; they 'assume a right, a title' to special treatment by other people, by institutions and by life in general, a title 'which in reality does not exist' (p.42), but which a person feels is due to him by virtue of his superior status. Internally, there is a similar coercive regime: what Horney calls *shoulds* (pp.64–85) are a constant battery of inner dictates which demand that a person *should* become the supreme being of his imagination, with utter disregard for 'what he can feel or do as he is at present' (p.67).

Failure to live up to the inner dictates leads to an inner turning against oneself or, as Horney calls it, the forming of the idealised self's counterpart, the *despised self*, and this will now become the target of anger. The resulting self-hate and self-contempt lead to self-belittling and self-frustrating mechanisms, and in extreme cases to self-destructiveness, of gross or subtle kinds (pp.110–154).

9   Horney uses the male pronoun throughout her books, except when discussing specific case studies.

The whole picture is made even more complex by the simultaneous existence of different life solutions, so that not only are there conflicts within each individual life solution between idealised and despised selves, but also conflicts between solutions. For example, a woman who is predominantly self-effacing will be driven to be subservient to others and will find it almost impossible to be expansive. She will thus tend to avoid any situations which involve assertiveness or competitiveness. However, if she also has a repressed expansive solution, she will be driven in the opposite direction to exercise power and control over others, and to excel in everything she does. This internal tug-of-war between opposing aspects of herself will result in a situation where whatever she does is wrong and she will be endlessly tormented. A person caught up in such a conflict may well move instinctively towards the detached solution which, Horney says, often serves to keep the conflict between self-effacement and expansiveness out of awareness. The task of therapy, for Horney, is to dismantle this complex intrapsychic development and to re-establish contact with the real self, thus setting healthy development in motion again[10].

Sarah's Story from the Horneyan Point of View

One of the criticisms which is levelled against Horney's theory is that the division into the self-effacing, expansive and detached solutions is reductive, that in the real world people do not correspond to types in this rigid way. Horney herself was aware that such a neat classification could be misleading and in her last book she was at pains to point out the dangers of seeing her three solutions as hard and fast categories. Her resort to a typology seems rather to have been an heuristic device, which would provide 'a means of looking at personalities from certain vantage points' (Horney 1951, p.191)[11]. She is aware that:

> …although people tending towards the same main solution have
> characteristic similarities they may differ widely with regard to the
> level of human qualities, gifts, or achievements involved. Moreover,
> what we regard as 'types' are actually cross-sections of personalities in

10   See Paris 1994, Part V, for a full account of Horney's mature theory.

11   As Dentith (1995, p.46) says of Bakhtin's typologies: '…their value…lies not in the detailed application of the categories he produces so much as in recognising the principles that underlie them.' This applies to Horney's too.

which the neurotic process has led to rather extreme developments with pronounced characteristics. But there is always an indeterminate range of intermediate structures deriding any precise classification (p.191).

Thus she prefers to speak of these 'solutions' as 'directions of development' rather than types, and in my discussion of case studies I would not wish to suggest that individuals can be understood wholly by reference to a Horneyan schema. However, certain observable characteristics and their consequences seem to be intelligible from the Horneyan point of view, and it may be useful to see what this theory has to tell us about them. In looking at the case of Sarah I want to consider the effects of expansiveness as a single solution to the problems of inner conflict.

Horney identifies three primary manifestations of the expansive solution. These are characterised by (a) narcissistic tendencies, (b) perfectionistic tendencies, and (c) arrogant-vindictive tendencies. Whilst there are important differences between these three manifestations, all of them 'aim at mastering life' (Horney 1951, p.212), and 'the individual prevailingly identifies himself with his glorified self' (p.191).

People who tend towards the 'arrogant-vindictive' solution are driven by a need for triumph over others, which makes them 'extremely competitive' (pp.197-198). They tend to exploit others and to frustrate their needs, and feel justified in this behaviour because they see life as a 'struggle of all against all' (p.200). In particular they justify their behaviour by reference to past hurts for which they are seeking retribution (p.201). They tend not to form close relationships, because gentle feelings have largely been repressed, and they tend to become independent and self-sufficient (p.204). Like all Horney's life solutions, this one carries with it large quantities of self-hate which are kept at bay by externalisation (p.208). This way of being has come about as a result of 'a hardening process' in early development, which was necessary in order 'to protect the child against the actions and attitudes of others'. This has resulted in the 'choking off of tender feelings' (p.210). This 'hardening of feelings, originally a necessity for survival, allows for an unhampered growth of the drive for a triumphant mastery of life' (p.203).

This description of development seems to be highly congruent with Sarah's account of her relationship with her mother. This was a difficult relationship: her mother was a domineering person and, as a child, Sarah had to erect a tough façade in order to protect herself from being overwhelmed. She calls this façade a 'front' and seeing this 'front' in the photo of herself as a young girl is upsetting. 'It is as if I was fronting up and saying: "Here I am, you can try to beat me but you know I'm pretty strong"'. In retrospect this front looks and feels false to her; she recognises that it is a defence and that underneath it there is a vulnerable child. She regrets the loss of the child, but sees that the 'fronting up' was necessary: '...that was what I was doing then in order to...exert my own identity against quite a strong controlling person'. As she grew into an adult, the front remained and became her dominant way of being: 'And then afterwards I think it kind of remained with me for a very long time, and then I suppose it still remains with me, and I suppose that then I began to feel, well, I did survive and here I am, the ringmaster [sic]. I'm doing it, I know I'm doing it. And there's a game in it.'

It is interesting, in terms of understanding Sarah's expansiveness, that she refers to herself here as the ringmaster when in fact her character role in 'The Circus' was that of mistress of ceremonies. The guidelines for the 'melody for two voices' exercise suggest that the self-character developed in the first stage should, in the second, be the first-person narrator of someone else's story in which the self-character is a player, but not the main player. Of course students are free to modify these guidelines, but it seems significant that in Sarah's story there is a considerable degree of confusion between the roles of ringmaster and mistress of ceremonies. Surely, in a real circus environment, it would not be usual for two people to be simultaneously in charge of a performance in the way Sarah suggests. A ringmaster is normally in overall charge of what goes on in a circus ring and I am assuming that this is the case here. The mistress of ceremonies, as portrayed, seems to be the lead figure in the particular event described and is therefore subordinate to the overall responsibility of the ringmaster. If the ringmaster represents Sarah's junior male colleague at work, in the transposition into the fictional story he has been elevated from a subordinate to first-in-command. And it is this position that the mistress of ceremonies clearly resents; she seeks to usurp the ringmaster's position, to gain power over him, even humiliate him, which indeed, by the end of the piece, she succeeds in doing.

Thus, metaphorically, Sarah has elevated a dominating male in her environment into an oppressor whom she has to defeat by usurping his power; in other words, in order to survive she has to *become* him. It is not surprising, therefore, that when talking about 'The Circus', Sarah habitually confuses the ringmaster and the mistress of ceremonies, and her identification with them. Sometimes she refers to herself as the ringmaster, sometimes as the *master* of ceremonies. Another time she cannot remember which one of them is supposed to represent herself. For Sarah, being in a powerful position seems to involve taking on a male identity.

The conflating of power with a male identity has echoes in Sarah's relationships with men from her childhood on. As a young girl she became fixated by pictures of Stalin, about whom she had sexual fantasies: 'I can never look at pictures of him with his hat and his moustache without sort of reliving this feeling.' She wonders whether he replaced her father in her imagination, as her father was 'quite absent' in her childhood. Stalin, of course, was an expansive personality *par excellence*, as the Horneyan biography of him by Robert Tucker shows (Tucker 1973 and 1990).

M, too, is represented in Sarah's novel as a powerful, idealised male. 'I think Epitaph…gave M a kind of mystical quality, that he was this kind of key figure in it…an adored figure'. This idealising of M was not something Sarah was aware of in her writing until it was pointed out to her by one of the other members of her writing group. Commenting on some sketches of M which Sarah had written in preparation for the novel, one of the male members of the group said that he wished he had had a girlfriend like the character in Sarah's novel, because her adoration and hero-worship must have made M feel invincible. The extent to which this had revealed itself in the writing without Sarah being aware of it: 'was almost a shock to me – because he [the group member] had understood something that I had never understood myself – I'd had to be told it'.

The group member also added that he could not believe that this representation was autobiographical because 'someone who, in the present, appears to be so much in control, could not possibly have put herself in that position in the past'. Indeed, the disparity, in Sarah's representations, between the power-hungry mistress of ceremonies and the narrator of the sketches of M is striking. Here is an extract from the latter. The narrator has just asked M the meaning of a particular Greek word:

> He smiled and said nothing. He stepped out into the road and hailed a taxi. He leant forward and rested his arm on the back of the driver's seat. Something was discussed at length and I forgot my question and stared out at the wide streets and frantic traffic. I was still learning the language and the place – looking for contexts. He took my hand, and rubbed my fingers and I rested against him. It didn't matter not to have an answer. It didn't matter not to know where I was going.

The taxi driver continued to talk. As he drove he turned his head and offered opinions to which M nodded and gave guttural assent or just tutted a negative. Like listening to a bedtime story. I relaxed to the rhythm and snuggled into his softness ('Mallaccas!').

As this example shows, once Sarah starts putting herself and her feelings more spontaneously into the story of M, she portrays herself as an extremely vulnerable and dependent young woman, completely at the mercy of the older and much more experienced person, self-effacing and powerless. As with the ringmaster in 'The Circus', in the novel she elevates M into a position of great power; she feels that 'I have to be sure the reader actually understands that this person was a really important person or a great person or great thinker or artist or whatever'. The novel is written:

> ...out of some kind of respect for him – appreciation. Yes, whatever the relationship was and whatever the reader might understand from the relationship between us, and whether it was exploitative, or whether I was into hero-worship, that was the way I was...what I learnt from him is now part of me and has given me a political perspective, some kind of understanding of what it is to be oppressed...

'Exploitation', 'hero-worship', 'oppression' – there is a sense here of an either/or: either you are weak and vulnerable and therefore liable to be oppressed, or you are the oppressor. The logical conclusion from this is that the only way to protect yourself from being oppressed is to become the oppressor. And in Sarah's life she is one or the other: as a child she is oppressed by her mother; as a young girl she longs for Stalin, the great oppressor of the Russian people; as an adult she oppresses others with her power. Even M, who taught her so much, is recognised as a possible oppressor, in the use of the word 'exploitation'. Opening herself up to someone much more powerful than herself, being wholly vulnerable, was, Sarah learned to her cost, a dangerous thing. That relationship wounded her considerably. She says that after it ended – as a naive young woman it took a considerable time for her to realise that M was not going to leave his wife and marry her – she was in a very bad state, under medication and almost on the point of physical and emotional collapse. Undoubtedly this experience would have reinforced Sarah's 'front': in order to protect herself from further damage she had to become the oppressor, to embrace the 'male' characteristics of power and control and therefore to repress her vulnerability and the gentler emotions.

Whilst Sarah's choice of an expansive solution was, to some extent, successful, in that it enabled her to survive and to establish herself professionally, this way of being had its problems. Her need for power and control led to tense situations in her working life and limited her ability to use herself in different guises in her fiction writing, for, as I have indicated above, in the expansive solution there is a taboo on the gentler emotions. I also had a sense that, in a more general way, Sarah was, as a woman, not entirely comfortable with her expansiveness. Indeed, it is obvious from the other case studies I discuss below, as well as from my own experience, that many women have a difficult relationship with the 'male emotions', by which I mean aggression and self-assertion.

A Horneyan psychotherapist, Alexandra Symonds, has done some interesting work on Horney's theory in relation to women, in the context of the changes brought about by feminism and women's efforts to break out of the traditional female role. Most women, she says, because of cultural pressure, 'develop the predominantly compliant, self-effacing character structure' (Symonds 1978, p.195). In spite of the changes brought about by the women's movement, the traditional stereotype is still deeply rooted, so that, for many women, their primary way of being continues to be self-effacement. Nevertheless, in spite of cultural conditioning, Symonds finds that 'a significant number of women...develop the predominantly expansive personality' (p.195). Expansive women are primarily career-oriented rather than oriented towards being girlfriends, wives or mothers. Most of those she sees in therapy have 'consciously rejected the typical feminine role as children because they did not want to be like their mothers, whom they saw as passive, compliant, and excessively dependent' (pp.197–198). However, whilst they have rejected the typical female role, they find that they are uncomfortable with their expansiveness, because opting for expansiveness has excluded the possibility of femininity. This may possibly be the case for Sarah, whose rejection of the typical female characteristics of compliance and dependence may have limited the satisfactions she can find as a woman. As I have said above, there is the possibility of an either/or mechanism at work here: expansiveness excludes compliance and dependence, and vice-versa.

One could of course argue, as no doubt many feminists still do, that if women are to take their place in a man's world, they have to repress their feminine tendencies and learn how to wield power in a male way, that it is indeed better to be the oppressor than the oppressed. But does the adoption of expansiveness necessarily imply the repression of feminine tendencies? In her discussion of Horney's expansive solutions, Symonds takes the view that Horney makes the characteristics of the expansive personality, viz. the orientation towards success and achievement, into wholly neurotic trends when, in fact, expansiveness can be regarded as 'part of a self-actualising process' (p.196). Whilst it is true that Horney regards expansive trends as essentially pathological, she does not regard all aggressive or assertive behaviour as expansive. She stresses again and again in her books the difference between healthy and unhealthy manifestations of the various characteristics she discusses, and she contrasts 'healthy self-assertion' with the pathological character of expansive trends. She would agree with Symonds that the ability to be self-assertive is a necessary part of being human. It includes '...openness to new ideas in oneself and others, the ability to be flexible and to change when necessary, the ability to take chances and to expand one's horizons...[Self-assertion]...is part of the process of healthy growth, autonomy, and self-realisation' (pp.196–197).

This certainly seems to me to be the case, but as noted above, defensive solutions tend to be exclusive of each other, so that from the perspective of the self-effacing solution common to women, anything even faintly resembling expansiveness looks suspect, as it threatens to undermine the integrity of that solution. Where a woman has adopted an expansive solution, it may not be possible for her to distinguish between expansiveness and healthy self-assertion and, in all likelihood, expansiveness will operate compulsively and indiscriminately. In ideal circumstances, taking the idea of flexibility of the psyche as a measure of psychological health, one would wish to have at one's disposal the possibility of being both assertive and unassuming when they are necessary in one's relations with oneself and with the outside world.

To sum up, then, in childhood Sarah chose to 'move against people', in Horney's terminology. As an adult 'moving against people' turned into expansiveness and became a way of life, a life solution. As a result of objectifying her expansiveness in the writing of 'The Circus', she seems to have been able to reassess it and to distinguish between its destructive aspects and healthy self-assertion. She realises that: 'it's not so bad to be organising and controlling in some ways, because you need that in order to function in life and in the job.' By learning how to suspend or shelve expansiveness as a way of being, she opens up the possibility of allowing other aspects of her personality to express themselves, in particular the gentler emotions, and this has enabled her to make changes, both in her professional life where she is learning to share power with other members of the team rather than to be in absolute control, and in the writing of her autobiographical novel where she can now tolerate the presence of her other less dominant voices. Thus, the writing of fictional autobiography has helped Sarah to move beyond entrapment in a single image of herself and to expand the possibilities for self.

Using Oneself as a Fictional Character – Jane's Story

Karen Horney's theory explains Sarah's difficulties of putting her feelings into her writing as a consequence of a dominant expansive self-image which placed a taboo on the expression of the gentler emotions. In discussing Jane's story, I use Horney's theory to understand her difficulties of using herself as a basis for fictional characters because of a conflict between self-effacing and expansive self-images.

Jane is of Anglo-Indian origin and in her early forties, married with two children. She has been writing since she was six, under the influence of her mother who was a published short-story writer, and when she joined the Certificate in Creative Writing she had been writing primarily traditional, non-autobiographical stories set in India. Some years earlier she had also written an autobiographical travel book based on a trek in Nepal.

Whilst Jane's stories were competent, she felt that her characters tended to be rather superficial and that the endings, which were always neat and determined by a fictional device, were 'cheating', 'a bit pat'[12]. She was attracted by writings which were psychologically more complex, such as those of Iris Murdoch, whom she admires for 'the obsessiveness of her characters, the obtuseness and stupidity and almost wilful self-destructiveness and destructiveness towards others'. Jane's own characters are 'pragmatic, down-to-earth and positive about life. They get on with it instead of anguishing about it.' She felt that in order to create more complex and psychologically compelling characters she needed to draw more extensively on her own experience. However, writing autobiographically was a problem for her because she felt she always came over 'very unsympathetically'. This was particularly the case with her travel book: '…everybody who read it said it didn't sound like me

12   Unless otherwise specified, quotations are from Jane's essays written for the Certificate in Creative Writing and two interviews I conducted with her.

and that I came over as this monster.' Autobiographical material was also harder to manage; less neat.

In spite of her demonstrable ability to produce interesting and readable short stories, she was not confident of her skills and was hampered by serious self-criticism, which sometimes brought her efforts to a halt for long periods. She spoke of the powerful critic in her head who was constantly looking over her shoulder and finding fault with everything she did. One of the reasons she gave for wanting to attend the course was to see whether 'writing is really what I want to do or whether it is an attempt to fulfil my mother's ambitions'. Clearly there was a problem here of drawing confidence from the efforts she was making and the work she produced.

The pieces of autobiographical fiction which she wrote during the course revealed a desire for closeness with significant people in her environment, but at the same time a deep uncertainty about the appropriateness of expressing emotion. The 'early memory' exercise resulted in 'Yellayah', which recounts a childhood journey by train from Bombay:

> Darkness, noise, rattle of metal, windows rattling. Lying in the dark feeling the country go by. My first taste of homesickness – a melancholy, sweetly sad feeling. The train rattles on through the dark – dumpety-dump, dumpety-dump, do as I say, do as I say, I'll do as I like, I'll do as I like, never again, never again, we're going away, we're going away, goodbye to Bombay, goodbye to Bombay. My thoughts fall into rhythm with it, my body relaxes into the jolting of the train from side to side. The dim yellow light flickers with each movement and threatens to go out.

The children are accompanied only by Yellayah, the Indian gardener from the block of flats where they lived in Bombay. Before the journey the narrator has never taken much notice of him, but now, in her homesickness, he begins to take on a greater significance:

> ...he has always seemed old and wrinkled: his almost black skin webbed with tiny white cracks, his feet big and flattened with splayed toes, his soles and heels cracked and dirty, his toenails yellowy brown and shrivelled like dried mushrooms. I don't remember him ever speaking to us. But in the dim flickering light of the cabin he seems different. He is wearing a red shirt and a loosely wound turban of yellow, instead of his usual dusty white. He smells strongly of earth, pungent spicy sweat and bidis. I find it comforting.

She admires the skill with which he takes water in a little clay vessel from the big earthenware pot, the mudka, and drinks it without touching the clay to his lips, and this seems to bring them closer together:

> He arches his head back so that the tendons in his neck stand out, and holds the pot at arm's length above his head so that a long stream of clear water pours straight down his throat...I want to touch him and this frightens me and makes me feel sick (extracts from 'Yellayah').

Here the desire for closeness borders on sexuality, evoking taboos and fears which the child does not understand.

Discussion of dialogue in an autobiographical setting resulted in 'Arrival' which portrays a meeting, after a long separation, between Jane and her father at his flat in India, whilst she is on holiday there with a friend:

> The lift creaks and wheezes its way up to the twentieth floor. Through the metal lattice gates I can see red splashes on the white walls where people have spat paan down the lift shaft. The round, polished brass plaque on the wooden door reads 'Institute of Human Potential: Body – Mind – Spirit'. Under the doorbell a smaller oblong one – old and tarnished – says 'Capt. B.P. Gupta, I.N. Retd'. It is the right place then. I knock on the door. A small dark-skinned Indian answers it. 'Yes?' he looks puzzled, his face absurdly screwed up like a monkey's. He is much smaller and thinner than I remember, and much more Indian. 'Hello, Dad.' 'Eh?' he is still looking blank. He glances past me at Baxter. 'It's me, Jane.' 'Yes, yes, come in.' His Indian accent is stronger too. He opens the door wider. I lunge at his cheek and miss as he steps back to let us pass.

The narrator has written from Kabul, letting her father know of her impending arrival and is clearly expecting to stay in the flat. It transpires very quickly, however, that there is a problem:

> '...it's this damn tenant of mine. I told the fellow my daughter is coming, I need the room, but the bloody fellow is still here.' 'Oh.' I understand now. We were supposed to be staying with him but he doesn't have a spare room. 'When is he going to leave?' I can feel rage and misery rising up in me. We are so tired – we haven't had a decent night's sleep or a decent meal since we left Greece nearly four weeks ago, but it isn't just that. It's the lack of welcome, the feeling – experienced so many times in my childhood – that he just doesn't

give a bugger, that his children mean less to him than strangers (extracts from 'Arrival').

After further lengthy explanations and excuses, the father hustles them out of the flat, saying that they should find themselves a hotel and a meal, and that they can all meet up sometime later during their stay. As the two travellers wait outside the flat for the lift, the narrator's pain and disappointment switch to anger: 'I feel such resentment, such rage, that I wish I could scream at him, curse him, tell him how much I hate him.' The narrator longs for some emotional if not physical sign from her father that he is pleased to see her after a gap of some years. However, his inability to engage with his daughter in this way or even to provide the minimum hospitality, confirms her lifelong experience of failed emotional connection.

Out of the 'life map' exercise Jane wrote the first chapter of a novel, which portrays the departure from India by boat of herself, her mother and sister. It opens with them standing on deck, looking down at the dock. All around:

> ...huge emotional scenes were going on – children screaming, women wailing and tearing their hair, men crying and embracing each other. Long strings of marigolds stretched from the deck rail down to the quay.

The narrator's father is down there, looking 'bored and embarrassed', occasionally waving half-heartedly. Her mother's lover, Commander, is also there, leaning on his red and black Chevrolet. The girls look backwards and forwards between the two men. As the ship begins to inch away from the quay, the emotional turmoil of the crowd explodes into a frenzy of shrieking: women faint, people throw garlands of flowers into the water, prostrate themselves in mourning at the loss of the motherland. The narrator's father, who has not even bothered to buy them a garland, leaves before the ship is out of sight. Unexpectedly, the narrator finds herself caught up in the emotions:

> I felt a stab of homesickness, and suddenly missed my father – not as he was, but as I had hoped he might be. My sister was running around the deck collecting all the blooms which had fallen from the garlands and throwing them into the water. They got caught up on the wake which was streaming out to both sides of the ship and bobbed violently away. I went down to our cabin and cried (extracts from 'Chapter 1').

The contrast here between the family's lack of emotion and the highly emotional scenes going on around them is striking, and the child feels instinctively that in order to express her own emotions she has to hide herself away.

These pieces of autobiographical fiction reflect a childhood environment where love and affection were not freely given and where it would have been unclear whether or not the child's own feelings were appropriate. A child in such an environment would not have received external validation for the authenticity of her own feelings and would therefore not have developed confidence in her natural way of relating to others.

Two autobiographically based short stories develop in more detail the theme of failed emotional connection in childhood and demonstrate its consequences. Both 'The Birthday Present' and 'How much is that Doggy in the Window?' feature a young, possibly eight-year-old girl as the main protagonist and narrator. In 'The Birthday Present' Anuja is a deeply introspective child of busy parents who seem unable to give her the affection or closeness she needs or to take time to satisfy her imaginative quest for knowledge. The action of the story focuses on Anuja's attempts to compensate for this lack by finding a person who will provide the emotional connection she needs. To her parents' dismay, she announces that for her birthday she would like a picture of Jesus, having in mind the one that hangs on the wall at nursery school, where Jesus is stretching out his hand to the viewer and smiling kindly:

> She had wanted a picture like that on her wall so that she could talk
> to him at night when she felt lonely because her mother was working
> in Bombay and only came home at weekends, and her father was
> often away at sea, and Rosie spent all her time looking after her baby
> sister and no-one ever seemed to have time for her. She could tell by
> Jesus's face that he would have time, that he would listen and care
> about how lonely she felt ('The Birthday Present', p.4).

She is disappointed when the picture her parents grudgingly give her is of baby Jesus cradled in the arms of an angel: '…a baby was no good at all. You couldn't talk to a baby. All they did was cry and make a fuss and then you got into trouble for doing something, or not doing something else' (p.6).

Anuja knows that people will love her if only she is good, but it is so difficult to know what 'being good' means: what seems natural or comforting to her often turns out to be 'bad' in the eyes of the grown-ups. When

Rosie, the ayah, catches her in her evening ritual of pleasuring herself before falling asleep and tells her that Jesus sees her doing it and will be cross with her for being dirty and wicked, Anuja realises again that she has failed somehow to be the sort of girl whom adults will love. So she becomes disillusioned with Jesus too; he is just another adult who does not understand her.

In her quest to obtain love and affection, Anuja moulds herself into the kind of person others want her to be: in Horney's terminology she *moves towards people*, becomes self-effacing. Self-effacement is central, too, in 'How Much is That Doggy in the Window?' where Sita, the main protagonist, also strives to be good, so that she will please her mother, who is portrayed as an irrational, immature woman, with a tendency to fly into a rage at the slightest provocation. When a blind beggar and his daughter sing and play the song of the story's title outside the block of flats where she lives with her mother and brother, Sita sees a prime opportunity for a display of goodness, and begs her mother to give her some money for them. In a magnanimous gesture, her mother gives her ten rupees, and Sita is thrilled by the impression this makes on the beggar's daughter, who smiles so kindly at her, and on the beggar himself, who declares that her mother is an exceedingly kind woman, blessed by Jesus. Not only does this provide Sita with proof of her own goodness, but she has also managed to transform her mother into a good person.

Over the next few weeks the man and his daughter return to play the same song; each time Sita gives them her mother's money and is happy because someone thinks that she and her mother are good, kind people. She would like to be friends with the girl, who is much nicer to her than the girls at school. But as the beggars come more frequently, Sita's mother grows increasingly angry and eventually refuses to give them any more money. Sita is mortified; each time she hears the violin scratching out the familiar song she cringes and hides herself away, and is relieved when the couple eventually cease to visit them. However, her failure to please makes her deeply unhappy and as she grows up, her experience of music is forever tainted by uncomfortable emotions.

The world portrayed in these stories is peopled by unpredictable, ambivalent adults whose love is not spontaneously available. The child narrators are in search of a person who will listen and understand, a person who will love them for themselves. Unrecognised for who they are, Anuja and Sita move towards people in their attempts to be loved. If love is not spontaneously forthcoming, then it must be because they are doing something wrong, because they are bad. They must find out how to please people, how to do the right thing, and then mould themselves into the kind of being that will gain them approval. But the adopting of a strategy means that they lose touch with their own individuality and authenticity or, in Horneyan terms, that they become alienated from who they are and this, the stories imply, will determine the course of their future lives.

The theme of failed emotional connection in childhood and the attempt to overcome it through self-effacing behaviour is a strong and recurring theme in Jane's autobiographical writings, which indicates the central role this way of being has played – and presumably continues to play – in her life. Whilst Jane no longer sees herself as predominantly self-effacing, and even finds her child characters rather 'goody-goody' and one-dimensional for her liking, self-effacing characters based on herself do not seem to cause her particular difficulties. One might say that they are safe and 'acceptable' self-representations, unlikely to evoke adverse reactions from readers. This is not the case, however, with expansive characters.

At the end of the second term of the Certificate in Creative Writing Jane presented for assessment a fictionalised extract from her travel book. 'From Yin Yang's to the Bardo Thodol' is set in the early 1980s and opens with the female narrator, Louise, and her American/Nepalese male companion, Hari, in Kathmandu, after a lengthy trek through Nepal. Constantly at odds with each other, both of them demonstrating a somewhat aggressive individualism, they head for Yin Yang's bar where Hari engages in deep conversation with another woman, and Louise finds herself isolated on the edge of a group of chatting acquaintances. In spite of her dislike of substances or behaviour which threaten to undermine her normal, rather rigid self-control, she succumbs to pressure to take a powerful drug, psilocybin, and in her drugged state finds herself dancing wildly and behaving uninhibitedly in public. When Hari takes her back to the hotel, she succumbs too to uninhibited and ecstatic lovemaking.

Louise is very different from the child narrators of the stories discussed above, and a much more successful mimetic characterisation than Anuja or Sita. Also, the writing generally in this story is much more lucid and open-ended; it trusts the imagery it employs to convey subtle changes in Louise's state of mind and is more daring in what it sets out to achieve. However, as I have said above, Jane felt uncomfortable with this representation of herself, because people who read the book found Louise an unsympathetic character. This might be a justifiable concern if Louise was so negative a character as to alienate the reader, but I do not think this is the case here.

The discomfort is, I think, more easily intelligible in psychological terms. If Jane's predominant strategy for obtaining love and affection in childhood is still a powerful (if unconscious) drive in her present personality, then her concern about the unsympathetic portrayal of herself in the travel book is not unreasonable. Whilst Louise cannot be said to be a 'monster' in any objective sense, she is certainly more complex than Anuja and Sita; she displays aggression and engages in behaviour which would not come under the category of 'goodness' or 'niceness' in their world. From the perspective of an idealised image of goodness, her behaviour certainly lets the side down.

The presence in Jane's autobiographical writings of contradictory images of herself is clearly very important in understanding her difficulties with using herself in her creative writing. We talked about this and she said:

> I think that was very strong as a child, that thing about always having to be good, that people have to approve of me. And then I went through a period of absolute anguish, I suppose [when I was] about 19 or 20, when I got to university, until I was about 30. I had this terrific conflict where I was trying to be good all the time, but then there would be these outbreaks of really appalling behaviour, because I was obviously trying to suppress everything in my character that didn't conform with the sort of goody-goody image. I found that very confusing and bewildering. And then from about 30 onwards I think I started to allow more of the aggressive/assertive side of me out, but perhaps didn't like myself very much for it, and I think over the last few years there has been more of a coming to terms with that, accepting that...

Nevertheless, she still worries that 'I am not managing to portray myself as acceptable'. What Jane means by this, she says, is that she is concerned to create characters with whom readers can identify, and people don't easily identify with aggressive female characters. I wonder whether this is generally true: one thinks of Emma Bovary, Lady Macbeth, Clytemnestra. Does the success of the writing depend on readers approving of, or identifying with, these characters? Perhaps, to an extent, but not entirely. Even if unlikable, these characters are powerful and fascinating fictional representations.

My feeling is that, whilst Jane's self-effacing solution has lessened over the years, it is still sufficiently active to interfere with the subtle processes involved in transposing autobiographical material into fiction. I would suggest that Jane still has a need to present herself in her writing in accord with the image of goodness which was so important to her in childhood, and when her writing reveals a more aggressive and complex picture of herself, the resulting self-exposure creates an uncomfortable tension. This means that using herself as a basis for fiction is problematical; it is easier to write non-autobiographical stories, where characterisation is more superficial, and where the literary devices and neat endings keep control over the material available.

In the current climate where, one sometimes feels, it is almost mandatory for women to be assertive, it seems strange to suggest that some women might have difficulty portraying themselves on the page in an expansive way. But changes in external conditions do not lead automatically or immediately to individual psychic change. The strong and long-term cultural preference for women to be self-effacing, particularly for a woman brought up in India, is deeply embedded in the female psyche, and change is a much more complex matter than simply giving women permission to be different. As Alexandra Symonds puts it: 'Helping a woman resolve her...fear of self-assertion, helping her to emerge with a more authentic identity to handle her hostility and the hostility of others, involves an additional layer of anxiety since she will differ from the expectations of the culture' (Symonds 1991, p.305).

There is a further complicating factor. Within the self-effacing solution, there is a taboo on self-assertion. Self-assertion is a characteristic of the expansive solution, which is diametrically opposed to the ideals of the self-effacing solution and often in conflict with it. To be assertive, the self-effacing personality has to undergo a complete switch to expansiveness, which means that the uncomfortable inner conflict, often heavily repressed, between these two opposing solutions, becomes activated, thus generating anxiety.

Early morning freewriting exercises in which Jane engaged during the course reveal expansiveness of the kind Horney describes, in the form of an arbitrary quest for greatness:

> Funny how I have always thought I'd make it – be exceptional. Life
> isn't bad now although I have to list things before I can FEEL how
> OK it is – nice house, lovely kids, happy marriage – but I wouldn't be
> satisfied with just that. I expect more – accomplishments, fame, riches.
> Not so much riches as success – Mum's legacy.

This powerful drive to be exceptional in life, the *search for glory*, as Horney calls it, is a preoccupation which goes back to Jane's childhood and continues to render real life disappointing: 'As children if we did a good drawing we would be "famous artists", if we wrote a story we would be " great writers"…I would rather be an unhappy "success" than a happy nobody'. Achievement, to have any significance, has to be on a grand scale, so that Jane undervalues her real efforts. This may well account for her uncertainty about whether she wants to be a writer and her inability to have confidence in what she has already achieved. It may also account for her desire, which also emerged in the freewriting, to withdraw into a state of inactivity:

> My dreams are rarely exciting… Sometimes I dream of business meetings – eight businessmen in grey suits sitting around a boardroom table and talking in monotonous voices. I like these dreams. I find them soothing. I don't have to get involved – I don't even listen to the conversation – I don't have to live – just survive. No that's the wrong word – too urgent – just exist. Like an amoeba – that's about the level of challenge I'm comfortable with. And yet when I'm awake I feel this urge to throw myself into things which I feel uncomfortable with.

Here there is a clear conflict between the desire to withdraw into an amoeba state, which is comfortable and soothing, where Jane can exist without having to be challenged, and the contrary desire for challenge, which is uncomfortable. Such a withdrawal, Horney's *detached solution*, would put out of action the contradictory tendencies towards self-effacement on the one hand and expansiveness on the other.

What Jane's writings reveal, then, are two powerful idealised images: that of the good child, seeking the affection of emotionally unreliable adults, and that of the great artist who will dazzle the world with her achievements. To put it another way, they reveal the self-effacing solution in conflict with the expansive solution. As these solutions are mutually contradictory and not achievable in the real world, the only course of action is to withdraw into detachment which, Jane tells me, she tended to do primarily in her teenage years and twenties. As she has got older, she says, she has become more expansive and worries less about it, but it is not surprising that confusion of identity resulting from a lifetime of inner conflicts continues to interfere with her use of herself in her autobiographical creative writing.

Writing out her contradictory self-images in autobiographical fictions has had a marked effect on Jane. She feels much more able now to recognise 'both my ability to write and my own self-generated commitment to be a writer', as a result of which her confidence is much increased. However, this has not been without its traumas. Engaging in the autobiographical exercises, she said, 'brought an awful lot of stuff up'. At the end of the first term she bought a car and suffered a series of panic attacks about driving it. She soon realised that the fear was not to do with the car: 'it was actually fear from my mother, my childhood, which had suddenly just come up in huge bursts and I couldn't understand it at all.' Later she also felt that there was considerable fear of taking up such a 'masculine [or expansive] activity' as driving. It is clear that, engaging in the writing had exacerbated the conflict between self-effacement and expansiveness, and this was having an impact on her life more generally. A number of counselling sessions helped her to talk about the fears and to overcome the panic, and since that time she has experienced a considerable opening up to an easier expression of emotion and a decrease in her need to keep everything under control. This had been helped by learning aikido and the Alexander Technique, and eurythmy, the Steiner dance which is said to be emotionally therapeutic, as well as by reading women's self-help books. But, she says: 'It started with the course. I found that first term very, very powerful...It has been almost a form of therapy.'

The decreased need for control has also had a marked effect on Jane's writing process. She feels that she is 'getting to grips with material which had always seemed too difficult for me before'. Since the course ended she has:

> started to work with things which are much more open-ended, that
> are just pieces, that don't necessarily have a beginning and an end and
> I was able to find them quite valid...they stood up as pieces on their
> own, whereas before I would have looked at them and thought well
> that is not a story, because it doesn't start anywhere or end anywhere.

What she is saying, in effect, is that she has started, in her writing, to accommodate the idea of chaos, rather than holding onto the safety of the neatly constructed entity. Further, she now feels freer to use herself in different guises in the text. For example, she successfully used herself as narrator of a story told to her by a friend, which she had been struggling for some years to write purely from his point of view. 'Suddenly', she said, echoing Sarah's comments in the previous section, 'it came into my mind that *I* am in the story.'

Karen Horney's theory makes good sense of the problems experienced by a talented writer in her attempts to deepen her fiction writing through the use of autobiographical material. The conflicts of identity described here seem to stem from a childhood environment where what Horney sees as the basic conditions for healthy development were not sufficiently in place. In order to feel loved and secure, the child had to take emergency measures by moulding herself into the sort of person she thought her environment demanded. This involved a move away from herself and the development of her real potential, and set in motion an intrapsychic process with a dynamic of its own. Because of this loss of contact with the real self, development of her potential was hampered, causing entrapment in images of self which interfered with the use of herself in the fiction writing. The confrontation with conflicting versions of herself in her autobiographical fictions has enabled Jane to break out of entrapment in cramping images of self. The resulting clarification of identity has brought about an increased freedom in her life generally, and an ability to use aspects of herself, in a more unconscious way, in her fiction writing.

Problems of Shelving the Critical Faculty: a Horneyan Understanding

Karen Horney's theory helps us to understand the difficulties that Sarah and Jane had with their writing. In Sarah's case, entrapment in an expansive image of herself meant that she did not have easy access to other aspects of her personality, aspects which she needed in order to convey the gentler emotions of the autobiographical narrator of her novel. She was also reluctant, until she engaged in the 'melody for two voices' exercise, to expose herself on the page in her expansive guise, as she was not entirely comfortable with her expansiveness. Jane found it fairly easy to represent herself in her self-effacing guise – although she did not approve of her self-effacing tendencies – but felt uncomfortable with representations of her expansiveness when other people reacted adversely to them. My own case is rather similar to Jane's, in that I was able to represent myself in my novel as self-effacing, as a perpetual victim, but unconsciously worked hard to keep out of view my repressed expansiveness and the dependency which allowed me to channel my expansiveness through my male partners. For all three of us, excessive control was a marked feature of our relationship with our self-representations, most perhaps in the case of Sarah, who placed herself on the page only reluctantly and in retrospect.

As I have said above, one of the main requirements of the creative process is flexibility within the psyche, which allows the critical and the creative faculties to collaborate with each other or, rather, the ability to shelve the critical faculty and to allow the 'imaginative body' to do its work. A need for excessive control – the dominance of the critical faculty – is bound to introduce an imbalance into the functioning of the creative process and may well give rise to blocks. For if the critical faculty cannot be temporarily suspended, the freedom of the imagination will be impaired. In my view, the writing difficulties experienced by Sarah, Jane and myself were the result of a problem with suspending the critical faculty.

From the Horneyan point of view there are three main, interrelated factors that are central to understanding the problem of shelving the critical faculty:[13] the inherent rigidity of the defensive character structure because of the conflicts between the different life solutions and the tendency to become entrapped in one dominant solution (Horney 1951, pp.310–311); the lack of self-confidence resulting from alienation from the real self (p.310); and the threat from the 'inner tyranny' represented by the pride system (p.118). Let me take these in turn.

As I said above, the defensive character structure comes into being in the first instance to defend the child against basic anxiety, which has been aroused by an environment that threatens the emergence of its individuality. As the defensive character structure develops and intrapsychic factors come into play, its function broadens, to provide also the defences needed to protect the adult from the increased anxiety and pain of inner conflicts, and the destructive effects of the pride system (p.297). There can be little flexibility within such a defensive structure: 'Rigid control through will power and reasoning is...[a]... strenuous means of attempting to bind together all the disconnected parts of the personality' (p.172). Where one particular life solution has become dominant, it will be rigidly adhered to. Loosening control means running the risk of being plunged into inner conflict, or of switching into one of the other life solutions.

Instead of the central organising agency of the psyche being derived from the real self, it will be determined by the defensive character structure and the compulsory narrative of shoulds appropriate to the dominant life solution. For example, if a man's expansive solution demands of him that he should be

---

13   Whilst Horney does not discuss problems of creative writing or writer's block as such, her chapter on 'Neurotic Disturbances in Work' in *Neurosis and Human Growth* focuses on 'creative work in the broadest sense of the word' (Horney 1951, p.310) and some of the examples are of creative writers.

powerful and controlling in all situations, then he will have difficulty bringing to life on the page a character based on himself who is weak and vulnerable and allows himself to be oppressed by others. He cannot allow his dominant image of himself to be suspended or shelved. Similarly, if a woman's dominant narrative of shoulds tells her that she must be good, then representing herself on the page as less than good contravenes the rules of her solution and will arouse anxiety. Or a character representing repressed tendencies can be portrayed accurately but condemned by the rhetoric. A dominant solution has to be adhered to rigidly, because it provides a much needed sense of identity which can, to an extent, sustain a person, in the absence of genuine self-regard (p.23).

In my own case, the dominance of a self-effacing solution made it impossible, without great struggle, to represent myself on the page as assertive and independent. Whilst in the rhetoric of the novel I wanted to show that my 1970s narrator had moved on and become more expansive, I could never achieve this. Again and again, my narrator's attempts to extricate herself from her dependency on Klaus come to nothing. She flirts repeatedly with an idealised detachment, taking herself off on her own and imagining that she does not need anyone, but this quickly dissipates, and she soon finds herself merging back into the relationship. Whilst she does not fulfil my authorial intentions, however, she is a much more authentic fictional entity than my 1980s narrator, who is represented as struggling heroically out of her dependence on Hugo but who, in retrospect, seems utterly contrived and inauthentic. Presumably, to represent myself at that time as a woman with the ability to assert herself and take responsibility for her life would have contravened my dominant self-effacing solution. In spite of this, when I read the novel now I can see that there is a subtle expansiveness running through the voice and actions of the 1970s narrator which has escaped censorship. But her expansiveness is not a tool in her quest for independence and responsibility; rather it is a means of ensnaring a person through whom to live.

For Sarah, her dominant expansive solution, which was largely kept out of awareness, prevented her from representing herself in her novel in the guise of a vulnerable young woman who fell victim to a rather unscrupulous older man. For in the expansive solution, weakness and vulnerability are not allowed. For Jane, it is the other way round; weakness and vulnerability, characteristics of the self-effacing solution, are more acceptable than expansiveness, which runs the risk of disapproval by others. Being locked into one particular Horneyan solution, then, or being in a conflict between different life solutions, can seriously interfere with fiction writing especially when the writing is autobiographically based.

The second factor I have identified as central to understanding the problem of shelving the critical faculty – the lack of self-confidence resulting from alienation from the real self – is a serious hindrance in a person's ability to engage in any creative pursuit. Throughout the whole of her theory, Horney differentiates between a healthy and an unhealthy development of self. In a healthy development, the real self – which at the outset is unknown, potential – grows and develops through good object-relating. The child finds people, situations and experiences that help it to develop its potential. This provides the child with a sense of its own worth, with a feeling of self-confidence, and an increased ability to make choices. In an unhealthy development the situation is much more complicated. The real self is lost sight of, so that self-esteem does not develop naturally. In its absence, emergency measures have to be taken. Self-idealisation occurs, and this has to be protected because, if it is undermined, its opposite pole, self-hate, will be evoked (p.112). The middle ground, where real self-worth and self-esteem would normally reside, is missing, thus allowing this see-saw to operate. One could say that alienation from self leaves a hole in the middle of the psyche. It is '…the subjective feeling of…being removed from [oneself]' (p.160). The self is decentred, moves away from its heart. Rather than a 'space for the imagination', a safe holding environment inhabited by benign presence, there is absence, or it may be filled with anxiety or be experienced as threatening and potentially dangerous, full of monsters, as Marion Milner describes it (Milner 1971, pp.35–44). As Trevor Pateman says: 'Imagination frequently fails us when the space which we are given in which to exercise it…creates a sense of anxiety rather than a sense of opportunity' (Pateman 1997, p.4).

This sense of anxiety in the inner space where the imagination functions is likely to be, at least in part, a consequence of the threat from the 'inner tyranny' represented by the pride system – the third factor I identified as central to understanding the problem of shelving the critical faculty. New writers often refer to a sense of danger or discomfort when trying to write, a powerful critic in the head who is constantly looking over their shoulder and finding fault with everything they write: 'The critical eye breathing down the creative neck', as one student puts it. This was certainly my own problem when I started to write fiction. The space within which my 'inner vision' lived was threatening, filled with anxiety, and often I preferred not to go there, even though I had a strong desire to write.

This sense of inner danger is a direct consequence of the pride system's capacity to inflict punishment for contravention of its rules, the failure to live up to the unrealistic expectations of the idealised image (Horney 1951, p.118). Thus, the space where creativity occurs and where contact is made with the developing self (Milner 1989, p.37) becomes difficult to enter, or may be completely blocked off. For me, trying to get in touch with my 'inner vision' often felt like prising apart the inner space by sheer effort of will, as if I were having constantly to lean against a heavy door which, if I relaxed my efforts, would swing back and slam shut. Needless to say, this was an exhausting process which made writing a tiring and dispiriting undertaking. For some people, the fear of inner torment is such that the desire to create has to be repressed: 'He does not embark on any serious pursuits commensurate with his gifts lest he fail to be a brilliant success. He would like to write or to paint and does not dare to start' (Horney 1951, p.107). Or if the desire to create is not repressed, the creative process will be wracked with anxiety or hampered by self-torment:

> ...a writer is inhibited in doing creative work because of several
> factors within himself which make writing an ordeal. His work
> therefore proceeds slowly; he fiddles around or does irrelevant things.
> Instead of being sympathetic with himself for this affliction, and
> examining it, he calls himself a lazy good-for-nothing or a fraud who
> is not really interested in his work' (pp.124–125).

For creativity to occur, there needs to be a capacity to be alone with the space within oneself (Winnicott 1958), and this can be done much more easily if that space is benign, if there is a sense that one is *present* to oneself in that space and, being present to oneself, that one can *work with* the doubts and difficulties which the creative process necessarily involves.

Shelving the critical faculty – a mechanism which, in the opinion of many writers and thinkers, is central to the creative process – is likely to be impaired in the presence of inner conflicts of the kind Karen Horney discusses. This is not to suggest that writers have to resolve their psychological problems in order to write, but that such problems are bound to interfere with the writing at different stages and in many different ways. As Horney says:

What these disturbances invariably...entail is a waste of good human energies: a waste of energies in the process of work; a waste in not daring to do the work that is commensurate with existing abilities; a waste in not tapping existing resources; and a waste in the impairment of the quality of work produced. For the individual this means that he cannot fulfil himself in an essential area of his life (Horney 1951, pp.327-328).

Therapeutic Dimensions of Fictionalising Ourselves

How does fictionalising ourselves help to alleviate difficulties with shelving the critical faculty? I would suggest that its main contribution lies in its power to provide insight into the inner life and to undermine the rigidity of the pride system. Writing fictional autobiography provides what one might call a 'safe diagonal', an oblique angle on problems of the self. Instead of having to tackle problems head-on and therefore running the risk of provoking acute anxiety and the mobilising of defences, we are provided with a means of identifying psychological problems through observing the way they manifest themselves on the page. For example, Sarah's writing brought into focus the fact that, as people had pointed out in the past, she was not present in her writing. This caused her to reflect on her need to control her self-representations by 'stuffing herself in' in retrospect, and on what this meant about her relationship with herself. Again, it was through Jane's writing of autobiographically based fiction that she became aware of the difficulties of using herself as a fictional character, and this led her to explore the conflicts of identity which underlay them.

Writing exercises such as 'freewriting', with its demand that we 'switch off' or suspend the critical faculty, or 'melody for two voices', which involves a gradual distancing of self through several levels of fictionalising, provide a means of evading the control of defence mechanisms whose role it is to keep out of awareness dimensions of ourselves which contradict our dominant solutions. Whilst the pride system's main strategy is to keep itself hidden, creating a playful metaphor of self shifts the emphasis onto a different plane, thus enabling us to see ourselves in a new way. As Sarah says about the creation of the mistress of ceremonies in 'The Circus': '...I allowed myself...to be placed in a position...where I...could be seen as a funny character....' But this light-hearted view also brought a more serious insight: that this way of being 'could also be seen as...quite dangerous...', potentially damaging to herself as well as to others. It was this particular insight which, I believe, was instrumental in undermining the dominance of Sarah's expansive tendencies and allowed her to re-discover the feelings associated with the more vulnerable side of herself.

The 'oblique angle' on self, which has the power to subvert inner defences, is a consequence of the essentially metaphorical nature of fiction. A straightforward autobiographical account of a situation, such as Sarah's usual way of behaving in team meetings, relies primarily on a *description* of people and events, a *telling* from the outside. A fictional rendering of the same situation will also rely, to an extent, on description, but it will rely to a much greater degree on *inference* from the action of the story and the behaviour of the characters involved (Gass 1979); in other words, it relies heavily on *showing*. Thus, in a fictional rendering, instead of standing outside of a situation and relating it from a distance, the writer is required to *enter into the experience* and to represent it from the inside and *with feeling*. When fictionalising ourselves, the requirement that we should 'show' rather than 'tell' means that we are forced to enter into *our own* feelings and emotions in a way which we may not be able to do simply by writing about the facts of our lives, and this has the effect of putting us in touch with dimensions of ourselves which are hidden or not easily accessible.

Writers on metaphor stress its power to bring us more readily into contact with our feelings and emotions (Lakoff and Johnson 1980; cf. Olney 1972), our 'primary process' material, in Freud's terminology. Murray Cox and Alice Theilgaard discovered in their therapeutic practice that, contrary to the traditional psychoanalytic approach, which starts from the surface and works inwards to the depths, working with the poetic image activated by metaphor enabled their patients to get in touch with the depths of themselves before stirring the surface (Cox and Theilgaard 1987, p.xiii). Because the metaphoric image is an indirect or oblique representation, it 'can serve as a container for feelings which are too overwhelming to be tolerated' (p.99). Metaphor's 'mutative' effect, as Cox and Theilgaard call it, is exerted 'by energizing alternative perspectival aspects of experience. This means that material which the patient has endeavoured to relinquish, avoid, or deny so that it is "safely" classified, categorized, and "filed away", appears again in the "pending action" file, in such a way that it can be tolerated' (p.99). Echoing Karen Horney's idea of entrapment in a particular 'life solution', Cox and Theilgaard refer to a state of imprisonment in a 'life-sentence...a descriptive life-theme, a psychological ground-base which lies so deeply within the personality that it is the equivalent to a musical key in which an individual's life-theme is orchestrated' (p.45). Finding an appropriate metaphor for a 'life sentence', they say, can act as a 'mobilizing motif' which can be instrumental in effecting change.

Apart from its role in providing an 'oblique angle' on self, a significant feature of metaphor from the therapeutic point of view is its dual nature. Whilst simile *likens* one thing to another ('My love is like a red red rose'[14]), in metaphor the thing being compared *becomes* the thing it is compared to ('Love is a growing or full constant light'[15]). However, in becoming the other it does not lose its original identity, rather it becomes *simultaneously itself and the other*. Sarah is aware of this double or metaphorical aspect of her fictional writing, this 'dual thing', as she calls it, which enables her to be simultaneously the leader of the team meeting and the mistress of ceremonies. As in the well-known gestalt mechanism of the duck/rabbit in visual perception (Hanson 1958), she can switch back and forth between the two different conceptions of herself. Instead of being entrapped in one all-embracing version of herself, she can engage in an *inner dialogue* which allows her to entertain other possibilities for self.

The most extensive discussion of the developmental nature of inner dialogue is to be found in the work of Mikhail Bakhtin. He points out that in order to know ourselves, we have to get outside of ourselves, to become 'exotopic'. The main way we do this is by 'appropriating other people's visions of us' (Holquist 1990, p.28). The writer is in a privileged position in this regard, in that he can create his own visions of himself on the page. However, because we can never get outside of ourselves completely or, as Bakhtin puts it, we can never be 'transgredient' to ourselves, our self-representations are contrived and do not correspond to any actual perceptions (Bakhtin 1990, p.37). Nevertheless, once these images of ourselves are objectified, we can, through a second-degree reflection, judge or express our relationship with that image (Palmieri 1998, p.50). This 'reflexive outsideness' (p.48) enables us to engage with ourselves at two removes, through two levels of objectification or through the 'double-voice'.

Fiction writing, Bakhtin maintains, offers a wide range of techniques for using the 'double voice'. Creating characters or first person narrators, he says, involves the creation of a 'posited author', an entity which sounds very

14   Robert Burns
15   John Donne

similar to Wayne Booth's 'implied author' (Booth 1991)[16]. The voice of this 'posited author' is not heard directly, but is 'refracted' through the voice of the other. Thus, we find out about the author through the dialogue with the voices of the narrator or character:

> Behind the narrator's story we read a second story, the author's story; he is the one who tells us how the narrator tells stories, and also tells us about the narrator himself. We acutely sense two levels at each moment in the story; one, the level of the narrator, a belief system filled with his objects, meanings and emotional expressions, and the other, the level of the author, who speaks (albeit in a refracted way) by means of this story and through this story (Bakhtin 1981, p.314).

In order to find the 'double voice' which brings us refracted knowledge of ourselves, we have to become 'polyphonic'. For Bakhtin, Dostoevsky is the prime example of a polyphonic writer (Bakhtin 1984)[17]. Rather than subordinating the characters and narrators in his novels to the authorial voice, Dostoevsky gives them as full and equal subject status as that enjoyed by himself as author, and enters into a dialogic relationship with them. In this way, the novel becomes a highly fluid entity, potentially chaotic and difficult to control. The writer, Bakhtin implies, has to have a high degree of openness towards the fictional entities he creates and must be prepared to be changed or deeply influenced by them. Thus, fiction writing demands a greater degree of psychic flexibility than would be usual in everyday life.

Echoing my discussion of 'shelving the critical faculty', Bakhtin portrays the novelist as someone who, in order to enter into the necessary polyphony of novel writing, has to suspend authorial control and to allow the characters and narrators he has created to develop a life of their own. Fiction writing, he says, gives an author a greater degree of 'surplus' than is the case in everyday life, by which he means a greater degree of knowledge of the characters and narrators he has created, by virtue of being outside of them (Bakhtin 1984, p.72). If he renounces that 'surplus' and engages in a dialogue with his characters and narrators on equal footing, then he has the possibility of *increasing his knowledge of himself*.

16   Re the 'implied author', see pages 161–165.
17   Elsewhere Bakhtin implies that the novel, unlike poetry, is intrinsically polyphonic (Bakhtin 1981, pp.275–300).

...the author utilizes now one language, now another, in order to avoid giving himself up wholly to either of them; he makes use of this verbal give-and-take, this dialogue of languages at every point in his work, in order that he himself might remain as it were neutral with regard to language, a third party in a quarrel between two people (although he might be a *biased* third party) (Bakhtin 1981, p.314).

This device frees the author from 'a unitary and singular language' and opens up the possibility 'of saying "I am me" in someone else's language, and in my own language, "I am other"' (p.315). Through this dialogue, the author is simultaneously himself and the other; from being singular, he becomes plural. When the narrators and characters the author creates are fictionalised aspects of himself, renouncing the 'surplus meaning' they already occupy in his psyche temporarily frees him from his customary singular vision of himself.

Sometimes Bakhtin, like Hélène Cixous, goes too far by suggesting that authorial control has to be not merely suspended but abolished altogether. At other times he states categorically that polyphony does not undermine overall authorial control:

The consciousness of the creator of a polyphonic novel is constantly and everywhere present in the novel, and is active in it to the highest degree... The author...is not required to renounce himself or his own consciousness, but he must to an extraordinary extent broaden, deepen and rearrange this consciousness...in order to accommodate the autonomous consciousnesses of others (Bakhtin 1984, pp.67–68).

What makes it possible for an author to do this is something akin to what I have been calling a 'writing identity':

It is as if the author has no language of his own, but does possess his own style, *his own organic and unitary law* governing the way he plays with languages and the way his own real semantic and expressive intentions are refracted within them (Bakhtin 1981, p.311; emphasis added).

For Bakhtin, this 'organic and unitary law' seems to be intrinsic to the writer. Running throughout his work there is a rather idealistic assumption that the writer has a natural ability to shelve authorial control and to embrace the polyphony of voices in his fiction:

> The novelist...welcomes the heteroglossia and language diversity of the literary and extraliterary language into his own work not only not weakening them but even intensifying them...It is in fact out of this stratification of language, its speech diversity and even language diversity, that he constructs his style, while at the same time he maintains the unity of his own creative personality and the unity...of his own style (p.298).

My research and experience have led me to the view that becoming polyphonic is much more difficult than Bakhtin would have us believe, that for many people it does not come naturally but as a result of a great deal of struggle. What I have been arguing is that a writer often has to *learn* how to do this; that what Bakhtin calls a writer's 'creative personality' is something which develops as a writer gets into closer contact with his inner life, his feelings and emotions, and finds a strong enough sense of his own identity to enable him to engage in the chaos of polyphony. The writer is often prevented from doing this because of difficulties of shelving the critical faculty and of allowing characters or narrators a life of their own. People who have opted for a single Horneyan 'life solution' are monologic, in Bakhtin's sense, in the custom of writing (and speaking) with one single voice. Engaging in the dialogics of fictionalising themselves forces them into duality or multiplicity, and this is likely to subvert the hold of their monologism and to open up greater possibilities for self. Increased psychic flexibility is likely, in turn, to improve spontaneous access to the unconscious, to facilitate the shelving of the critical faculty and to make engaging in creative work less problematical.

One could say that fictionalising ourselves, letting go of the usual controls we exert over our self-representations and allowing new versions to emerge, forces a *confrontation* with ourselves or, as Cox and Theilgaard call it, a 'metaphorical confrontation with self' (Cox and Theilgaard 1987, p.45), in which aspects of ourselves with which we have not been readily in touch, or which we have a vested interest in keeping hidden, become visible in a refracted form. Engaging in a dialogue with these aspects of ourselves and becoming more tolerant of them is likely to undermine the need for control over our self-representations and to facilitate a greater degree of flexibility in the creative process.

CHAPTER 3

Fictionalising Significant People in Our Lives

The Voices of Others in Our Personal Narratives

My discussions in Chapter 2 focused around the confrontation with ourselves which writing fictional autobiography can bring about, its potential for providing insight and for increasing the dialogue between different aspects of the personality. In the present chapter I discuss the role of fictional autobiography in facilitating a dialogue with the voices of significant people in our lives, such as our parents and siblings, voices which exert a powerful influence over our views of ourselves and our relationship with the past.

One of the questions I asked students in the questionnaire was whether writing fiction based on their past had helped them to discover things about their parents or siblings that they did not know before. The answers to this question were copious and fascinating. Well over half of respondents reported that they had either discovered new knowledge about their relations with their parents or siblings, or that the writing had helped to consolidate existing insights. By far the most significant response was the sense of having found a new perspective on parents which fictionalising allowed them. One person says: 'I wrote a brief thing…about my mother and saw her coming across as someone I usually protect myself from seeing, i.e. a domineering, manipulative sometimes rather unpleasant person. In my everyday life I see her as vulnerable and I'm indulgent of her bad behaviour.' Another says: 'I have gained insight into my father, in the sense that I am able to see him as a man with the same hopes and disappointments as other people. Previously he was always my father who gives me a hard time!' For many, this new perspective led to increased empathy towards parents. One says:

'Walking back through memories of childhood my father appears more than I would have guessed…[they] illustrate a love and hope that is there that I hadn't considered in this way before.' Another says: 'I discovered that what I believe to be true is not necessarily what others believe to be true regarding the same events…I attach less blame to [my parents] for much of the hurt in my childhood.' For another, seeing people and events from perspectives other than her own freed up her emotions, so that she was able sometimes 'to view part of the past more benignly or with even greater anger!'. The result of these new perspectives and increased empathy was, for some people, an improvement in family relations beyond the writing. As one puts it: 'It humanised [my parents]. It triggered me to talk to them about stuff. Things we hadn't discussed in years.'

The gaining of a new perspective on parents, the increase of empathy for them and the consequent improvement in real life relationships beyond the page were all part of my own experience of writing my second novel, *New Town Blues*. This novel tells the story of a family – a mother, father and daughter – who live in a new town called Farley, and is loosely based on myself and my parents and certain events in my early life in my home town Crawley. The story is told in the third person from the points of view of the three main protagonists. All three are unhappy people, frustrated in their attempts to find fulfilment in their lives, largely because of traumatic events in their pasts, the memories of which have been repressed.

When I began writing, I had it clearly in mind that the novel was going to be an indictment of the 'cultural desert' of new town life, as well as of my parents, from whom I was at that time estranged. In the course of the writing, however, the plot and the characters began to take their own direction, became progressively more fictional than autobiographical, and the negative ending I had planned turned into a positive one. In particular, the character of Donald, based on my father, against whom I harboured intensely angry feelings, is the most sympathetically portrayed of the three main protagonists.

The writing of this novel was a very important factor in my finding a more empathic and workable relationship with my parents and an acceptance of Crawley as my home town, both of which helped to consolidate my identity. My ability to suspend the critical faculty and let the characters develop a life of their own, rather than controlling the narrative, as I had tried to do in my first novel, *Stages*, was clearly important in allowing this new, more empathetic perspective to emerge. This development was no doubt facilitated by the long struggle to find a first-person writing voice for *Stages* and the increased confidence and stronger sense of identity which resulted. Of considerable importance also was the psychotherapy I was undergoing at the same time, which meant that I was delving back, simultaneously on two fronts, into childhood memories and my relationship with my parents.

The two case studies I discuss in this chapter, of Jennifer and Jessica, are further examples of how fictionalising our parents and siblings can have a therapeutic effect, not only on our relationship with internal images of them, but also on the real-life relationships with them. These case studies differ from those of Sarah and Jane, neither of whom consciously set out to explore themselves through writing fictional autobiography and whose insights into themselves and into the difficulties with their writing came by chance rather than by design. Both Jennifer and Jessica stated explicitly at the outset of the course that theirs was a quest to create a personal narrative that might help them to make better sense of themselves and their lives. Both of them identified particular problems which they sought to address: a sense of being psychically fragmented in the case of Jessica; unresolved resentment against members of her family in the case of Jennifer. Thus the emphasis in this chapter is much more on autobiographical creative writing as a therapeutic rather than artistic undertaking (although in the case of Jessica there are tensions between the two).

The theoretical approach I adopt here is more straightforwardly object-relational, drawing on the psychodynamic theories of Donald Winnicott and Christopher Bollas (although the theory of Karen Horney is relevant in the case of Jessica). In addition, there is a new theoretical element here. Both Jennifer and Jessica use the term 'personal narrative' when talking about their autobiographical quests, and this usage makes an important link with recent work in psychology, notably that of Jerome Bruner on narrative as a mode of self-understanding (Bruner 1986, 1990). Bruner distinguishes between 'paradigmatic' knowing and 'narrative' knowing (Bruner 1990, pp.11–43). By paradigmatic knowing he means a type of knowledge which aims at truth and relies on theories, argument, analysis and the testing of hypotheses; in other words, on logical or scientific modes of thinking. By narrative knowing, he means a type of knowledge which aims at verisimilitude and looks for meaning; it arises out of the stories people tell themselves and each other about their own experience. Storytelling as a means of communicating goes back to the very earliest times, but it is the scientific or paradigmatic mode of understanding which has become dominant in the modern world.

However, in the last twenty years or so the importance of narrative as a fundamental mode of human understanding has again been recognised and is now well established in philosophy, psychology, psychotherapy and the social sciences (McLeod 1997, pp.28–31).

A narrative, whether in its original literary context or in its applications in other disciplines, is normally distinguished from a story. A *story* is an event or a series of events which finds its form in a *text*, a verbal or written representation of the events. *Narration* is the act of telling or writing, the act of creating a text out of the story (Rimmon-Kenan 1996, pp.2–3). The storytelling capacity is present in all cultures; it can be identified as appearing in infants at about the age of three (Neisser 1993, p.5), although there also seems to be a pre-verbal narrative capacity observable in younger infants (McLeod 1997, pp.32–33). Much of our everyday thinking and planning and remembering and daydreaming is done in narrative. In order to understand what we are doing or saying, we require a context and that context, more often than not, is a narrative one (MacIntyre 1981, pp.192–194). An action, such as why a person has committed a crime or, at a more mundane level, why a person is standing waiting for a bus in the morning, becomes intelligible within a narrative sequence. It provides a plot – a beginning, a middle and an end – and a way of understanding the relationship of the different elements of the story to each other. It is also simultaneously backward and forward looking, drawing on what has gone before and anticipating what is to come. It is therefore a structuring device which situates events in time and allows for the bringing together of past, present and future within a loosely constructed framework, thus providing meaning and stability.

For Alastair MacIntyre, understanding who we are involves understanding the stories into which we are born – or, put another way, of understanding the rough drafts, authored by others, which make up our own narratives (MacIntyre 1981, p.201). This is clearly of relevance to my discussions here. However, I would not wish to imply, as writers such as Donald Polkinghorne do, that life narratives are the primary or even the only basis of personal identity and self-understanding (Polkinghorne 1991). Rather, I would incline more to the view of Ulric Neisser (1988) who sees narrative as one amongst a number of different ways of knowing the self.

One of the important functions of personal narratives is that they enable us to make sense of stories which deviate from the norm. In this sense they operate as a means of problem-solving (McLeod 1997, pp.36–38; Bruner 1990, pp.49–50), and this is particularly relevant to my discussions in this chapter. In setting out to create a personal narrative, both Jennifer and Jessica implicitly (explicitly in the case of Jessica) ask the question: 'How did I come to be the person I am today?' Embedded in this question are a number of further questions: 'Why am I not comfortable with myself the way I am?' and 'What story will make sense of myself and my discomfort?' There is therefore an expectation that by finding a story which makes sense of the past, they will feel more at ease with the present and be able to proceed into the future with a more solidly based sense of self.

The idea that narrative is an important mode of self-understanding provides the framework for this chapter. In the case of Jennifer I explore the significance of narrative point of view, particularly the narrative technique known as 'free indirect discourse' or 'dual voice', for finding a voice for significant others. In the case of Jessica I discuss the significance of finding a narrative form for a fragmented sense of self. In both instances I make comparison with Virginia Woolf's writing of fiction and autobiography, and its relation to self. Also of relevance here is the idea of 're-writing' personal narratives, which is a development, within counselling and psychotherapy, of the thinking of Bruner and others. The assumption is that if the way we have been authored by others has left us with self-narratives which are oppressive or inappropriate, then speaking them or writing them differently may provide a means of re-formulating self in such a way that we become more comfortable with ourselves. I have found these ideas very fruitful in thinking about the therapeutic role of the *process* of writing fictional autobiography. I discuss the therapeutic role of fictional autobiography as a *product* in Chapter 4.

Finding a Voice for Our Parents and Siblings – Jennifer's Story

Jennifer is in her late fifties. She has a successful marriage, with grown-up children and now a grandchild, and this, she says, has been the most important thing in her life. Nevertheless she has always regretted that she did not go into higher education when she left school or make a career: 'I feel I wasted a lot of potential by not having guidance or even expectations, or anything like that.'[1] As a child, she displayed a considerable aptitude for botany, but in keeping with the ethos of her time, she was not encouraged to

---

1   Unless otherwise stated, quotations are from Jennifer's essays written for the Certificate in Creative Writing and two interviews I conducted with her.

pursue a career in science, and the options suggested by the girls' grammar school she attended were limited to teaching or nursing. She recently took a degree in English as a mature student, for which she gained an upper second, and this has to some extent compensated for her lost opportunities. However, when Jennifer first attended the autobiography course there were still 'unresolved resentments' about not having had the opportunities which her brothers had, to study beyond secondary education and to make a career.

Jennifer came to the course hoping 'to develop ideas for a narrative based on my own life'. As she had just spent several years writing essays, her prose style was rather academic and she was concerned to develop 'a freer, less formal style'. Freewriting proved particularly valuable here; she found it liberating to discover that she could write for a fixed period of time without a preconceived subject matter or structure.

The 'early memory' exercise was valuable in enabling Jennifer to fill gaps in her past through imagination. In the interview she refers to a fragment of wartime memory which she used as the basis for a story. She and one of her brothers were on their way back to school after lunch when the air-raid siren sounded. She remembers being in a neighbour's garden and not knowing whether to go home or on to school, but does not remember what decision was made. In the story, she replaced her brother with a friend, Kathleen, who was 'becoming important in forming a narrative', and took them home, where they hid in the Morrison air-raid shelter, an event familiar from many other occasions. The resulting story is thus a composite of disparate bits of experience, rather than the experience of that particular occasion. However, the finished piece somehow *feels* true, although 'I am not sure whether it is true or not…and when I was writing it I was not sure whether I was creating it or remembering it'. It has now 'gone in as a memory', and she does not feel any desire to go back and change it. She describes this process as 'tidying things up and you can then put it in a drawer which says "finished" and you don't have to go back to it because you have worked your way through it'.

This exercise made Jennifer aware of the extent to which the viewpoints of her parents, brothers and other significant people were shaped by her own perspective. She now felt that if her story were to have any validity, it 'must have more than one voice speaking, so that other viewpoints could be more forcefully stated. Perhaps it would also be useful to allow these voices to comment upon one another and upon the reliability of their narratives.' A tape-recorded interview was particularly useful here, Jennifer having chosen to interview the brother nearest in age to her, with whom she had never before discussed their childhood. Mark reacted with great enthusiasm to the idea of the interview, which gave rise to a short story entitled 'The Chalk Carving'. This dramatises Mark's memory of an art class at school where the boys' task was to carve a sculpture out of a piece of chalk they had gleaned from a nearby quarry:

> The chalk pit was steep and crumbling, but not big enough to be really dangerous. Of course, everyone needed a piece of chalk from the very top and the air was filled with the noise of sliding chalk and yelping boys as they were carried back down to the bottom, struggling to keep their balance as if they were on skates. At the end of the lesson, each boy had found a piece of chalk which he considered suitable for his purpose. Some staggered under the weight of huge boulders while others had pieces small enough to go in their pockets: 'hardly big enough to carve an acorn', thought Mark. His choice was in between these two extremes. He showed it off to his friend Brian, who was struggling to force an awkwardly-shaped rock into his trouser pocket: 'This is gonna be a Red Indian chief, with a feathered headdress. See, that bit can be his big nose, like an eagle. He can be called "Golden Eagle"' ('The Chalk Carving', pp. 1–2).

Under the guidance of his teacher, Mr Knight, Mark works hard to prise out of the rock the head of his Indian chief, but just as he is making progress, the nose falls off. Mr Knight sympathises and suggests turning the sculpture into a cat, but again disaster strikes and the head falls off. Mr Knight surveys the damage:

> 'Mmm, let's see. You know, I'm sure you could salvage something from this bit. Perhaps a frog – yes, I'm sure you could make it into a frog.' Holding the two pieces, he gave Mark what he hoped was an encouraging smile but, as their eyes met, they both began to laugh. Mark's laughter was partly fuelled by embarrassment and partly by a sense of the ridiculous, as he envisaged the chalk growing smaller and smaller as more pieces fell off. Perhaps it would finish up like the acorn he had seen in the pieces of chalk chosen by some other boys (p. 5).

Mark eventually ends up with a tortoise which, in the class exhibition, has to be propped up on another piece of chalk, because one of the legs falls off.

The experience of relating and writing up this memory had a transformative effect on the relationship between Jennifer and her brother. When he read the story, he was 'absolutely delighted' and since then he has taken to telephoning her regularly, to tell her about other things he has remembered. These discussions have been 'more revealing of my brother's early emotional experiences than any previous conversations we have had. As a result I have found myself becoming far more understanding of his viewpoint and less resentful of the unfairness I felt as the only girl.' These experiences have changed Jennifer's whole perspective on her brother:

> I actually feel now that I never really knew him before. He is two and
> a half years older than me…I really hadn't any idea of the way he saw
> the world when he was a child, because you don't talk to each other
> about that sort of thing…I don't know whether he feels he
> understands my viewpoint better, but I certainly understand his.

The task of writing a story based on her brother's experience, which involved thinking herself into her brother's head '…made me realise *emotionally* what I already knew intellectually, that one's own past is a construct and that those we shared it with have their own construct which is often very different from ours'.

This experience also changed her perspective on her own resentments. Through engaging in a dialogue with her brother, hearing that he too felt underprivileged in certain respects as a child and looking at that early situation from his point of view, she began to understand that the fault was not necessarily with her brothers, but inherent in the ethos of their time, when 'boys were the ones who were going to be the breadwinners, boys were the ones who were assumed to be the most intelligent…and that you cannot really blame mothers and fathers and brothers for believing what was generally assumed to be the fact'.

Jennifer then went on to use this new perspective on her resentment as a theme in the 'melody for two voices' exercise where 'the self of the narrator…comments upon the way the life and character of the younger self were affected by the structure of the society in which she lived'. The piece opens with the narrator looking at a photograph of her younger self:

> The girl in the photograph is pretty and her eyes sparkle with health.
> She is sixteen and is consciously presenting this picture of carefree
> youth for the camera, hoping that the photographer will be
> sufficiently impressed to put the finished photograph into the window
> of his shop ('Melody for Two Voices', p.1).

It is a 'two-dimensional black and white image' which, however, does not deceive the narrator, whose memory colours and fleshes out the subject of the photo into the living, moving, more complex self of her early years. Whilst the girl in the photo is 'not unintelligent' and 'quite well educated', she is 'now working as a GPO telephonist', a job way beneath her capabilities:

> The trouble with Jennifer is that, having had the misfortune, as she
> sees it, to have been born a girl, she feels that any possibility of a real
> career is denied her. This viewpoint has been thrust upon her by her
> parents and her brothers, conforming to the ethos of the time. Mark,
> who is two years older than her, is a trainee engineer for the GPO,
> and it is his enthusiasm for this work that has encouraged Jennifer to
> apply for work as a telephonist. Of course, it was unheard of in the
> 1950s for girls (or women) to be employed in any technical capacity
> and so Jennifer, who studied physics, chemistry and maths to 'O' level,
> must be content with working the switchboard, while her brother,
> who failed his eleven-plus and went to secondary school, becomes an
> engineer (pp.1–2).

Jennifer's job is regarded as no more than a stop-gap between schooling and marriage; the most important thing is for her to make the most of her appearance, so that she attracts a good man. The young Jennifer wishes she were a boy and resents the situation in which she finds herself, but the older narrator realises that:

> …what Jennifer really wanted was not to be a boy but to have a boy's
> opportunities, privileges and self-esteem. Yesterday she would often
> think: 'Why wasn't I born a boy?' Today I think: 'Why was she not
> treated equally with her brothers?' (p.4).

Thus, Jennifer's resentment at not having been able to go into higher education or develop a career is placed in a different context, where painful feelings and emotions are ameliorated by the appeal to adult reason. It is also separated off from the people to whom it has long been attached, so that those relationships can be reassessed.

The work on these various writing tasks and the insights which resulted began to suggest a shape for Jennifer's narrative: if it was to be a valid representation of the past she inhabited, then it would have to be 'multi-voiced', not only giving expression to her brothers and parents, but to herself at different stages of her life. From one of her early morning freewriting sessions arose the image of herself 'as a participant in a circle dance', which she felt could be used 'as a metaphor for the shifting relationships within my group of family and friends'.

By the end of the autobiography course, Jennifer had achieved a great deal: the writing was becoming more fluid, a possible shape for her narrative was emerging and, unexpectedly, her 'unresolved resentments' against her brothers were being addressed. She had 'a number of ideas on how to present my characters' and intended 'to continue writing short pieces based on these characters and their experiences in the hope that they will begin to interact to form a narrative'. The emerging themes of her writing seemed to be 'emotional and spiritual growth and increased understanding between some of the characters', and an important background to their experiences was 'the changing structure of their society and their differing responses to it'.

The pieces of fiction Jennifer submitted for assessment at the end of the second term of the Certificate in Creative Writing reveal steady progress towards giving voice to different members of her family and showing 'increased understanding' between them and herself. Jennifer's relationship with her elder brother, Simon, was highly problematical when they were children (he was eight years older and often very cruel towards her), although as adults they have talked a lot more than Jennifer and her brother Mark, and the relationship is now 'less of a problem'. Nevertheless, on and off during her childhood, particularly in response to various tormentings to which she was subjected, Jennifer was convinced that when she grew up she was going to kill Simon, and this motif figures largely in the short story 'The Decision'.

It is set in the home of Simon and his wife Caroline. It is his sixtieth birthday and his sister Alison (representing Jennifer) and her husband David are the only two other members of the family remaining after the party. A lot of alcohol has been consumed, and everyone is tired and inebriated. David is the first to retire to bed, leaving the other three talking in the living room.

This opening section is in the third person, primarily from Alison's point of view. She observes how gentle and kind her brother is towards his wife Caroline, who has recently suffered some kind of mental breakdown. This view of him contrasts strongly with Alison's memories of him when they were children, when 'he had been neither kind nor gentle to her' ('The Decision', p.2). In the course of the conversation Simon says that his daughter Melissa reminds him of Alison, to which Alison replies sharply: 'I hope you didn't terrorise her the way you did me when I was little' (p.3). This introduces tension, which Alison hurries to dispel, saying that she has forgiven him by now, but as she finishes her drink she:

> asked herself whether she really had forgiven Simon. She remembered her helpless fury at being unable to defend herself against him. He was so much older and bigger than her but, as well as that, he possessed that special quality so highly valued in the family (especially by mum) – he was a boy.

The old resentment at the privileges and unfair status of her brothers flares up, although it is quickly tempered now by an adult understanding that 'these advantages were not inborn or god-given, but that all those years of being treated as superior to girls made them believe they really were superior' (p.3).

Caroline now goes up to bed, and Alison and Simon are left alone. He pours himself another drink; he knows he shouldn't indulge, he tells Alison, because he suffers from angina, but he has the pills to cope with it; he pats his trouser pocket reassuringly. They talk about Caroline and her apparent inability to take charge of herself. Alison accuses her brother of patronising his wife, of preventing her recovery by over-solicitousness. She spouts feminist sociology at him, gleaned from her recent sojourn at university as a mature student, and this makes him angry. They argue and Alison finds herself threatened physically, her back against the door. The encounter recalls an occasion from their childhood when she was similarly threatened:

> 'Look, Alison, I've got some icing sugar for you. Open up'. Simon is smiling at her. With his blond wavy hair and turquoise blue eyes he looks guileless and charming. It is 1942 and sugar is rationed. Alison once stole some icing sugar from the store cupboard, when mum was at work, and now she recalls the lovely instant sweetness as the fine powder dissolved on her tongue. A spoonful would be a real treat, but she has learned to be suspicious of Simon's 'treats' (pp.7–8).

Six-year-old Alison, vulnerable but learning from experience, refuses to co-operate. The more stubborn she is, the more pressing Simon becomes, until she starts to cry, and he is able to force the contents of the spoon between her lips. Of course it is not sugar, but bicarbonate of soda, and as Alison rinses the disgusting taste from her mouth she vows 'that when she grows up she will kill him' (p.9).

Now, confronted with her adult brother, who has ceased to be the big, tough bully of her childhood, she meets his eyes, stares him out and he backs off; she is no longer the little sister at his mercy. They start to clear up the debris from the party and she takes a tray of glasses into the kitchen. When she returns, Simon is in the armchair, 'his face grey and his forehead greasy with perspiration', his frightened eyes gazing at her. His hands scrabble at his trouser pocket in an effort to retrieve his angina pills, but he cannot reach them.

The story now switches to Simon's point of view. He can see Alison standing by the door, watching him. He needs her to get the pills out of his pocket, but cannot communicate this. He regrets getting angry with her earlier; as the blackness of unconsciousness encroaches, it seems to him that they have always argued, ever since they were children, although there was a time, he recalls, when she doted on him, followed him everywhere, wanted to play, but she was too small, too young. Then he went to the grammar school and everything changed. He was a scholarship boy from a council estate, constantly harassed and tormented by the fee-paying prep school boys. It was the end of his childhood; he had to learn how to cope. There was no time for his little sister.

When Simon emerges from the blackness, he finds Caroline, David and Alison bending over him. 'Alison's face was white and expressionless. In her hand she held the container of pills' (p.13).

In this story the main protagonist, Alison, acting as spokesperson for the author, seems to be seeking a balance between resentment and forgiveness. The resentment is still there, inadvertently slipping out in the course of conversation and in the memories which, figuratively as well as literally, have left a bitter taste in her mouth. But the inclusion of Simon's point of view, portraying him sympathetically, dramatising what must have been for him extremely painful circumstances at school, shows that the character of Alison, and presumably also the writer, can now appreciate the difficulties her brother experienced as a child. This appreciation provides a new perspective from which the author can view her own resentments, and this new perspective enables her to find, in fictional form, a satisfying resolution to an old problem. Thus in the story, in spite of the fact that as a child Alison vowed that she would kill her brother when she grew up, when an opportunity arises in her adult life, she does not take it, although her hesitation reveals that a powerful inner conflict is being confronted.

The work Jennifer submitted for assessment at the end of the Certificate in Creative Writing consisted of the first two chapters of a novel under the title *Art Silk*. Chapter One opens with Alison (here again representing Jennifer) clearing out her mother's council house after her death. She has found, wrapped up in tissue paper, a dress which she remembers her mother making when Alison was about six years old. It spills out, '…fragile and faded, like a shed snakeskin. Its soft sheen lights up the empty room in the empty house' (*Art Silk*, p.1).

Alison reminds herself that it is not correct to call it a dress; it is a 'frock', as her mother used to say, and that the art silk out of which it is made did not mean, as she had imagined as a child, that this was 'artistic, colourful, glamorous silk'. 'Art silk' was short for artificial silk: 'a deliberate ploy by manufacturers and retailers to persuade people that they were buying something special, "arty", bohemian, rather than a cheap substitute for the real thing' (p.1).

Alison recalls her mother making the dress, her delight at the finished item and her eagerness to wear it to the pub on the Saturday evening her husband Joe came home from the factory just outside London, where he was helping in the war effort. In spite of his weak chest, he had cycled the fifty-mile journey and was not keen to go out on one of his infrequent weekends at home. But his wife pressed him and he succumbed. After they had gone out, Alison, indignant at having been left alone with her two older brothers, crept out of the house in her night-dress:

> The dewy grass in the front garden was cold and wet on my bare feet, but it was not as dark out here as it was in my room. I'd always hated the dark. Anyone could creep up on you in the dark. Out here, you could see the moon. I followed the grass path between the flower beds, wondering what to do next, when I saw the man from next door and his wife climbing their front steps. 'Hello, what are you doing out here like that? Where's your mum and dad?' 'Up the pub.' 'Well, you'd better come indoors with us. Look at her, the bottom of her nightie is soaked. Come on, we'll warm you up.' 'Mum said she wanted some pleasure'. 'Oh, did she now?' said Mr. Pierce, taking me by the hand (p.9).

Chapter Two is from the point of view of Alison's mother, Rosemary. Using an approach remarkably similar to that adopted by Jessica (see below), Jennifer adopts the perspective of Rosemary looking down from heaven after her death. Watching her daughter sifting through her things, she is surprised that it is Alison who is undertaking this task, rather than Toby, the younger of the two boys. Alison

> was never really family-minded. Couldn't wait to get away. Seemed to prefer the company of strangers. By the time she was sixteen I hardly saw her, except for meals, and sometimes not even then. She was such a lovely child too, always so happy and smiling and eager to please. Then suddenly, when she was about three or four years old, she got sulky, telling tales and pouting, always pouting. I remember I once asked her: 'Why aren't you my happy, smiling little girl any more? Why are you always moping around and complaining about everything?' She didn't answer me (p.10).

Rosemary wishes she could ask her now, as Alison sits stroking the frock her mother made all those years ago, and the frock reminds her of that incident when Alison left the house that night she and Joe had gone down the pub. She had been longing to show off her new dress and they were not out for long. When they got back, Simon, their eldest boy, was still up; he said the other two had been very quiet. But when Rosemary went upstairs to check, Alison was not in her bed. Alarmed, they prepared to alert the police, but just then there was a knock on the door and Stanley Pierce from next door was there with Alison in his arms:

> 'Hello there, saw you were back. We found her wandering about in her nightie. Frightened to death. Said you were up the pub, something about wanting some pleasure. She's alright, we've given her some cocoa to warm her up, but she wouldn't let us bring her back until you came home. Said Simon would hit her when he found out she'd sneaked out. I've been watching out for you, 'cos I knew you'd be worried. Who'd have kids, eh?' (p.12).

Rosemary remembers being relieved, but embarrassed in front of her neighbour. She picks Alison up and takes her back to bed. As she comes downstairs to see Mr Pierce out, she notices that where she had cuddled Alison to her, there is a cocoa stain, right on the front of her new dress.

These two chapters, in the voices of the two women, convey mutual resentment and a lack of understanding, as well as an awkward class divide, presumably brought about by Alison having moved away from her origins. The adult Alison remembers how, once she was at grammar school, she 'lost respect for her [mother's] abilities, felt embarrassed by her accent' (p.5). Thinking of her in her bright frock, remembering her 'joyful physicality, her childlike delight in her own allure', she feels 'pity and shame' (p.5). The *double entendre* of the title 'Art Silk' also reflects this discomfort.

Whilst the characters of Alison and Rosemary and their interrelations do not mirror exactly Jennifer's life story, she feels that through them she is exploring her relationship with her mother which, of her significant relationships, she finds 'the most difficult of all': 'I think in a way, from my own point of view rather than from a creative point of view, I am trying to understand what kind of person [my mother] was.' The story of the dress has been created out of 'little flashes of something I remember my mother wearing', tied in with memories of watching her make dresses. Her mother was 'a very complex' person: 'In some ways she was extremely feminine and in another way she would much rather have been a man and despised all things feminine.' Jennifer feels that her own problems with sexual identity have been affected by this: '[It] jumped out at me when I actually wrote a description of her and when I read it through I thought: I am not talking about her, I am talking about me. Is that because I am putting what I feel onto her or is it because I am very similar to her? It is difficult to disentangle it.'

Trying to sort out who her mother is for her is also a way of trying to understand who she is herself, of trying to discover *her own truth*. Her perspective on her own truth has changed considerably in the process of writing; she recognises now that what she has always regarded as the 'truth' of her past, is not necessarily the same as her brothers' 'truths'. This was brought home to her when, in the conversations with them, she realised that her mother was an entirely different person for them 'especially for [my] older brother, because she was a young married woman [when he was a child] – it was before the war – it was before she'd had all the problems with my second brother's illness'. So that whilst 'we are brothers and sisters...we had different parents'.

This recognition that she and her brothers each have different truths, different versions of their collective past, has enabled Jennifer to work through her unresolved resentments: 'I can think, well that is true – what I have always remembered is true, but it is only part of the whole truth, and so there are other things which are true, that change the perspective of my truth, so that I feel I have resolved certain things.' In *Art Silk*, which Jennifer describes as 'a quest narrative': 'Alison is searching for the "truth" about her mother. She is also searching to reconcile her past with what she has become, for the "truth" about herself.' As with her explorations of her brothers' versions of the past, Alison 'finds more than one past and more than one truth', which reveals the fallibility of her own version. Alison's ability to see her mother in a different light, to understand her version of the past, helps her to move towards 'a kind of forgiveness'. Her mother, in turn, looking down from the spirit world also re-evaluates her daughter's actions and attitudes, so that there is a kind of reconciliation, albeit at a distance.

When I talked to Jennifer again some six months later she reported that she had not continued with the novel. This was partly because of misgivings about the possibility of upsetting members of her family, by producing a novel which, whilst not an actual representation of the family, would be close enough to give rise to aggravation. More important was the feeling that the writing she had done had already laid to rest some of her resentments. She had done 'a lot more thinking and also I've done a lot more talking with my brother Mark'. These discussions had given Jennifer a certain sense of satisfaction, because he was now voicing relatively mild criticisms of their mother, which indicated that what Jennifer saw as his rather idealised perception of her had undergone change. Talking to Mark had 'rounded out lots of problems in my mind about this feeling of resentment that I had'. This meant that, whilst she had not done any more writing, '...the thinking and the talking and the general reassessment has been done'.

This reassessment of the old resentments and laying them to rest seems to have given Jennifer a stronger sense of her own identity:

> I was reading this about…mutual forgiveness. I feel in a way [that] that's not necessary any more, because I think, as Popeye says: 'I am what I am' and a part of what I am is obviously what sort of life I've had, and there's no point going around blaming yourself for things that you might have done which were not necessary, were perhaps reactions to the way things were happening, but partly I mean not to go round blaming other people but to think, well, perhaps if I was brought up that way, she's got as much to blame for me being what I am as I've got [for] being what I am…

Thus it is no longer a question of finding someone to blame. Nor is there any longer a need for forgiveness; what began on the page as a fictional exploration of different points of view from the inside has moved into the real world of relationships where she can now negotiate her position face to face with her siblings, and the closer relationships with her brothers are clearly of great value to her.

I asked Jennifer whether she felt that fictionalising her autobiographical material rather than attempting to write a more straightforward 'factual' autobiography had made a difference. She replied:

> ...if I'd been trying to tell everything from my point of view I think it would have been much more difficult for me...knowing that there were other strands to it that I wasn't actually putting forward. And so in a way letting the other characters speak was a way of giving myself permission, if you like, to put my point of view, because I felt it's okay for me to slag off saying what a terrible life I'd had...if I can let the other people come in and say, yeah but hang on, look, this is it from their point of view..., otherwise I suppose I would feel that I was being unfair...

She also added that if she were to try to write a straightforward auto-biography: 'I wouldn't put in nearly so much in the way of how I felt...'. I believe that it is this, more than anything, which has enabled Jennifer to move on in her self-understanding. Whilst at the outset she understood intellectually that the oppression and lack of opportunity she suffered was a consequence of a gender bias in the family and social ethos of her youth rather than the ill-will of any particular member of her family, it was only writing the story in a fictional guise and from several different points of view that enabled her to enter into the experience *with feeling* and to acquire a different kind of knowledge of it.

Therapeutic Dimensions of the 'Dual Voice'

It is clear from Jennifer's own words that finding a voice for significant people in her life, namely her mother and brothers, had a profoundly therapeutic effect on her own sense of identity and enabled her to resolve some of the resentment she was harbouring from her childhood years. The connection between personal identity, creative writing and the relationship we have with significant people in our lives is the theme of Luann McCracken's essay on Virginia Woolf (McCracken 1994). She discusses Woolf's quite different sense of personal identity as revealed in her early and late autobiographical writings, and the link between this and Woolf's relationship with her mother. Both the early autobiographical sketch 'Reminiscences' (begun in 1907; Woolf 1989a) and the late one 'A Sketch of the Past' (written in 1939; Woolf 1989b) deal with the death of Woolf's mother, but approach it in very different ways.

'Reminiscences' is 'striking for its impersonality. There is a narrative "I", but that narrative persona is more an observer of the effects of events than an experiencer of them' (McCracken 1994, p.292). There is a 'literal absence of an individualised identity or an identity of [Woolf's] own' (p.294). McCracken finds the cause for this lack of identity in Woolf's inability to separate from her mother. She draws on Nancy Chodorow's object-relations approach to understanding the mother–daughter bond, which suggests that the girl child has an intrinsic difficulty in forming a sense of separate identity because she is of the same sex as the mother. Boys, on the other hand, are 'required to engage in a more emphatic individuation and a more defensive firming of experienced ego boundaries' (Chodorow 1978, pp.166–167; McCracken pp. 295–296). However it arose, Woolf's lack of individualised identity has a profound effect on her writing identity. Because she has not separated from her significant others, in particular from her mother, and found an identity of her own, she cannot put her emotions into the writing.

In 'A Sketch of the Past' Woolf 'includes herself in what she describes' (p.293), including her *feelings* about her mother's death. She is able to be present to herself on the page, to celebrate her past relationship with her mother; in other words to assert 'a positive identity that allows relationship' (p.303). Arguably this has been partly facilitated by her writing *To the Lighthouse* (1927), about which she said: 'I wrote the book very quickly; and when it was written, I ceased to be obsessed by my mother. I no longer hear her voice; I do not see her' (Woolf 1989b, p.90). Through fictionalising, she had found a workable objectification of her mother, which allowed her to be separate, but also to retain her as a valued object in her psychic world. By the end of her career, McCracken argues, 'Woolf has approached a balance between past and present; her sense of self admits both identification with the central mother-figure and separation from her', and this more solid sense of identity leads to a more solidly based writing identity, which enables her as a writer to 'merge with the identities of others through imagination' (McCracken 1994, p.291).

There is a strong link here with what has happened in the case of Jennifer. Through imagination Jennifer has managed to separate herself from troublesome and unworkable versions of her brothers and her mother which inhabited her psyche from childhood on. As characters in her own fiction, they played a role which kept in place an unhelpful version of the past. By creating fictional stories around these characters and empathically inhabiting their lives for a while, she has freed them from the inhibiting constraints of her fixed version of events and given them an opportunity of telling their own versions. The re-written versions have now been reabsorbed, so that the reasons for resentment are no longer relevant.

Something similar happened, too, in the writing of *New Town Blues*. As I have said above, my intention when planning the novel was that it should be an indictment of new town life and of my early family environment. In the event, through giving voice both to my father and mother in the guise of the characters Donald and Joan, and through exploring from their points of view their own difficult pasts, I wrote a much more sympathetic story than I intended. Having written the novel, I found that I had a much stronger sense of belonging, not only to my home town Crawley but to my family, both of which I had previously rejected. In other words, I had re-written and then re-embraced troublesome parts of my life story which were vitally important to me in developing a stronger sense of my own identity.

These three different examples of the strengthening of identity through giving voice to significant others highlight the importance of finding an appropriate point of view from which to tell one's story. This was clearly of great significance to Jennifer in starting to write her autobiographical novel. She says several times that it was vitally necessary for her to allow other members of her family to tell their own stories. She became aware from her reading of Ronald Fraser's *In Search of a Past* (1984) how diverse were different people's versions of the same historical events. For example, it was particularly significant for her to realise that she and her brothers had 'different mothers'. When, as a result of Jennifer's discussions with her elder brother, he began to bring their mother down from the pedestal on which he had always placed her, Jennifer had a sense of relief. Not only were her views changed by her brothers' stories; theirs, in turn, were changed by hers.

The possibilities for experiencing other people's points of view became clear to her when she was transcribing her brother Mark's school story. Writing it up from his point of view gave her 'a feeling of going into somebody else's life', whilst still retaining her own perspective:

> I was partly looking at him from my point of view as an adult and I was partly him. I could feel and I could see what was happening to him and I very much entered into the way he felt, but I was also looking at him and analysing how he felt and why he felt that way. It was very much a dual view as I was writing it.

This *dual view* is also present in the piece Jennifer wrote in response to the 'melody for two voices' exercise. She wanted to show the reader that whilst her resentment 'shows clearly in some of the pieces I have written', she also understood the reasons for the resentment. In the exercise she tries to show how her present self, with its increased understanding, 'interprets the past differently from the self living through it'. Thus, in the opening paragraph, we get two different perspectives:

> The girl in the photograph is pretty and her eyes sparkle with health.
> She is sixteen and is consciously presenting this picture of carefree
> youth for the camera, hoping that the photographer will be
> sufficiently impressed to put the finished photograph into the window
> of his shop. Looking at this representation of my youthful self, I am
> tempted to believe in the two-dimensional, black and white image that
> it portrays but, as my memory colours the photograph and adds the
> third and fourth dimensions, the girl returns to life, and I can watch
> her as she leaves the studio and catches her bus back to her parents'
> house on the edge of town ('Melody', p.1).

Here, the author is closely identified with the narrator and relates to her past self both in the first and the third person. By using the present tense she inhabits the past and the present simultaneously, so that she can move easily in and out of her different 'selves'. A similar approach is used in the novel *Art Silk*, where the first-person narrator, again closely identified with the author, moves in and out of her present and past perspectives on her relationship with her mother:

> The dress spills out of its tissue wrappings, fragile and faded, like a
> shed snakeskin. Its soft sheen lights up the empty room in the empty
> house. Mum's favourite dress.

> Correction. It is not a dress, it is a frock. 'My art silk frock'. It's not
> only fashions in clothes that change. Words date us just as surely. As I
> grew up I sloughed off the language of her generation, as well as
> many of her attitudes and beliefs. She changed too but words like
> 'frock' surfaced from time to time, betraying her preference for the
> days when she was young, modern, desirable.

> As a child in the 1940s I thought that 'art silk' meant artistic,
> colourful, glamorous silk. I was in my twenties before I discovered
> that 'art' was short for artificial. Cynical by then, I saw the shortened

form of the word as a deliberate ploy by manufacturers and retailers to persuade people that they were buying something special, 'arty', bohemian, rather than a cheap substitute for the real thing.

I pull at the seams, opening them out, to remind myself of the original colours of the fabric, before sunlight and wear faded it. The neatness and strength of the work remind me how much effort Mum put into the making of that frock. I was six years old at the time and loved to watch her at her sewing (*Art Silk*, Chap. 1).

For her novel, Jennifer wanted to develop further her idea of a 'dual view' and to create a *multi-voiced narrative*. The early drafts had been written in the third person, with an omniscient narrator, but she then felt that it was inappropriate to represent the conflicts within her family through a single voice which was essentially her own adult perspective. She decided to adopt a third-person narrative written from the points of view of each of the main characters as 'a useful compromise between the omniscient narrator and the "restricted viewpoint" of the first person narrator'. However, she was aware that it was important for each of the voices to be distinctive and she was having difficulty achieving this. The voice of her *alter ego*, Alison, was the closest to hers and the one in which she felt most fluent. The voice of Rosemary, representing her mother, was causing more difficulty. These difficulties clearly forced Jennifer to change her mind again, because the pieces of the novel I have seen consist of a first-person 'melody for two voices' from Alison's point of view and a restricted first-person narrative from the point of view of Rosemary after her death. As Jennifer did not continue with the novel, it is not possible to say whether this latter approach would have been successful overall, but her attempts to find an appropriate point of view for her personal narrative are interesting. They highlight the difficulties of finding a workable relationship, on the page, between author, narrator and character when one is writing autobiographically, difficulties which have a psychological as well as a literary dimension.

In his influential essay on point of view Norman Friedman lists a range of narrative positions, each of which allows a different degree of authorial presence. In *editorial omniscience* (as in George Eliot's *Middlemarch* [2]) the 'author will not only *report* what goes on in the minds of his characters, but he will also *criticize* it' (Friedman 1955, p.1172). In *neutral omniscience* (as in

2   Some of these examples are Friedman's; others are my own.

Flaubert's *Madame Bovary*) we do not get the author's visible intrusions, but the author's voice still dominates; he does not *speak through* his characters (p.1172). All versions of first-person narration deny the author any direct voice in the proceedings and he has surrendered altogether his omniscience regarding other characters (p.1174). In *I as witness* (as in Scott Fitzgerald's *The Great Gatsby*) and *I as protagonist* (as in Salinger's *The Catcher in the Rye*), 'the reader has available to him only the thoughts, feelings and perceptions' of the narrator (pp.1174–1176). In *multiple selective omniscience* (as in Beryl Bainbridge's *A Weekend With Claude*) the author is even further distanced from the narrative voice. Here the 'story comes directly through the minds of the characters as it leaves its mark there'; there is no-one to summarise and explain the thoughts, perceptions and feelings passing through the characters' minds (p.1176). In *selective omniscience* (as in Arthur Schnitzler's 'Lieutenant Gustl') 'the reader is limited to the mind of only one of the characters' (p.1177), whose voice is sometimes rendered in the first person, in stream-of-consciousness or interior monologue. The *dramatic mode* (as in Hemingway's 'Hills Like White Elephants') and the *camera* (as in Robert Coover's 'The Sentient Lens') dispose of mental states altogether, the former corresponding to a stage play where 'the information available to the reader…is limited largely to what the characters do and say', the latter presenting 'without apparent selection or arrangement, a "slice of life" as it passes before the recording medium' or camera (pp.1178–1179).

Thus, Friedman's categories move from a position where the author is visibly and firmly in charge of his narrator's or character's views and behaviour, through a progressive disempowering of the author, to his total exclusion. The key factor here is the *distance* between the author and the narrative voice. Apart from authorial omniscience, all the other points of view require that the author's identity is to a greater or lesser extent suspended. Indeed, according to the fashion in novel writing which developed strongly from Henry James on, the more the author's identity is repressed, the better the fiction. This, however, will not fulfil Jennifer's aim. She is attempting to find a narrative perspective which enables her to combine her *present* understanding of her past with various episodes from her past *in the way she experienced them at the time*, together with the different versions which other members of her family have of those episodes from the past. This means that she needs a perspective which gives her a voice as author/narrator, but at the same time she must not be seen to impose her version of events on the characters and narrators, including herself as a character from the past. In other words, she needs to have simultaneously both closeness to and distance from her narrative perspective. As Jennifer herself realises, omniscience will not achieve this. First-person point of view provides a very limited perspective (although, as I said, Jennifer opts for this in the submitted drafts). Of the remaining categories in Friedman's taxonomy, it is *multiple selective omniscience*, where 'the story comes through the minds of the characters as it leaves its mark there', which would seem to offer the appropriate perspective. But Friedman says that here the author is even further distanced from the narrative voice than in first person narratives (p.1176). Is this true?

Friedman's paper was written before the systematic discussion in English of *free indirect discourse* (FID). This is neither the direct speech of a character, nor the straightforward indirect speech of a character as reported by the narrator. It is an indirect form of speech, in that the third person is used, but instead of the thoughts or words of the character being transposed into the narrator's words, they *retain the actual words, personal tone, gesture and often the idiom of the character.* To do this, the narrator 'places himself...directly into the experiential field of the character, and adopts the latter's perspective in regard to both time and place' (Pascal 1977, p.9). In so doing, however, *the narrator is not obliterated*; he retains his own 'objective position' (p.6). He is:

> always effectively present in free indirect speech, even if only through
> the syntax of the passage, the shape and relationship of sentences, and
> the structure and design of a story; usually, of course, he also appears
> as the objective describer of external events and scenes and of
> psychological processes, and as a moral commentator. Above all,
> perhaps, as the agency that brings multiple and complex events into
> relationship with one another and leads them to an end that
> establishes, even if without explicit comment, an all-embracing
> meaning (p.137).

For Bakhtin, free indirect discourse is one of the most important examples of 'double-voiced discourse' which gives the novel its characteristic *heteroglossia* or 'multi-voicedness':

> It serves two speakers at the same time and expresses simultaneously
> two different intentions: the direct intention of the character who is
> speaking, and the refracted intention of the author. In such discourse
> there are two voices, two meanings and two expressions. And all the
> while these two voices are dialogically interrelated, they – as it were –

know about each other (just as two exchanges in a dialogue know of each other and are structured in this mutual knowledge of each other); it is as if they actually hold a conversation with each other (Bakhtin 1981, p.324).

The rhetorical effects of this dialogic narrative technique are several and are well demonstrated in Doris Lessing's story 'One Off the Short List' (Lessing 1979, pp.220–247)[3]. Here the main protagonist Graham Spence, a minor TV presenter, has a compulsive need to seduce certain women of note, so that he can cross them off his mental list. The story recounts the case of one such pursuit, of set designer Barbara Coles. It is told in the third person from Spence's point of view, the narrator going in and out of his mind to give us both an inside and an outside view of events. In the following extract Spence, having insinuated himself into Barbara Coles' flat, is trying to work out how to get her into bed:

> Now a problem. He wanted to be closer to her, but she was fitted into a damned silly little chair that had arms.[3] If he were to sit by her on the floor...? But no,[4] for him, the big bulky reassuring man, there could be no casual gestures, no informal postures. Suppose I scoop her out of the chair on to the bed?[2] He drank his coffee as he plotted.[1] Yes, he'd carry her to the bed, but not yet (Lessing 1979, p.237).

As Helen Aristar Dry points out, this brief extract contains no less than four styles of thought representation: (1) the narrator's summary of the character's thoughts; (2) the character's sentences in his exact words (free direct discourse); (3) some of the character's words interpolated into the narrator's report (FID); and (4) the character's thoughts transposed to third person (FID) (Dry 1995, p.99). Using FID means that 'there can be many textual gradations between unequivocal representation of the character's voice and uninterrupted narrative exposition' (p.99).

The value of this technique, which is a form of *multiple selective omniscience*, lies not only in its ability to create a rich ambiguity of narrative voice, through simultaneous access to a number of different points of view, but also in its ability to evoke empathy with characters who outwardly might not be very appealing. Giving the reader an inside view of Graham's suffering (that

3   I am indebted to Helen Aristar Dry's discussion of Lessing's story (1995).

he is driven to use sexual dominance to compensate for a sense of professional failure) and the extent to which he is himself a victim of family pressures and societal demands, goes some way towards countering the assumption that he is simply a boor who preys on successful women (pp.102 and 108).

In terms of what Jennifer is trying to achieve in her autobiographical novel, a richly ambiguous, multi-voiced text which evokes empathy would be particularly useful. First, it would allow her simultaneously to inhabit her characters and to have narrative distance from them. Second, it would encourage her as reader of her own text to empathise with characters towards whom she feels intrinsically antagonistic. Whilst Jennifer is not fully aware of the possibilities of FID, she moves intuitively towards it in her various attempts to find a workable point of view and achieves something of its effects. Indeed, her metaphor of the circle dance suggests a *series* of dual voices, in the sense in which it was used by Arthur Schnitzler in his play *Reigen* (1900). In Schnitzler's version, each scene revolves around the act of intercourse between two characters, and is linked to the next by one of these two characters engaging in intercourse with one of the two characters in the next scene. The circle is completed when one of the characters from the last scene has intercourse with one from the first. The use of intercourse as the linking act is apt here, with its connotations of simultaneous merging and separateness. In Jennifer's formulation it is not sexual merging which is the key, but 'increased understanding between some of the characters', an increased overlap, even merging, of points of view, a willingness to be changed by the encounter with another, without, however, a complete loss of identity. It is this temporary merging of points of view within a context of overall narrative control which allows Jennifer's 'truth' to be 're-written' or reformulated, so that a new and more workable 'truth' can emerge.

Whilst these points of view are, in one sense, the voices of others, they are also an integral part of who she is. In psychoanalytic terms they are the voices of her object world and part of her self-identity. As Christopher Bollas says: 'The concept of self... [refers] to the positions or points of view from which and through which we sense, feel, observe and reflect on distinct and separate experiences in our being (Bollas 1993, pp.9–10). He goes on to say that 'one crucial point of view comes through the other who experiences us' (p.10). What he is referring to here is the object-relations view that, from childhood on, aspects of ourselves are brought into being through our relations with other people, largely before we are able to reflect on the process and often in ways which are problematical to us. Throughout life, the psyche retains traces (or 'the shadow') of those significant encounters. These traces may be felt, but unthought, and part of the work of psychoanalysis is to facilitate 'the emergence into thought of early memories of being and relating' (p.3). Thus, the analysand may find himself, in his free associations, 'speaking with the voice of the mother, or the mood of the father, or some fragmented voice of a child self either lived or withheld from life' or, on the other hand, 'speaking *to* the mother, anticipating the father, or reproaching, exciting or consoling a child – the child self of infancy, in the midst of separation at age two, in the oedipal phase, or in adolescence' (p.1).

One of the most important ways in which significant figures from childhood continue to 'cast their shadow' in later life is in the way we manage the self as an object. By 'objectification of the self' Bollas means the way we constantly engage in dialogue with ourselves; negotiate, within what he calls 'intrasubjective space', between the different areas of the self such as our instinctual needs and desires, our superego prohibitions (p.42). In the evolution of the relation to the self as object it is the ego which plays the crucial role. Bollas's understanding of ego is that it is a development of an innate 'internal structuring tendency' (p.50). From the first hours of life the infant internalises 'rules communicated to him from the mother and father about the handling of the instinctual drives and needs' (p.50). This process continues throughout childhood, whilst the infant is 'the object of parental empathy, handling and law' (p.51). In adult life the way we handle ourselves as objects derives from the way we were handled as infants:

> Our handling of our self as an object partly inherits and expresses the
> history of our experience as the parental object, so that in each adult
> it is appropriate to say that certain forms of self perception, self
> facilitation, self handling and self refusal express the internalised
> parental process still engaged in the activity of handling the self as an
> object (p.51).

It is a form of 'knowledge' which is written into ego structure, but which is consciously unthought; it is part of the 'unthought known'.

As we have seen, Jennifer's self-writings contain narrative representations of significant features in her early relationships with her mother and her brothers: the mother's preference for her sons over her daughter; the cruelty inflicted on her by her elder brother; his abandonment of her when he went to grammar school. These narratives are split off from the historical events which brought them into being and have developed a life of their own in Jennifer's inner world, where they have become internally oppressive. If left at the level of the 'unthought known', these narratives will continue to play themselves out in Jennifer's inner world. They form a layer of experiencing which is not changed by the changing of external conditions, e.g. by the death of the mother. They are also not changed (as Jennifer found) simply by a better understanding of the historical circumstances in which boys had greater opportunities than girls.

For Bollas, it is in the psychotherapeutic encounter that 'the person's narrative relation to himself as an object' can be reported and reflected upon (p.60). It is an opportunity to consider, together with the therapist, certain assumptions and attitudes towards the self. For example, 'the point of view which the patient reveals in his narration establishes crucial aspects of the transferences to the self as object' (p.61). Apart from this 'telling' or narrating aspect of analysis, there is, Bollas observes, a 'showing' aspect. In his attempt to bring the unthought into being, the analysand will use the analyst 'mimetically'; he 'lodges himself inside' the analyst, compelling that other to experience his (the analysand's) formative object relations. In this sense, the analysand *creates a character* which is simultaneously himself and the other, *a dual voice* which enables him to speak, in dialogue with the analyst, the unthought part of himself and to develop a stronger sense of identity. In engaging with herself as object through her writings, Jennifer uses *the page* instead of an analyst as the means of objectification. If it is the 'unthought', or unreflected upon, nature of her significant past relationships which has allowed them to continue to function in a damaging way, then by drawing them out and *thinking* them with her adult consciousness, inhabiting them on the page through the dual voice, she is re-contextualising them in such a way that they belong to her present rather than her past. Thus they become less troublesome and an integral part of her present, reformulated identity.

Finding a Form for a Fragmented Identity – Jessica's Story

The case of Jessica bears a certain similarity to that of Jennifer. Jessica is a professional woman in her mid forties who has undergone psychotherapy. Like Jennifer, she was aware from the outset that she was using her writing as a method of self-exploration, although she also very much wants to write what she calls 'quality fiction'. Also like Jennifer, Jessica achieves a sense of resolution in finding a fictional voice for her mother, but the main focus of her quest is to find a form for her autobiographical novel, which she has difficulty doing. This difficulty seems to be strongly linked with what Jessica refers to as her 'splitness', her sense of being psychically fragmented.

Since the age of fifteen, Jessica has been:

> consciously engaged in the task of finding a narrative that would offer some sort of account of my development as a person. It was difficult for me and those around me to understand why someone who appeared to have everything (looks, brains and wonderful parents), could be so depressed and anxious and have such low self-esteem'[4].

According to Jessica, her problems stem from the disruptive influence of her older sister, who suffered a fall as a baby, cracked her skull and became epileptic. The mother's guilt about the accident and the need to compensate for it by an over-tolerant attitude towards the child resulted in Jessica's sister developing into a difficult and unruly person who polarised the family into two opposing camps: Jessica and her father versus Jessica's mother and sister. This split alienated Jessica from her mother and sister, who were seen as 'dark people', and meant that she identified wholly with her schoolteacher father, which led to a valorising of masculine hard-headedness in her attitude towards books and studying, to the detriment, she feels, of her female identity. Also, because her sister was seen as 'bad', Jessica felt that she had to be 'good', which meant that aspects of herself which were not in accord with this ideal had to be repressed. The resulting splits in her personality have interfered with her ability to learn or to retain her learning, and have left her with a feeling of being out of touch with aspects of herself. She also describes herself as having 'strong control needs', of being perfectionistic and guilt-ridden about her past. She would like her personal narrative to help her identify the cause of her problems and to assuage her sense of guilt; ideally, it will be a single, all-embracing piece of work which will encapsulate the 'truth' of her predicament.

During the autobiography course Jessica wrote a number of straightforward autobiographical pieces. 'Sisters' records what must have been a typical episode in Jessica's early home life. It opens with the narrator, aged about ten, cowering in the bathroom in retreat from the physical battle between her father and her sister:

---

4   Unless otherwise stated, quotations are from Jessica's essays written for the Certificate in Creative Writing, the two interviews conducted with her, and her unpublished M.Sc essay written in 1991.

In the silence I kneel on the cold lino floor of the toilet, following the grainy, swirly pattern of waves and spirals. I have stopped breathing. The toilet becomes my pew and I pray, not that she is all right but that he won't have to go to prison. This time I think he has killed her and I cannot bear the thought of life without him. Please God, let him be spared. It's not his fault. She provokes him, always. Calls Mum names. He's got to do something. He can't let her get away with it, can he? ('Sisters', p.1)

The incident has been sparked off by some minor everyday remark made by mother to daughter, missiles have been thrown and father is bent on physical punishment. The narrator's role in life is determined by these daily occurences:

She [the sister] was bad; there was never any doubt in my mind about that. And I? I had to be perfect. The message was there in the air that I breathed. Implicit in the way she was treated. She was bad through and through, the murky background against which I must shine, the shadow that set me in relief. She was dark and I was fair. She was ugly and I was pretty. She was an idiot, an imbecile, a brainless dolt and I was clever. I was born in a fortress impregnable to changes of perception or adjustments to the shading. There was a perfect balance between black and white, bad and good, which had to be maintained at any cost to prove it was not their fault. *They* were not bad (p.3).

In 'Visitation' the sisters are older; the narrator, married and newly pregnant, is at home when her sister arrives unexpectedly on the doorstep:

She stands at the door with two bulging carrier bags. Christ, she wants to stay. How can I get out of this? Her hair is flat and greasy as it was when we were children, not the backcombed beehive she sported during the 60s and even through the 70s. Gone too are the white stilettos, worn regardless of season or weather. She wears low-heeled, sensible shoes and a battered suedette coat that's gone shiny at the cuffs ('Visitation', p.1).

Reluctantly, the narrator invites her in, gives her tea, hoping that she will go soon. But she is still there when husband Geoff arrives home for supper. Her presence evokes the threat of violence, a reminder of the abuse the narrator suffered at her sister's hands when they were children:

> I couldn't touch one of her dolls to reach one of mine in the toy box;
> couldn't walk on her bit of carpet to get to my bed; couldn't exist
> without apologising for it. 'Ask my permission, beggar who begs for
> everything,' went the chant. And at night, just as I was drifting off
> into sleep, 'Fuckabugger dear, you're going to die,' a whispered cackle
> in my ear (p.1).

'Bevendean' is a very different piece, still first person, but this time consistently in the past tense, rather than the mixture of past and present that characterises the other two. The narrator, an educational professional, is on her way to see the new head of a primary school in the housing estate of the title. She is hot and harrassed, with just ten minutes to grab a lunchtime sandwich and, cynically surveying the parade of shops, she does not expect to find suitable sustenance there, let alone courtesy. To her surprise, all the people she encounters, the old man and his wife in the newsagent's who direct her to a café, the woman who serves her in the café, smile at her and are helpful. These unexpected kindnesses puncture her brisk, cynical façade and, as she sits in her car eating her sandwich, she recalls a previous visit to the school when she was still a trainee, doing educational research with young children:

> I usually worked in the medical room but one day I was moved to the
> Library. I set up my equipment: the tape recorder, the Mr Men box,
> the 'stimulus items', and had time to spare before my first child (or
> 'subject' as I had learnt to call them) was due. Another hot autumn
> afternoon, light streaming in, catching the dancing motes of dust, a
> just discernible scent of pine and the stronger mushroomy smell of
> new red carpet. Picture books were displayed around the room on
> free-standing shelves arranged to form little snug areas, with bean
> bags and rugs and cushions, so cosy. Loud cheerful colours trumpeting
> out the message that this was a place where reading was meant to be
> enjoyed. I found my eyes were pricking. Soon there were tears
> ('Bevendean', pp.2–3).

Memories flood in, of being a natural, spontaneous reader at the age of four, before reading became something to be achieved and resistances set in. Sitting there in the car, she realises that the refusal to read was a wilful stubbornness on her part, a self-destructiveness that had deprived her of joy.

These three pieces are all quite different in tone. In 'Sisters' the young narrator, trying very hard to be good, as a counterbalance to the 'bad' sister, is portrayed as frightened and vulnerable, in her childhood omnipotence taking on the burden of guilt for a situation which was not her responsibility. In 'Visitation' the adult narrator is nervous but tougher, concerned to get rid of the unwelcome visitor. In 'Bevendean' both sides of the narrator are visible: the hard, somewhat brittle façade giving way to reveal a vulnerable, damaged person underneath.

Reviewing these three pieces in her first essay, Jessica sees them as part of her larger project to create a single narrative that makes sense of her life, but feels that her writing 'is more effective if I focus on specific episodes'. She is aware that the pieces are quite different in style and that the first two contain frequent changes of tense. However, 'this kind of zig-zagging backwards and forwards between past and present, or more and less immediate experience, is something that I shall probably retain in my longer piece of work…'. 'Bevendean' seems to her to be a microcosm of how the longer work might turn out, and the overall theme – that of 'a family, mother, father and two sisters, and the evolution of their two very different personalities as a result of the roles assigned to them' – is 'fairly clear'. There is a major worry, though, about letting all the material go into one work, which would preclude the possibility of developing it in more fictional forms later.

These pieces of writing, then, show Jessica identifying and portraying different aspects of her personality, different versions perhaps of the way she sees herself: the 'good' girl of her childhood, the stronger but wary wife and mother, the tough carapace of the professional woman masking the vulnerable, wounded person underneath. There is an indication in 'Sisters' that she would like to hold her parents responsible for her plight, but an awareness in 'Bevendean' that her own refusal to co-operate with external reality has damaged her profoundly.

By the end of the second course of the Certificate a significant shift is visible. 'Splitting' is an episodic piece, written in the third person, with the main protagonist, a teenager at school, now identified for the first time by name. Sarah is bold, self-destructive and openly destructive of others, particularly of those she perceives to be weaker than herself, the maths teacher for example: 'She wanted to inflict harm and poor Miss Mamby was such a natural victim, with her sticking out teeth, bad breath, and bristly chin. Miss Mamby, ex-missionary, was too nice ('Splitting', p.3).

Cruelty also plays a significant role in Sarah's relationships with 'best' girlfriends, whom she nevertheless loves passionately. With boyfriends too, she is equally ambivalent, the conflict between her desire for closeness and her fear of intimacy rendering her cold and unfeeling in the face of their 'hopeless falling in love'. Sarah knows she is troubled, that 'without [God's] goodness to bind her', she might 'split into hundreds of fragments': '…she was much more of a wreck than Miss Mamby, but no-one was going to destroy her. She felt hollow and bogus, permeated by a vague fear of not being all right, which she never confessed to anyone…' (p.4).

Her moments of release are occasional out-of-body experiences, which happen unexpectedly, 'as if whatever it was that held her down had been unzipped, like a pantomime costume, releasing her to rise to a worry-free domain' (p.1). The experience recalls a show she once saw, where a performer dressed as a lion had opened himself up and revealed himself as a man. The idea had excited her, with its opposite possibilities: 'how wonderful if a mere person could give birth to a raging, roaring lion!' (p.1).

When reading this piece I was confused as to whether Sarah represented Jessica's sister or Jessica herself; the overt destructiveness was more in keeping with what I had heard and read about the sister. I raised this with Jessica, saying that I was surprised she had portrayed herself as similar to her sister. Her reply is interesting: 'I think that is the point really…I can tolerate that idea now. At one stage I couldn't tolerate that idea at all…because the family was polarised'.

This piece of writing then seems to have provided a vehicle through which Jessica was able to express the 'bad' side of herself, the side which she could not express in childhood because of the need to be 'the good daughter'. The image of the pantomime lion, a consciously fictional device, is also significant in its neat representation of another side of the personality waiting to be released, or of an authentic interior self floating free of the shackles of a split and troubled persona.

Another piece of writing from the second course is also important in what it achieves for Jessica on a personal level. One of Jessica's deepest regrets, she says, is the lost opportunity for a close relationship with her mother. In 'Desire' she records an occasion where her need for intimacy with her, which (like reading and other things she might have enjoyed) she denied herself for most of her childhood, is temporarily fulfilled, when Sarah persuades her mother to spend the night with her:

> They brought down the spare mattress, giggling as they wrestled with its bulk, negotiating the narrow staircase, bending it to go around the corner in the hall and through the door into the living room.
> Together they lifted the settee to one side and pushed the telly into the alcove, which left just enough space if they wedged the mattress

against Dad's desk. They looked directly at one another and smiled
big open smiles. And all the while, Sarah was willing it to be all right.
She wanted this with such clarity ('Desire', p.1).

Whilst there is clearly a genuine need here for closeness, the 'desire' of the
title seems to have other, less worthy motives. With father away in London,
this is an opportunity for Sarah to interfere in the mother-sister dyad from
which she feels excluded (here, again for the first time, the sister is given a
name – Alex); there is also a strong implication that Sarah is using her mother
for her own ends, as she seems to do most of the time:

> Somehow, after the usual telly and homework, she had managed to
> say to her mother, as if it were the most natural thing in the world,
> 'Let's sleep down here tonight.' Her mother had laughed her tinkly
> laugh, but Sarah could see that she was pleased. She knew that Sarah
> despised her. Sarah was daddy's girl. She used her – to provide meals
> for herself and the gangs of friends she seemed to attract; to do her
> washing and ironing; to set her hair for Saturday night; to test her on
> her homework – but she did not love her. It was him she loved
> (pp.1–2).

This was Jessica's first piece of fiction to treat of her relationship with her
mother, and it demonstrates a deeply ambivalent attitude towards her. It gives
voice, however, also for the first time, to her mother's feelings, albeit in the
third person (there is a brief section which expresses the mother's resentment
of Sarah's intimacy with her father). In fact, up to this point the majority of
Jessica's writing has been from her own point of view, whether in the first or
third person.

Two things, then, have happened in the writing of these two pieces: first,
a moving away from 'the facts' of Jessica's experience, in the conscious use,
for the first time, of imagery (the unzipping of the pantomime lion) and,
second, the giving of voice to another member of the family. These developments indicate a willingness on Jessica's part to loosen her control on her
own material (in the interview she frequently refers to the need to keep
things under control and the fear of 'mess' and 'chaos') and to allow it to find
its own shape, which points to a growing acceptance of the voices emerging
in the writing, even though the things they are saying may not be to Jessica's
liking.

By the end of the final course of the Certificate Jessica has the beginnings
of a continuous longer narrative which begins to look and sound like a novel.

The characters of Sarah and Alex, who figured in the earlier short pieces, are still there, but most significantly Jessica has now been able to write extensively from the perspective of her mother. In the first chapter, the mother of the family is looking down from heaven just after her death. The family is congregating at the house for her funeral. Her two daughters are there, Sarah, the younger of the two, married but at university now; and Alex, the difficult, older child, about whose future her mother worries most. Eddie, her husband, is also there, looking tired and shattered.

In a similar way to Sarah's out-of-body experience in 'Splitting', the mother is relieved to have escaped from the heaviness of earthly life; she feels light as a feather, young and carefree. From this vantage point she understands all kinds of things of which she was previously unaware: that because of Alex's greater needs, she neglected Sarah; that because she did not know how to assert her own rights and desires, she allowed herself to be used by others. She recalls with pleasure the time she and Sarah slept together on the living room floor, whilst aware that Sarah despised her; she recalls too the times when Sarah stole her husband from her and, from this safe distance, reprimands Sarah for it. Most of all, though, she wants the family to know that she tried her best, that she wants them to remember her as a good mother. The chapter has a light touch; the narrator is sympathetically portrayed and is herself sympathetic towards those she has left behind.

Chapter 2 is in the third person, but from Alex's point of view. She has bought, with money filched from her father's wallet, a new kitchen knife and is dicing a loaf, in order to feed the blackbirds. There is something slightly manic and unpredictable about her, a subtly conveyed potential for violence lurking beneath the surface: in the thoughts which fill her head as she slices or as she passes amongst her father's delicate living room furniture on her way to the French windows; in her anger at the way 'her' blackbirds allow themselves to be outwitted in the scramble for the bread by the hated starlings[5].

Chapter 3 is Sarah's chapter. It flashes back to her father's grief at the loss of his wife and Sarah's sense of power over him as he weeps on her shoulder. She is outwardly hard and unfeeling, her mother's demise not apparently causing her grief; it is 'a gift', providing her with a legitimate reason to take time off from her studies and go on a train journey without feeling guilty,

---

5   The original version of this chapter was written whilst Jessica was attending a previous creative writing course of mine.

although implicitly we are shown that this stance masks deeper and much more painful feelings.

Each of the chapters conveys a different set of emotions, a different perspective on the family relationships. All three female protagonists (the father is not yet developed as a character) are complex characters explored from the inside. The mother demonstrates insight and understanding; she is no longer the 'flat character' of 'Desire', but has been expanded, through empathy and imagination, into a thinking, feeling person with a distinct voice. Alex, too, is portrayed as being capable of expressing gentler emotions in her relations with the blackbirds, 'her blackies'.

The final essay makes clear the progress Jessica has made during the year. A long piece of autobiographical fiction is beginning to take shape. Its focal point is the death of her mother and its aim is:

> to put the record straight for myself, my dead mother and my
> estranged sister. Writing enables me to say things or show things that
> it has been impossible to share with any members of my family. It's a
> way of me saying that I understand and accept and maybe even
> forgive; I am also asking to be understood, to be accepted and to be
> forgiven.

The style of writing has developed out of the short pieces written earlier; particularly important has been the more extensive use of imagery and the introduction of a magical realist perspective which, Jessica says, has the effect of circumventing her tendency to be too analytical and controlling. Also important has been the new skill of writing from the point of view of her mother and developing her voice further. Free indirect discourse, used in two of the three chapters, provides an appropriate perspective from which to portray the main protagonists; as I have said in my discussion of Jennifer, it strikes a workable balance between closeness to and distance from her characters, and has the power to evoke empathy.

Jessica envisages the novel taking shape out of a number of discrete, self-contained pieces (perhaps fifty in all), for which she will seek a linking principle later. This loose but definite sense of structure makes it possible for her to relax her need for control over the developing work and to allow for temporary uncertainties. The formulation of a discrete project has also allowed different themes arising out of Jessica's story to separate themselves off: 'sisters, mothers and daughters; daughters and fathers, are the more obvious ones. Confusion over gender identity and living with mental illness are others…emotional barriers to learning' and the 'struggle for personal integration'.

A number of important developments, then, have made it possible for Jessica to progress towards a personal narrative that makes sense of her predicament: the building up of a body of fragments; the writing out and identifying of different aspects of herself; the giving of voice to members of her family; the finding of a shape for the whole narrative. As the project grows and becomes more defined, a 'virtuous circle' of increasing confidence comes into effect: the need for control loosens and the fear of using all the material in one go decreases.

With regard, however, to Jessica's original aims for her narrative, it seems that she is not so much identifying *the cause* of her predicament or finding *one single truth* which makes sense of the past; rather she is identifying and reassessing the various narratives which make up her own inner world in the present: her own as well as those of other significant people in her life. This reassessment involves revising unsatisfactory or troublesome narratives which were formulated in childhood or adolescence and which have taken on a life of their own in adulthood. In this sense the *reparation* involved is directed not so much towards the members of Jessica's family, for as she admits, her formulating of a kinder narrative will not change the way those people feel: her mother is dead, her sister would not be able to appreciate Jessica's empathy with her plight, and Jessica's father 'has his own preferred narrative'. It is an internal process which allows Jessica to re-shape or re-write her version of her past in such a way that she can *show* what happened, without apportioning blame. Reformulated in this way, the past becomes less painful or troublesome.

When I talked to Jessica again some nine months later, she had done no writing at all since the Certificate ended. She was taking lessons in operatic singing and was excited by performing and the increase in self-confidence it brought about. Having at first said that she agreed with my summary, Jessica went on to say that she did not feel there had been any *personal* development during the course. There had been a development *in the writing* and she was particularly pleased with the introductory section of the novel which gave her mother a voice. I had a sense that there was a certain perversity at work here, as Jessica had previously talked a great deal about her quest for a narrative which would make sense of her difficult life and the desire for forgiveness, and she had charted her progress towards this in her two essays.

Now she preferred to look at the writing purely from the technical point of view.

When I showed Jessica the transcript, she agreed that what she had said there did seem to '…imply progress of some sort…'. She then went on to say, in an attempt, I think, to clarify what she was trying to do in her writing, that she felt her story was 'quite interesting', particularly in that 'there are…anomalies in me…that need to be explained…':

> …I don't have a sort of nice even profile…some things I find terribly difficult and other things I find really easy…there are big deficits and peaks and troughs…I don't mean through time, I mean in my ability now. I mean there are certain things that put me in a state of panic and they are really quite small insignificant things that I can't do, or that I don't know. This knowledge thing, I suppose that's one thing I still feel I haven't quite got to the bottom of…

Jessica is alluding here to the first interview, where she talked about her 'learning difficulties', a theme which she wrote about in 'Bevendean': 'I have a lot of difficulty taking in any information…That is something I am still working on, trying to get an account of it, because it still puzzles me; I am an intelligent person, but I don't feel intelligent'. She also refers to herself as 'hugely ambivalent about success, so much so that I tend to sabotage anything I do'.

This problem of not being in touch with her own learning, of being able to learn or retain some things but not others, and of being ambivalent towards her own success, is clearly an important theme for Jessica; indeed I would suggest that it is her *central theme* and that it is intimately connected with her sense of being split which appears so often in conversation and in her fiction. In fact, she says this herself in the first interview: '[splitting] is my main theme really…not being integrated. Not being able to accept different parts of myself'. From this perspective, Jessica's quest for a personal narrative is not so much a way of making sense of *her past* (although it may be important for her to understand how the splitting came about), but of *creating a sense of unity in the present*. This is also confirmed in the first interview, where she says: 'I am looking for a shape really…It has to do with coherence really'.

Jessica sees her splitness as primarily between the male and female parts of herself. Her male side manifests itself, she says, in a relentless drive for success and aggressive conquest. This aggressive, ambitious side of herself is thwarted, however, by guilt feelings: 'Any achievement of mine is automatically tinged with guilt', and by the ambivalence towards her success mentioned above, which often leads to self-sabotage. Her achievements have been done 'to impress' rather than 'in a search for the truth', and usually this meant impressing men. 'I do things for the wrong reasons', therefore 'it is all contaminated' and she feels no ownership of it. Sometimes she feels as if her knowledge is locked away in isolated compartments.

Jessica ascribes this conflict between her drive for success and her guilt feelings about it, to her sense of having gone beyond her father in professional terms and of therefore displeasing him. This would make sense against the background of Jessica's conviction as a child that, in order to prevent her parents from feeling guilty about the damage done to Jessica's sister, Jessica had to be the good child, the perfect child. By going beyond her father, exacerbating what she describes as his already low self-esteem, she is not living up to the ideal she set herself as a child: to protect him from pain. Jessica's male side also manifests itself, she says, in predatoriness in human relations, the need for herself and others to be perfect, and in 'enormous control needs'. Little things people do, such as a gesture which Jessica does not like, can completely change her attitude towards them.

A piece Jessica wrote in response to the 'melody for two voices' exercise portrays a powerful conflict between predatory masculinity and idealised goodness. 'Conference' has, for the first time – in spite of Jessica's conscious identification with her father – a first-person male narrator. He is an academic who has just shifted his field of work from experimental psychology to child development and is attending a conference, not primarily out of interest in the subject matter, but in the expectation that he will find someone to go to bed with. Hilary, his wife, has just given birth to their son Gabriel, and he feels excluded from the 'nauseating intimacy' of the mother–child relationship, so he feels justified in his pursuit, although a little guilty for having left her alone so soon after the baby's birth.

On the very first evening he sees precisely the woman he wants sitting on a stool in the bar: '…one of those honey blonde, willowy English beauties; an angular face, good bones and that almost translucent waxy skin that glowed without being greasy' ('Conference', p.1). Everything about her is soft and sensuous, the gentle colour of her clothes, the sheen of her stockings: she is 'perfect…a dream' (p.2).

Without hesitation, he propositions her and, to his surprise, she follows him to his room without a word. The sexual act is related in a wholly explicit and rather clichéd, 'hard porn' fashion, appropriate to the coarse, unfeeling character of the narrator. For the narrator it is a superlative experience – 'the fuck of a lifetime' (p.2). Afterwards, he expects her to roll away and light a cigarette; instead she holds him close, caressing and kissing him. Uncharacteristically, he is overwhelmed by tenderness, instantly 'falls in love', and has visions of leaving Hilary and spending the rest of his life with this 'perfect woman'.

When he wakes in the morning, she is not there. But he happily gets up and dresses in anticipation of seeing her at breakfast. As he crosses the foyer, he catches sight of her. To his surprise she looks completely different, wearing a scarlet jumper and long black leather coat, quite out of keeping with the soft image he has of her. Worse still, she is obviously on the point of leaving, because she is loading her things into a taxi. He feels devastated and betrayed. As the taxi pulls away, he feels as if: '…a part of me was severed. I was never going to let anyone treat me like that again' (p.3).

In this piece, the narrator is shown switching suddenly out of his callous predatoriness into an idealised romanticism. His devastation at what he regards as the betrayal of his finer feelings is, the reader inevitably feels, only what he deserves. At the outset he was in search of sexual gratification, pure and simple, and so, presumably, was the woman. There was no indication that she wanted anything more, or that her behaviour after sex was unusual. Her gentleness, however, triggers in him the switch from one extreme way of being to another. When he realises that he has been misled, he is furious, and promptly switches back to his dominant way of being. Only now, this tough, unemotional carapace will have become even more rigid than it was before. Having allowed his vulnerability to be exposed – the very thing that his hard façade is there to protect – he will not easily let his defences down again.

Jessica identified strongly with this character's sudden shift from predatoriness to falling in love: 'That exercise was based on me…I really enjoyed that.' She says that she is aware of her tendency towards predatory conquest of this kind, which she associates with males, but that she is 'deeply ashamed' of it. She also says that 'there is a large part of me that believes in…the whole falling in love thing that is beyond rationality', and that she finds it 'quite hard to tell the difference between fantasy and reality'.

She refers to this inner polarity as 'a capacity for worship' on the one hand and 'total dominance' on the other. These two conflicting sides of her personality, which represent two quite different attitudes to life rather than typically male or female attributes, are intelligible in Horneyan terms as a conflict between expansive and self-effacing solutions. The expansive seems to be uppermost and finds easier expression in the fiction (e.g. in the character of Sarah) than the self-effacing. What Jessica describes as her 'learning difficulties' might well be a consequence of this inner conflict. Her dominant expansiveness drives her to use her knowledge to do 'great things', to achieve glory, rather than for self-fulfillment. For the self-effacing side, the mere idea of public success is anathema and must be torn down.

The situation is complicated by what could be interpreted as a second Horneyan conflict, within the dominant expansive solution itself. A piece of writing called 'The Crystalline Tower' is referred to in both interviews. It is based on a dream and contains two powerful and opposing images. One is the tower itself, which is made of glistening white ice, and which seems to represent the heights to which the narrator aspires. The other image is of menstruation, blood-soaked knickers kept hidden under the stairs, and seems to represent the messiness of the narrator's 'actual self'. The desire to reach the tower and inhabit its clean, pure coldness, is perhaps a way for the narrator to keep herself above the messiness of herself. But the tower is an unreliable structure:

> ...[it] collapses, the tower always collapses...I have endless dreams about climbing up scaffolding and then it starts rocking and creaking and there's nothing underneath. I just have to fall and you know it's like 'who the hell do you think you are up there anyway'...it's like sort of sabotage going on down below or I've just gone too far...into the stratosphere almost.

The 'search for glory', well captured in the repeated imagery of climbing a tower – the drive to actualise the expansive idealised image – is, in Horneyan thinking, just one side of the pride system's see-saw; on the other side is the despised image, self-hate and self-contempt. One cannot have the one without the other.

When I asked Jessica to describe her conscious image of herself she said: 'I do see myself as vulnerable, but I see myself as inadequate really, more than anything, this is when I'm feeling bad...when I'm feeling good I think I can do anything, I get this total omnipotence...and it's just ridiculous.' The two sides of the see-saw are clearly visible here: a sense of inadequacy on the one hand, and total omnipotence on the other. Being immersed in the messiness of self-hate and self-contempt is clearly painful, so that the search for glory, the quest for external acclaim, is compulsive and difficult to relinquish. But as the dream indicates, the search for glory is ultimately fruitless: it is a hollow structure which cannot serve as a basis for genuine self-esteem.

It is not surprising that Jessica has in the past attempted to create structures to keep her above the messiness of fragmentation. She describes philosophy, which she chose for her first degree, as 'clean and pure, divorced from the grubby and complex reality of my family life'. It is controllable, gives her a framework. She cannot cope with knowledge which is messy, like politics, she says, that you come in on in the middle. It mirrors the messiness of her own lack of integration.

Writing an autobiographical novel is also, Jessica says, 'putting some order on [the mess]...'. But writing a novel, I say, indeed engaging in any creative activity, requires being able to confront mess (Milner's chaos). She replies that she *is* confronting the mess 'by doing things in bits'. By this she means that the only way she can move towards a shape, a structure, for her fragmented sense of self is by creating a narrative that is itself fragmented. As noted above, the chapters for the novel were each written from a different point of view: first-person narrative for her mother, and FID for the voices of herself and her sister. She was clearly very pleased with the first, but expressed concern that the character based on herself was not very sympathetic. It is the expansive side of her personality and she hopes that 'the more vulnerable side will come out [later]'.

It is what Jessica describes as the vulnerable, gentler side of herself which seems to be connected with a sense of authenticity, and which represents the middle ground between the extremes of expansiveness and the idealisation of romantic love. This gentler side appears infrequently in the pieces of writing I have seen, but it is there in 'Bevendean', where Jessica begins to have sympathy with her 'actual self' which has been damaged not only by the family but also by herself. External factors have helped this middle ground to emerge. Singing has taught her that 'it's all right for me to actually enjoy myself'. It validates who she is, something which was missing from her childhood:

> Anything I did that was good always had the other side to it...[it was]...taking something from her [the sister]...or from my mother...being attractive was taking something from my mother...being academic [was] a slight to my father...there's never this feeling that things were celebrated. They were shown off to other people but not celebrated.

She talks several times about the longing to be seen: 'What matters more to me than anything is the feeling that I can be *seen and loved*'. Presumably, this means seen and loved *for herself,* rather than being used for other people's purposes, and being able to express herself freely in front of an audience which appreciates her is liberating. Also, in the past five years, partly as a result of having become a mother, but also of close involvement with women attending an M.Sc course, she has, she says, started accepting her gentler, female side more readily.

As this authentic middle ground continues to grow, the inner conflicts may well diminish. In any case, Jessica's awareness of her inner conflicts has already been beneficial in itself. She says that accepting that she is a split person has been an important part of her development and that there is more of a dialogue now between the different sides of her personality: 'I'm getting there…I mean in my life there is definitely progression towards integration. I mean there are some things that are always going to be there, I will just have to acknowledge them and accept them.'

In the light of Jessica's background, it is not surprising that she did not build up sufficient confidence in herself to form a solid basis for growth and that she became fragmented. Her desire for integration is clearly a major driving force in her life and her quest for an integrating narrative is a part of that drive. In spite of Jessica's own misgivings, I do believe that the work she has done on her writing has helped her both to understand and to grapple with her inner conflicts. Whilst at the moment singing is providing 'more immediate rewards', I hope that in time she may return to her writing and find a satisfying shape for herself on the page.

Becoming Authors of Our Personal Narratives

As we have seen in the case of Jennifer, finding an appropriate narrative perspective from which to write her story was an important factor in clarifying her own identity. A similar phenomenon is present in the case of Jessica, who also moves towards a coherent self-narrative by finding a first person voice for her mother and a 'dual voice' for herself in the guise of Sarah. In both cases, but particularly in the case of Jessica, finding a form or structure for the narrative is also of significance. Jennifer at first strives to link together the different voices of her narrative using the metaphor of a circle dance, but later opts for the theme of clothes and their colours. Jessica talks about assembling 'fifty or so discrete, self-contained pieces' which she would combine at a later stage.

All four women, at some stage in their work for the Certificate, discuss or struggle with the problem of form or structure for their autobiographical novels. Of course, there are technical difficulties in finding a form or structure for any novel, but finding a form for an autobiographical narrative comes with its own special difficulties. Where an autobiographical narrative is striving to give coherence to a fragmented sense of self, the difficulties, I would suggest, are likely to be even greater.

There is a good deal of discussion of fragmentation of personality in current thinking about the self. With the decline of the unitary model of the self, the model of self as fragmented has become dominant. This is particularly so amongst feminist writers, who see the unitary model as appropriate to men and the fragmentary model as appropriate to women. Estelle Jelinek, for example, when discussing the 'identity image' that occurs in women's autobiographies, says:

> In contrast to the self-confident, one-dimensional self-image that men
> usually project, women often depict a multi-dimensional, fragmented
> self-image coloured by a sense of inadequacy and alienation, of being
> outsiders or 'other'; they feel the need for authentication, to prove
> their self-worth (Jelinek 1986, p.xiii).

Autobiographical fiction by men also frequently presents fragmented self-images and the theme of the outsider. One need only think of the writings of Hermann Hesse and Albert Camus. It may well be that the social or cultural pressure for women to occupy multiple roles – wife, mother, housekeeper, lover – has made them more *aware* than men of the different aspects of their personalities, but this does not mean that men are fundamentally more unitary than women, simply that they have been defined as such by the social context.

There is also an assumption, in the current claiming of fragmentation as a model of identity for women, that it is a wholly positive thing. Cora Kaplan, for example, sees the acceptance of the 'inherently unstable and split character of all human subjectivity' leading to the 'potentially hopeful incoherence of female identity' (Kaplan 1986, p.226).

This celebration of fragmentation as the new model of the self arises out of the psychoanalytic theory of Jacques Lacan. For Lacan, alienation from self is a natural state of being, an unavoidable consequence of the development of self-consciousness. The 'I' comes into existence at the *mirror stage*, the moment – somewhere between the ages of six and eighteen months – when the infant, which up to now has been in a state of oneness with the mother, without an individual identity, sees its reflection in a mirror and is jolted into a realisation that it is separate (Lacan 1949, p.1). What the child sees, however, is a delusion; it wrongly assumes that the image of itself in the mirror is the reality of itself, when in fact it is a product of its own invention. This identification of the I with the spectral image, which Lacan describes as the forming of a primordial imago, is centrally important for Lacan in that it not only establishes 'a relation between the organism and its reality…or… between the *Innenwelt* and the *Umwelt*' (p.4) and is crucial to the development of the child's motor co-ordination, but it leads to the 'assumption of the armour of an alienating identity which will mark with its rigid structure the subject's entire mental development' (p.4). The problem arises because the mirror stage occurs prior to the development of the self, or the subject, in the 'dialectic of identification with the other' (p.2), i.e. in the child's relation with people and the outside world through language. Thus the self is created at two different levels: at the level of the imaginary and at the level of the symbolic. The resulting rift in the self is permanent. It means that the adult human being is irretrievably fragmented and wracked by the desire for the original narcissistic object, its own unattainable reflection. This inevitable self-alienation leads to neurosis and makes itself known in later life through images of what Lacan calls the 'fragmented body' which appear in dreams and works of art (the paintings of Hieronymus Bosch are singled out as a prime example) (pp.4–5).

In Horneyan thinking, whilst there is a considerable awareness of the psyche's multiplicity, psychic *fragmentation* is neither inevitable nor desirable. The concept of *alienation* is central here too, but it is a state of deformation of character, an unnatural state of being which can, to an extent, be alleviated. From a Horneyan perspective: '…the belief that the self is inevitably deriva-tive, inauthentic, and fragmented is a product of inner conflict and self-alienation, which is then generalised as the human condition' (Paris 1994, p.215). Psychic fragmentation brought about by inner conflicts can be unbearably painful. People suffering from it often attempt to relieve their pain by measures such as *compartmentalisation*, where 'a person disconnects conflicting currents and thereby no longer experiences conflicts as conflicts' (Horney 1951, p.185). This can bring the sufferer a 'feeling of unity', but at the expense of the repression of large parts of the personality (p.185). Com-partmentalisation may also involve frequent switching from one defensive solution to another, with the resulting inconsistencies of behaviour, as in the Jekyll and Hyde story (p.190).

Amongst contemporary writers on the self, it is Jane Flax who takes issue, most significantly, with the celebration of fragmentation as the new model of the self. Psychic fragmentation, she says, is 'a painful and disabling' state which renders impossible the 'registering of and pleasure in a variety of experiencing of ourselves, others, and the outside world' (Flax 1990, p.218). She is referring here specifically to people with whom she works who suffer from 'borderline syndrome', but she implies that psychic fragmentation can be similarly painful and disabling in whatever degree. 'Those who celebrate or call for a "decentered" self', says Flax, 'seem self-deceptively naive and unaware of the basic cohesion within themselves that makes the fragmentation of experiences something other than a terrifying slide into psychosis' (pp.218–219). A person who is psychically fragmented has great difficulties using 'the transitional space in which the differences and boundaries between self and other, inner and outer, and reality and illusion are bracketed or elided' (p.219). This is likely to make everyday functioning, i.e. human relations and relations with self, including the ability to work and create, exceedingly difficult.

For writers, psychic fragmentation may have a detrimental effect on their ability to structure their writing. For Norman Friedman, it is the stability of the narrator's position which ensures the unity of a work of fiction (Friedman 1955, p.1165). If a writer's psyche is fragmented in such a way that there is a shaky sense of identity, it may well be difficult to maintain a stable narrative position (especially if the narrator is autobiographically based) that will give coherence to a longer piece of work, such as a novel. Virginia Woolf again provides a useful example here. In her book on Woolf's writing practice, Sue Roe draws attention to Woolf's sense of being split up into different parts (Roe 1990, pp.37–39). In order to write she had to let go of her fragmented, everyday self or 'Virginia' – her 'actual self' in Horneyan terminology – and to immerse herself in what she called her 'writing I'. But this 'writing I' was extremely fragile and difficult to maintain; it necessitated isolation and withdrawal from the world, and contact with people undermined her ability to write (pp.39–40).

Woolf's method of structuring her novels was complex. Rather than 'centering' them, as Henry James did, through the narrative perspective of a particular character (James 1934, pp.37–38), she focused on an object as the centrepiece of a novel. This worked well in some of her writings, notably the lighthouse in *To the Lighthouse* (1927) and an oil lamp in *Between the Acts* (1941). Writing *The Waves* (1931), however, caused her extreme distress. She wanted to combine the points of view of six different characters, but found that '…the novel changed when the perspective changed' (Roe 1990, p.31). In the early drafts she tried using a moth and a flowerpot as the focus, but later abandoned this and tried instead to use abstract blocks of colour as perceived by one or other of her characters: 'a purple ball hanging', 'a vast slab of pale yellow', 'a slope of purple vallies' (Roe 1990, p.30), but that still left her with six different perspectives. In the final draft she interleaved the six perspectives with a series of 'Interludes' from the point of view of Bernard, one of the characters, who temporarily stands outside of the narrative and reflects on it as a whole, but this does not, in Roe's view, result in cohesion: 'If neither Virginia Woolf nor the fictitious story-teller, Bernard, is able to reassemble [the] fragments into a "better" story, this leaves the six speakers, Bernard included, in a state of exposed fragmentation' (Roe 1990, p.108).

Roe's view is that *The Waves* is 'about the difficulty of finding a shape or framework for desire, without resorting to the putting on of a carapace of social convention, obligation and constraint' (p.109), but it could as easily be about the difficulty of finding a shape or framework for a fragmented sense of self with which Woolf herself was so obviously concerned. Indeed, at times in the 'Interludes' Bernard seems to be acting as a spokesman for the author's own desire for unity: 'if I had a pencil and a sheet of paper I could draw the design of my life…and it would be seen that those innumerable scenes depend from a thin black line which is what I call (provisionally) myself' (Woolf 1976, p.657; Roe 1990, p.30).

From the evidence which Sue Roe puts forward, there is little doubt that Woolf achieved a sense of identity from her fiction writing. However, this does not seem to have carried over into her life beyond the writing to provide her with a better integration of her fragmented self. Her writing process, which involved submergence in her 'writing I', provided an escape from the fragmented 'Virginia' and hence temporary relief from psychic pain. But this imaginary structure only worked as long as a novel was in progress. As soon as it was finished, she was again vulnerable and unstable. When there was stability in her external life, she could contain herself between novels. But when her external life also became unstable, as it did during the Second World War, the anxieties became overwhelming and impinged not only on 'Virginia' but also on the relatively secure space of her 'writing I'. Sue Roe sees the failure of Woolf's ability to hold on to the sense of identity achieved through her writing as a major factor in her suicide (Roe 1990, pp.40–42).

It does not follow from this that finding a form for oneself on the page cannot be therapeutically helpful. Whilst Woolf certainly seems to have been trying to find a stronger sense of identity through her writing, at least at the level of the imagination, she does not seem to have consciously set out to use her writing as a therapeutic exercise. Indeed, she was very concerned to distinguish strictly between her art and any therapeutic benefits it might have had for her: 'To use writing as an art, not as a method of self-expression' (Woolf 1928, p.79). Woolf was, of course, strongly influenced in this view by the aesthetics of her Bloomsbury companions Roger Fry and Clive Bell, who drew a sharp and extreme distinction between the emotions and feelings experienced in life and those experienced in the presence of a work of art. The intuitive, subjective response to works of art which they called 'aesthetic emotion' was something elemental, independent of time and place, and of almost religious significance. The artist's role was not to express himself but to sacrifice himself to the great cause of producing 'significant form' which evoked aesthetic emotion (Bullen in Bell 1987, pp.xxi–l; Fry 1909). This philosophy of art may have been part of the problem for Woolf of being able, ultimately, to draw psychological support from her writing, although, as noted above in the discussion of 'Sketch of the Past', she acknowledges the therapeutic benefit gained from finding a satisfactory form for her feelings about her mother in *To The Lighthouse*.

I am reminded, when thinking about Woolf's reluctance to explore the therapeutic benefits of her writing, of Jessica's desire to push aside her previous clearly stated purpose of trying to make sense of herself through her writing, in favour of just wanting 'to make a work of art'. There is bound to be a tension between the two goals and perhaps inevitably one of them will suffer at the expense of the other. Woolf, of course, managed to write some highly regarded fiction in spite of her problems of identity, and that may well be possible for Jessica too, but perhaps it is important for a writer to be clear, as Jennifer seems to have been, about which of the two goals she is pursuing at any one time.

In *A Healing Art*, which discusses a number of successful autobiographical novels written out of a need to cope with psychological crisis, Marilyn Chandler emphasises the role of autobiography as giving form, centre and shape in narrative to what she calls the 'protean self' (Chandler 1990, p.136). The autobiographies she includes tend not to use the traditional narrative structures, the *linear*, with its beginning, middle, and end, or the *circular*, where the beginning already anticipates the end (pp.163–4). Instead, the authors' sense of fragmentation and awareness of the possibilities of postmodern forms lead them to attempt more complex structures. Elie Wiesel's *Night* (1981) 'presents a disjointed series of images, isolated representative moments, associatively connected, that accumulate but do not imply progress toward a culminating epiphany...' (Chandler 1990, p.144). Christa Wolf's *A Model Childhood* (1983), with its intermingling of past, present and future into an eternal present 'refuses to sustain the fiction that she writes from a stable vantage point' (Chandler 1990, p.141). Yet these novels do convey to the reader a solidity, 'a satisfying symmetry that offsets fragmentation and offers a familiar reassurance in the end' (p.141). To borrow the term Kim Worthington uses in her discussion of postmodernist fiction, the fragmentation that the novels represent does not result in *'radical unreadability*, the wholesale rejection of the orderings and connections of narrative' (Worthington 1996, p.29; emphasis added). A good postmodernist novel, even if employing anti-narrative fictional devices, remains intelligible, 'because its flaunting of the rules is understood' (p.29). Its *lack* of structure is also its structure, because it continues to be held together by the firm hand of the author who created it. In finding a narrative form for the fragmented self through fictional autobiography, the writer has the possibility of creating his or her own *readability* on the page.

The key factor in creating readability of the fragmented self is the achieving of authorial control. This may develop over a period of time. The simple act of placing oneself on the page, even through jottings in a diary or journal, is already a first step in taking charge of the chaos of oneself. Developing those jottings into a story which makes sense is an assertive act which can bring genuine self-esteem. As Chandler says: 'As a writer gains distance from an experience, his rendering of it tends to become increasingly articulated, patterned and imaginative' (Chandler 1990, p.153). Choosing a fragmented narrative form to convey a fragmented sense of self seems logical, although difficult to achieve. One of Jessica's problems with finding a form was the profusion of themes; yet another was her fear that she would use all the material in one go. But having fixed upon a principle of organisation, the uncertainty seemed to fall away. As Chandler says: 'A principle of organisation constitutes an implicit statement of value. To decide in what terms the story shall be told means defining what is important about the story' (Chandler 1990, p.144).

When I look again at the beginnings of Jessica's novel, what strikes me as most important is that it is her mother's perspective which has become the focal point, and it is this with which she is most pleased. In her discussion of narrative point of view, Rimmon-Kenan rejects the term 'point of view' as implying a primarily visual perspective. She prefers the term 'focalisation', which she borrows from Genette (1980) and which she broadens to include 'cognitive, emotive and ideological orientation' (Rimmon-Kenan 1996, p.71). The choice of Jessica's mother as the central narrator of the novel (so far she is the only character written in the first person) certainly provides a strong visual perspective, for in the opening section she is looking down from heaven, with a god's-eye-view, which gives her, and *only* her, access to the minds of all the other characters in the story. She also provides a strong *emotional* bias to the novel, in that her attitude is mellow, sympathetic, forgiving, even though, as quickly becomes clear from the subsequent third-person sections through the consciousness of Sarah and her sister, Alex, the family's history is a tangled web of powerful negative emotions. She acts as a sort of guardian angel of her troubled family, spreading her wings over them and binding them together. In this sense she becomes a *crucial focalising device* for the developing narrative, providing its fragmented parts with a firmly rooted structure. For Jessica as writer, I would suggest, the sense of comfort and satisfaction she derives from finding this role for her mother is a fictional fulfilment of her desire to be *seen*: to have someone who sees all of her, her good parts and her bad parts, and accepts her for what she is.

Jennifer, too, gives her mother the role of godlike first-person narrator, looking down from heaven after her death with sympathy and forgiveness on her wayward daughter. Whilst Jennifer's overall theme for the novel has become clothes, the most important item of clothing, around which the early part of the novel focuses, is the art-silk dress her mother makes and Alison's re-discovery of it years later. Thus, in both of these attempts at creating a personal narrative, the mother has become the central structuring feature.

This is very interesting if considered from the point of view of object-relations theory. For Winnicott[6], being *seen* by the mother is crucial if the infant is to develop healthily as an individual. In the very early stages of a child's life, self is potential rather than actual (Winnicott 1960a, pp.17–18). The baby has no sense of itself and others as separate. When it cries because it

---

6   I am indebted to Adam Phillips' summary (1988) of Winnicott's theories.

is hungry, the breast appears magically; the baby is creator of its own world. This sense of omnipotence is a necessary first stage in self-development (Winnicott 1960b, p.145). In order to 'feel real' a baby needs the mother's face to act as a kind of mirror (Winnicott 1967, p.111). In the very early days of the baby's life, Winnicott believed, the mother should be totally absorbed by the infant so as to reflect back to it how it feels; the mother's role is to give back to the baby the baby's own self, so that its 'true self', which at this stage is only potential, has a chance of developing. This needs to be done in such a way that the baby's omnipotence is not challenged. If the child gains confidence in its sense that the external world behaves in accord with its own needs and wishes, gradually it will be able to abrogate its omnipotence and develop a relationship with the world through objects (Winnicott 1960b, p.146).

If the mother is continually preoccupied with other things, e.g. talking to someone else whilst she is nursing, the baby will not be able to get something of its felt self back from the environment; it will not develop a solid basis of self to enable it to move from apperception (seeing oneself) to perception (seeing others as objects). If the mother only gives to the infant what she herself feels, then this is likely to lead to the infant's compliance, the attempt to fit in with the mother's self, and the development of a 'false self' which acts as a defence against the integrity of the 'true self'[7]. In Winnicott's thinking, then, self-identity requires an internalisation of the mother's sight of the child, so that, as it grows into an adult, it can become its own mother, mirroring itself back to itself: 'being seen... is at the basis of creative looking' (Winnicott 1967, p.114)[8].

Whether or not Jennifer's and Jessica's mothers failed to be 'good enough mothers' in Winnicott's sense is not possible for me to say. What seems clearer is that both Jennifer and Jessica, for whatever reasons, lost touch with or perhaps even banished their mothers fairly early on from their role as good internal objects, and that this must have left painful gaps in their psyches. By empathically inhabiting their mothers and writing them back into their personal narratives in fictional form, Jessica and Jennifer reintroject an

7   Where Horney identifies three basic strategies of defence in the child which lead to alienation from self, Winnicott sees only one.

8   Lacan's notion of the 'mirror stage' is not, as Winnicott thought, similar to his own (Bowie 1991, p.23). As I said above, for Lacan the mirror image reflected back to the child is false and fragmenting, rather than a validation of its authenticity.

important parental figure into their object world. This helps to give shape to their inner world, to create an internal holding environment that is a friendlier space, less alien, and easier to occupy, both generally and with regard to creativity.

Whilst, then, for some people, as the example of Virginia Woolf shows, finding a form for self through fiction writing may provide a temporary imaginary structure which they inhabit whilst the novel is in progress and which is likely to collapse when it is finished, for others it can constitute a move towards coherence for the painful fragments of self and therefore play a role in the development of a stronger sense of identity.

Fictional Autobiography and Narrative Therapy

In this chapter I have been looking at the use of fictional autobiography, first, to 're-write' the voices of significant others who are part of one's object world and, second, to find a form for a fragmented sense of self through the use of a focalising device, in this instance a parental figure 're-written' and reintrojected into one's object world. Both these examples of re-writing self-narratives are much more akin to what might go on in a counselling or psychotherapeutic context than in a creative writing course: personal narratives are consciously being explored for the light they can throw on present discomforts. I will therefore conclude this chapter by comparing the work Jennifer and Jessica have done and my interpretation of it with a growing trend in psychotherapy and counselling towards a narrative-based approach and the use of writing, which takes its impetus from the work of Michael White and David Epston, family therapists working in Australia and New Zealand.

Drawing on the analogy of social organisation as a text, White and Epston follow Foucault in believing that the normal state of being situated in language and discourses, which are constructed by society and accorded a truth status, results in subjugation. These discourses, which are a form of power, determine the way people live within a particular society and the way they think about themselves and their lives (White and Epston 1990, pp.18–20). Being immersed in stories written by others often makes people's experience problematic, forcing them to seek therapeutic help: '...persons experience problems, for which they frequently seek therapy, when the narratives in which they are "storying" their experience, and/or in which they are having their experience "storied" by others, do not sufficiently represent their lived experience' (p.14). A narrative approach to therapy encourages people to identify or generate their own alternative stories through which they find new meanings that are 'more helpful, satisfying, and open-ended' (p.15).

White and Epston call their approach a 're-authoring therapy':

> A re-authoring therapy intends to assist persons to resolve problems by: (1) enabling them to separate their lives and relationships from knowledges/stories that are impoverishing; (2) assisting them to challenge practices of self and relationship that are subjugating; and (3) encouraging persons to re-author their lives according to alternative knowledges/stories and practices of self and relationship that have preferred outcomes (Epston, White and Murray 1992, p.108).

The first step is to encourage clients to 'externalise' the problem, to see it as an entity in its own right – a 'dominant story' – rather than as an intrinsic part of themselves or their relationships (White and Epston 1990, p.38). Separation from this dominant story, which has been shaping their lives and relation-ships, enables them to 'identify previously neglected but vital aspects of lived experience – aspects that could not have been predicted from a reading of the dominant story' (p.41). They call these 'unique outcomes'. Having identified unique outcomes, clients are encouraged to generate new stories within which the unique outcomes will acquire new meaning. The new story is called a 'unique account', and clients are encouraged to reflect on the impli-cations which the new story might have for their relationship with them-selves, with others and with the original problem. These implications are for-mulated into 'unique redescriptions' of self and others. Clients also explore the 'unique possibilities' which this new knowledge of themselves might offer in their lives, and they are encouraged to 'identify and recruit an audience to the performance of new meanings in their life', usually family members or friends (White and Epston 1990, p.41). The use of an 'audience' is centrally important to White and Epston's narrative approach and distin-guishes it from the use of narrative in psychoanalysis. In the latter, they say, the problem is seen as 'mainly "in the head" of the client' (Epston, White and Murray 1992, p.110), and this is limiting: '...it is not sufficient simply to change one's own picture of oneself privately; one must in addition have a convincing picture to show others' (p.111). Through the performing of new meaning around unique outcomes clients 'revise their relationship with the problem' and this enables them to re-author or re-constitute themselves, each other, and their relationships, according to alternative stories or knowledges (White and Epston 1990, pp.63, 75).

Writing plays an important part in White and Epston's approach. It may take the form of a letter from therapist to client summarising the story which the client and therapist have devised together in the session. Sometimes clients respond with a letter of their own, or the contents of the letter become the subject of the subsequent session. Alternatively, clients are invited to record their own stories, whether on video or audiotape, in letters or in stories of various genres (p.163). Whilst there is no conscious use here of fictionalising as a means of exploring self, clients are encouraged to enter into stories with their experience and imagination, take these stories over and make them their own (Epston, White and Murray 1992, p.100).

The similarities with the work done by Jessica and Jennifer in their self-explorations are several. There is a considerable amount of externalis- ation or objectification involved in their self-writing, of themselves and of their problematic relationships with others. Whilst it would not be true to say that their aim is to externalise the problem as such, there is certainly in both cases the emergence of a 'dominant story'. Both of them enter into their stories with experience and imagination and make them their own. They take representative scenes from the past and expand them through imagination. They step into the characters who inhabit their psychic worlds. Re-inhabiting them, not as the child or the young person they were, but as an adult, enables them to bring to bear all the accumulated insight and experi- ence which comes with age. In so doing, they subvert their existing knowledges and literally re-write them. This results in the identifying of new knowledges in the sense in which White and Epston use the term, i.e. a new way of looking at a given situation or relationship. A good example of this is Jessica's realisation that whilst she has always tended to see her sister as 'bad' and herself as 'good', she and her sister are in fact quite similar. Writing this down for the first time she finds quite shocking.

As to the question of audience, this is a central part of Jennifer's project, where the co-authoring of stories with her brothers and subsequent discus- sion of them has the effect of changing *their* truths as well as her own. Perhaps, too, the quest for a personal narrative in the form of a fiction which might be published and presented to the outside world is in itself a desire for audience although, in the case of Jessica, this is unlikely to be with members of the family.

My approach to understanding the work Jennifer and Jessica have done differs, however, from White and Epston's approach. In linking the work of my students to a psychodynamic theory I am, in Bruner's phrase, using the paradigmatic mode rather than the narrative (Bruner 1986). As McLeod says in his recent summary of the field of narrative therapy, in psychodynamic approaches: '…the therapist will not work with the story itself but will use the narrative to gain access to what are considered to be more fundamental emotional or behavioural structures… [such as]…object relations' (McLeod 1997, p.55). Working at the level of such fundamental emotional or behavioural structures as object relations, bringing about what one might call a 're-structuring of the psychic furniture', is, in my view, of primary importance in eliciting lasting psychic change. From White and Epston's case studies it is clear that there is a strong behavioural element to their approach, which aims to work on the immediate problem without reference to underlying psychic structures that might be problematical. This raises questions in my mind about the long-term effect of such short periods of therapy as some of those described. It also raises questions about the kind of client with whom this work is likely to be successful. It has been noted that White and Epston work largely with clients whose stories have become 'fixed in place by family structures' or reinforced by long-term involvement with mental health professionals (McLeod 1997, p.89). It may be that their approach may not be so effective with people who do not fall into this category and who may be more familiar with externalising or reflecting on themselves.

My use of the idea of re-writing personal narratives or 're-authoring' also differs fundamentally from that of White and Epston. Their use of this term, drawing as it does on Foucault's theory of power/knowledge, implies an *empowerment* in a person's functioning in relationships and in the outside world generally. If a person's story has been authored by the language and discourse of others, then adopting an *authorial* stance where one has not done so before, enables her to *take control* of her story, to re-write it in her own way, and to acquire her own power within a power-oriented world. Thus White and Epston's focus is wholly outward-looking, concerned with the external world and a person's ability to act within it.

In the psychodynamic context in which I am working the focus is much more inward-looking. The self and its story have been *co-authored* by the dialogue between a person's real or true self, and family, culture and society. A person's authorial stance in relation to the story of the self is a product of that dialogue, as are the voices and points of view of her object world. In a malformation of personality of the kind that Horney describes, where a person has adopted a 'life solution', the authorial stance is likely to be omniscient and controlling, and to a considerable degree unreflected upon. Re-authoring in this context would involve a person dismantling her dominant authorial stance, so that she can re-evaluate and re-work the characters and narratives of her object world, and thus create a version of her story that sits more comfortably with her own 'idiom', in Bollas's sense. As this process proceeds, not only will her narratives have changed and become more comfortable, but so too will the nature of her authorship. Rather than omniscient, imposing rigid control over the characters and their storyline, it will become more Jamesian, allowing the characters and their narratives to have a life of their own; or even postmodern, tolerating, as Bakhtin advocates, many different points of view, and indeed many different 'truths', within the text of the self. If, as has been suggested, the self can be thought of as a kind of novel (albeit a 'bad...cluttered and undisciplined' novel) (Carr 1985, p.115), then we need to be able to tolerate within ourselves rival world views, many different truths, and hold them together with an authorial stance which is not rigid or fixed, but solidly based and flexible. Writing fictional autobiography, I believe, by subverting our 'monologic' authorship, helps us to move towards a more flexible authorial self, and this in turn helps us to develop a stronger sense of identity and a greater facility for engaging in creative work. Thus, it can provide us with a valuable tool for use in a therapeutic context. I discuss this idea further in the next chapter.

CHAPTER 4

Fictional Autobiography in Self-Therapy and Psychotherapy

It is clear from the previous chapter that that there are strong similarities between the therapeutic work Jennifer and Jessica have done through writing fictional autobiography and the work done by clients in narrative therapy. The majority of students responding to my questionnaire were also of the view that there are strong similarities between writing fictional autobiography and the psychotherapeutic process. For many, the main similarity was the opportunity fictional autobiography provided for focusing on oneself, for objectifying self and self-experience, and thus for obtaining new perspectives on, and increased insight into, self and others. Here is a typical comment: '[Fictional autobiography] gives one the space and permission to focus on oneself. It allows one to work through ideas about one's identity and one's intrinsic worth as a human being. It allows reflection from a safe distance – without incurring judgement on one's life.' Another important similarity was the way fictionalising one's own material brought about engagement with feelings which may have been blocked off: 'It enables you to look at a problem or a situation and in turning that into fiction you have to look at your feelings towards it which can often lead to a greater understanding....' Conversely it could provide distance and a framework for painful feelings, thus making them more manageable, and sometimes providing cathartic relief from trauma: '...when happenings are hurtful and difficult to acknowledge, writing about them, clothed in the disguise of fictional characters is a positive therapeutic process.' Several people mentioned a link with their own therapy: 'Almost all the themes I pursued [in my writing] have arisen during various activities undertaken as part of my own therapy.' Some saw psychotherapy and fictional autobiography as working together: 'It seems to me that therapy and writing autobiographical fiction are very closely linked and each can in a sense "feed" off the other.' This latter

152

comment echoes my own experience of the fruitful crossover between writing autobiographically based novels and undergoing psychotherapy which I referred to in the introduction.

What, then, are the possibilities for using autobiographical creative writing as a tool in self-therapy or self-analysis or in psychotherapy or psychoanalysis[1]? Writing as part of a writing apprenticeship, where the main purpose is to develop work which might eventually be publishable, is surely going to be very different from engaging in writing for the purpose of gaining insight into oneself? This chapter addresses a range of questions which arise when we move fictional autobiography out of a creative writing context and into a therapeutic one.

In comparing the re-writing of self-narratives by Jennifer and Jessica to the practice of re-authoring in the counselling work of White and Epston, my emphasis was on the writing of fictional autobiography *as a process* that enabled the writer to adopt a new authorial stance in relation to her inner world. In this chapter I explore the potential of fictional autobiography *as a product* that might be used as a self-reflexive tool in psychotherapy or self-therapy. I discuss the similarities and differences between the writing of fictional autobiography and engaging in psychotherapy, consider what a psychoanalytic approach to autobiography would consist in, and discuss the idea of transference in this context and the advantages, from the therapeutic point of view, of writing down and crafting one's narrative rather than just speaking it. I also include a brief overview of existing therapies that employ creative writing.

Fictions of the Self in Autobiography and Psychotherapy

One of the most striking similarities between writing autobiography and engaging in psychotherapy is that both involve working with fictional narratives of the self. It used to be believed that when we wrote autobiographically we were revealing or discovering the truth of the self. This belief is epitomised by Rousseau's opening resolve in his *Confessions* 'to set before my fellows the likeness of a man in all the truth of nature, and that man myself' (Rousseau 1782, p.1). In more recent times the idea that we can write the

---

[1]   From here on I use the terms psychotherapy and psychoanalysis interchangeably, on the assumption that psychotherapy can be thought of as a less intense, less frequent and theoretically more catholic psychoanalysis.

truth of the self has become problematical. Freud and psychoanalysis have shown us that what we take to be the truth of the self is often a lie; things we say about ourselves are often a means of diverting our own and others' attention from things we are hiding (Sprinker 1980). Research into memory reveals that as much as we might strive for accuracy in remembering ourselves in the past, this may not be possible. As Ulric Neisser says, autobiographical remembering is a complex, many-layered procedure that involves:

> (1) actual past events and the *historical self* who participated in them;
> (2) those events as they were then experienced, including the individual's own *perceived* self at the time; (3) the *remembering self*, that is, the individual in the act of recalling those events on some later occasion; and (4) the *remembered self* constructed on that occasion (Neisser 1994, p.2).

This means that: 'The self that is remembered today is not the historical self of yesterday, but only a reconstructed version' (p.8), a mixture of fact and fiction, or even on occasion a complete fiction of our imagination (p.6).

Poststructuralism has also highlighted the multiplicity of selves involved in speaking or writing about ourselves. As Roland Barthes puts it: 'the one *who speaks* (in the narrative) is not the one *who writes* (in real life) and the one *who writes* is not the one *who is*' (Barthes 1966, p.261). Even before words are committed to the page, there is, as Derrida maintains, an essential and unbridgeable gap, *différance*, between the words we speak and the 'trace' written in the unconscious by society and history (Derrida 1978, pp.196–231). Therefore we cannot assume a mirroring of psyche and text; even when we are speaking or writing about ourselves in the present, we can only know ourselves at several removes.

Thus, we are much more aware now that the moment we put pen to paper when writing about ourselves, we are writing a kind of fiction. Autobiography's designation as fiction, however, does not imply that it has no validity as truth. For contemporary writers on autobiography, the autobiographical enterprise continues to be a quest for the truth of the self, but that truth is more in the nature of a subjective or 'personal truth' rather than 'objective truth'. As Georges Gusdorf says: 'In autobiography the truth of facts is subordinate to the truth of the man' (Gusdorf 1980, p.43). And the truth of the man, and of course of the woman, will be a truth *in the present* rather than a truth in the past or a truth for all times. For the writing of autobiography is always done through the perspective of our present consciousness. As Janet

Varner Gunn says: 'Autobiography, at the level of perspective, involves a certain mode of self-placing in relation to the autobiographer's past and from a particular standpoint in his or her present' (Gunn 1982, p.16). Indeed, as Paul John Eakin suggests, the present has a crucial role to play in *creating* our truth as well as in enabling us to discover it: '…autobiographical truth is not a fixed but an evolving content in an intricate process of self-discovery and self-creation' (Eakin 1985, p.3). This means that the only kind of truth which we can hope to find through autobiography is provisional and specific to the present moment, and will therefore change over time.

The idea that our truth is a kind of fluid and ever-changing fiction is also implicit in current thinking on the psychotherapeutic process. Freud was already aware of the possibility that many of the stories his patients told him about the past had been amplified and elaborated into fictions, and that it was these fictions which were responsible for the continuation of their symptoms. According to James Hillman, through the writing of his case studies Freud invented a new genre, somewhere between fiction writing and science (Hillman 1983, p.5), which Hillman calls the genre of 'therapeutic fictions' (p.13). These are not fictions written by the patient, but the analyst's written version of the patient's story that has been created between them during the analysis: the patient and the analyst are 'two authors…collaborating in a mutual fiction of therapy, though conventionally only one of them will write it' (p.16).

The text here is literally a written document, and its content will, naturally, be more the analyst's version than the patient's. However, in current psychoanalytic thinking, the idea of a written text is also used as a metaphor for the spoken content of the analytic relationship. Thus Spence: 'The patient's history is…a constantly changing story that the patient is writing and rewriting, together with the analyst, inside and outside the analytic hour' (Spence 1985, p.81). When a patient comes into therapy, she has a version of her story which she will tell the therapist. The patient is locked into a particular version of her past which is not working, so that she cannot make sense of her current life. The therapeutic process involves re-shaping or re-writing that story in collaboration with the therapist. Depending on the theoretical orientation of the therapist, whether he is Freudian, Jungian, Kleinian, or whatever, he will interpret the patient's story according to the plot implicit in that orientation. A Freudian will see the 'universal plot' of the Oedipus complex, and a good deal of attention will be paid to the relationship with the mother or the father. The patient may resist the therapist's version of her story; sometimes the new version will be no more healing than the original. Successful therapy 'is...a revisioning of the story into a more intelligent, more imaginative plot' (Hillman 1983, pp.17–18).

For some of those who regard psychotherapy as the revisioning of a story, the question of truth does not figure largely. For Adam Phillips, who adopts a poststructuralist approach, the 're-written' story of a patient is a more workable rather than a more true version of the one with which he came into therapy (Phillips 1993). For Peter Brooks, however, narrative truth is "true" insofar as it carries conviction' (Brooks 1994, p.60). Again he is not talking about 'objective truth', although confusingly he uses the term 'historical truth' to denote a person's conviction that something is 'true to the *experience* of the past' but which may be 'the experience of fantasy...just as well as what we usually call fact' (p.60; emphasis added)[2]. Nevertheless, for Brooks, a narrative can be more true than less, and there can be 'faulty narratives' which stand in the way of self-understanding and the finding of meaning. Psychotherapy will not provide us with 'a final narrative truth...[but]... analyst and analysand work together dialogically in an effort to create... narratives that may achieve a provisional but crucial truth' (Rickard in Brooks 1994, p.9).

There is, then, a strong similarity between autobiography and psycho-therapy in their central concern with fictional narratives of self and the personal or subjective nature of our own truths. There are, of course, also dif-ferences, some of which are explored by Adam Phillips (1994). Whilst acknowledging that autobiography and psychotherapy are both ways of telling the story of the self and that both deal in fictions, he concludes that they are very different, even opposite activities. In psychotherapy the story of the self has to be deconstructed, to become unreadable, in order to be read and interpreted. Autobiography, on the other hand, is a process of finding a

---

2   Opinion is divided on what Freud meant by 'historical truth'. Freud's archaeological model (Freud 1938) implied that there was a grain of truth in every memory, and psychoanalysis was seen as a 'science that retrieves genuine fragments from the past and constructs essentially valid scenarios of ancient events' (Neisser 1994, p.6). Donald Spence (1982) counters Freud's idea of historical truth. Peter Brooks maintains, however, that Spence's opposition between 'historical truth' and 'narrative truth' is wrong. Referring to *Moses and Monotheism* (1937–39), Brooks says that Freud regarded historical truth as opposed to 'material truth', i.e. 'truth substantiated by observable events or verifiable facts', and accorded 'historical truth' the same status as 'psychic truth', i.e. 'that which is true for the subject, whether its origins be real or phantasmatic, that which belongs to his understanding of his own story' (Brooks 1994, p.74).

shape for the story of the self, finding a beginning, a middle and an end (p.68). So whilst psychotherapy aims at a sort of controlled fragmentation, autobiography seeks to impose order on the fragmentation. From this point of view, psychotherapy could be seen as a prelude to autobiography: it would create the necessary conditions for the creation of a new story of the self through autobiography, but autobiography would not itself be a psychotherapeutic exercise (p.69).

Phillips is assuming that autobiography means a published book about a person's life, written for a wide audience, whilst psychotherapy is an unrecorded and private conversation between two people. He is also assuming that one does not set out to write autobiography with a view to curing oneself of psychological problems, whereas a person enters into psychotherapy, if not for a cure, then at least for relief from debilitating symptoms. But is he right in these assumptions? Can one set out to write autobiographically, not primarily for publication (although this may be a by-product), but with the specific intention of trying to understand oneself better? And if so, what sort of autobiography would facilitate this approach?

The Possibilities for a Psychoanalytic Autobiography

There has been in recent years a good deal of discussion of the possibility of incorporating the methods of psychoanalysis into the writing of autobiography, and thus making out of autobiography a means of self-analysis or 'autopsychography' (Sturrock 1993, p.258). However, the prevailing view is that attempts to do so have not been successful. For Christine Downing, the problem lies in the conventional structure of autobiography: 'the usual chronologically ordered arrangement of outward events misses the point' (Downing 1977, p.212). For her, a psychoanalytically informed autobiography would take into account what Freud called 'primary process material', i.e. the material deriving from the id, in the form of dreams, fictions and myths.

John Sturrock is also of the view that autobiography is hemmed in by the chronological model. This results in an end product which is a 'counterfeit integration of a random life into a convenient fiction' (Sturrock 1977, p.55). If autobiography is to provide a vehicle for therapeutic insight, it requires 'a revaluation less of the past than of the present, the moment of writing' (p.55). This could be done, he says, by adopting a thematic or free associative approach, and he holds up the example of Michel Leiris as 'the new model autobiographer'.

Leiris (1901–90) was an art critic, anthropologist and poet associated with the Surrealists who is best known for his autobiographies *L'Age d'homme* (1939) and *La Règle du Jeu* (1948–68). These he wrote using the technique of free association within a Freudian framework, with the aim of curing himself of problems of impotence and masochism, which his psychoanalysis had not relieved. In *L'Age d'homme* (ET *Manhood* 1992) Leiris takes as his focus a double portrait by Lucas Cranach the Elder of Lucretia and Judith, and the stories of these two women as reported by Livy and the Old Testament respectively. Lucretia is the wife of a high-ranking Roman who is raped at knife-point by her husband's friend, a member of the Roman royal dynasty. The morning after the rape, Lucretia tells her husband and father what has happened and, overcome by the shame of it, stabs herself to death before their eyes. This act incites the Roman people to rebellion against the royal dynasty, causing their downfall. Judith is a virtuous widow living in the city of Bethulia, which is under siege by the Assyrian army under the command of Holofernes. To save her people, Judith seduces Holofernes in his tent and, whilst he is in a drunken stupor, cuts off his head. With their general slaughtered, the Assyrians raise the siege and flee.

Common to these two stories is the theme of self-sacrifice in a great cause, a theme which underlies Leiris's project: in the 'great cause' of ridding himself of his emotional and sexual problems, he 'sacrifices' himself by revealing to the reader in great detail the most intimate secrets of his failed sex life and of the punishment he visits on himself for his failures, in the form of self-woundings and attempts at suicide. In line with Sturrock's call to 'revaluate the moment of writing', Leiris puts the emphasis not on past events themselves but on the language he chooses to describe them, 'concentrating on certain salient words or groups of words in the certainty that these will show themselves to be privileged points of entry into his past' (Sturrock 1977, p.58). Not only does he organise his volumes of autobiography by association of ideas (and sometimes of words) instead of by chronology, but he 'deliberately follows those networks of association which will cause him the greatest unease' (p.58).

This approach, however, fails to cure Leiris of his emotional and sexual problems. Sturrock's view is that this is because 'language is never the possession of any individual, so that to employ it is to be alienated from the self' (p.58). As language is one of the few media through which we *can* access the self, this does not make sense as a reason for failure. Indeed, as Kim

Worthington says, autobiography comes closest to bridging the gap between self and language (Worthington 1996).

In my view there are several reasons why Leiris fails to cure himself through the autobiographical act. First, the idea of a cure is unrealistic; the more modest aim of gaining insight into his problems would have been more manageable. Second, he does not, at least in *Manhood*, take the necessary next step and analyse his writings from the psychoanalytic point of view; rather he indulges in a form of acting out. Third, if, as Sturrock suggests, the point of the exercise is to 'revaluate the present', then the psychoanalytic perspective Leiris adopts is not the most appropriate. A strictly Freudian approach encourages a preoccupation with the past, with the *origins* of disorder, rather than with trying to understand the mechanisms which hold the disorder in place in the present. It also makes sex and aggression the primary focus of exploration, which means that other relevant factors are likely to be over-looked.

Like an obedient Freudian analysand, Leiris sticks closely to the rules, showing us again and again how gruesome incidents in his innocent early life laid the foundation for his behaviour in adulthood. In so doing, he creates for himself not a way out of his dilemma, but an expression, albeit finely wrought, of his self-hate and self-disgust. As Susan Sontag says in her foreword to *Manhood*, the book is: '...a manual of abjection – anecdotes and fantasies and verbal associations and dreams set down in the tones of a man, partly anaesthetised, curiously fingering his own wounds' (Leiris 1992, p.viii).

As I have said above, a psychoanalytic theory which puts the emphasis on the present is the theory of Karen Horney. Whilst Freud's theory is *diachronic*, explaining the present in terms of the past, Horney's theory is *synchronic*, seeking to explain psychic phenomena in terms of their *function* within the present character structure. This does not mean to say that the past is disregarded; the present character structure has evolved out of the past, but it has developed into 'an autonomous system with an inner logic of its own' (Paris 1994, pp.120–121). Horneyan analytic technique involves directing the patient's attention to the structure of the defence system. It aims to motivate the patient to fight the battle against the pride system by becoming aware of all the aspects of the defensive structures: '...his search for glory, his claims, his shoulds, his pride, his self-hate, his alienation from self, his conflicts, his particular solution – and the effect all these factors have on his human relations and his capacity for creative work' (Horney 1951, p.341). This is not an awareness of how these things operate in the abstract, but 'of the *specific* ways in which these factors operate within him and how *in concrete detail* they manifest themselves in his *particular* life, past and present' (p.342). This awareness is also not just intellectual knowledge but an emotional experiencing (p.342). A Horneyan approach to self-analytic autobiography or 'autopsychography' would put the emphasis on using the writings to throw light on the present structure of the psyche, through increasing intellectual understanding and emotional experiencing of the defences in operation. How would one go about this? A brief consideration of the work of Bernard Paris, who for many years has been applying Horney's theory to literature, will help us to answer this question.

Paris's work is multi-faceted, but one of his main concerns is to throw light on the psychology of the author primarily through an understanding of the author's relationship with his or her fictional characters. He focuses his attention exclusively on realist fiction, such as the plays of Shakespeare and the major nineteenth-century novels of writers such as Dickens, Eliot and Austen (Paris 1974; 1978; 1991a; 1991b; 1997). Unlike many literary critics, he sees mimetic characters as whole rather than partial human beings, as 'round characters' or 'creations inside a creation', as E. M. Forster called them (Forster 1979, pp.73-80; Paris 1997, p.7). He believes that, using Horneyan theory, they can be understood in terms of their inner motivations and defences just as if they were real human beings with a life of their own. When they are so understood, it becomes clear that authors are faced with a dilemma. Either they have the choice of 'allowing their characters to come alive and kick the book to pieces', or of 'killing [them] by subordinating them to the main scheme of the work' (p.10). Most great realist authors, Paris says, remain true to their psychological intuitions and allow their characters to live out their lives at the expense of their creators' own intentions. However, this often leads to a conflict between character and plot, a conflict that can be particularly revealing of the author's psychology. Sometimes this conflict is discernible in the author's rhetorical treatment of the characters' experience (p.10). By rhetoric, Paris means 'the devices an author employs to influence readers' moral and intellectual responses to a character, their sympathy and antipathy, their emotional closeness or distance' (p.11). Whilst authors often have an intuitive grasp of their characters' psychology, they often misinterpret them. Horneyan analysis reveals that: 'Writers tend to validate characters whose defensive strategies are similar to their own and to satirise those who have different solutions' (p.12).

Apart from conflicts between the characters and the author, Paris has also observed that there are often, in realist fiction, inconsistencies in the author's rhetoric itself. When reading Thackeray's *Vanity Fair* in the 1960s, he was puzzled by the thematic contradictions he observed there, and was reminded of a passage in Horney's *Our Inner Conflicts* which says that 'inconsistencies are as definite an indication of the presence of conflicts as a rise in body temperature is of physical disturbance' (Horney 1946, p.35; Paris 1997, p.5). By applying Horney's theory to novels such as *Vanity Fair*[3], Paris began to see their thematic contradictions 'as parts of an intelligible structure of psychological conflict' of the author (p.5).

By interpreting psychologically both the mimetic characters themselves and the rhetoric surrounding them, Paris believes that it is possible to build up a picture of the *implied author* of an individual work and, by applying this analysis to the writer's *oeuvre* as a whole, to build up a picture of what he calls the *authorial personality*:

> When the rhetoric consistently glorifies characters who embrace a particular solution while criticising those who have adopted others, it reveals the implied author's own defences, repressions and blind spots. In works where the rhetoric is inconsistent…it reveals the implied author's inner conflicts (p.13).

Paris further believes that by analysing the implied authors of individual literary works and the authorial personality of a writer's *oeuvre*, using Horneyan theory, one can then go on to use the texts 'as a source of insight into the inner life of their creator' (p.13)[4].

What is this 'implied author' which Paris seeks to analyse from the Horneyan point of view? The term was coined by Wayne Booth (Booth 1991, pp.67–77). As a writer writes, Booth says, he 'creates not simply an ideal, impersonal "man in general" but an implied version of "himself" that is different from the implied authors we meet in other men's work' (pp.70–71). For Booth this is an inevitable effect of fiction writing, for there is no such thing as a neutral presence in fiction. The author will always imbue the work with certain values, and the reader will create an image of the author on the

3   See Paris (1974) for his discussion of *Vanity Fair*.
4   There are many examples in Paris's work of how he goes about his analysis. The interested reader might usefully start with his latest book *Imagined Human Beings* (1997).

basis of those values. They may not necessarily be identical with the values of the real life author. Indeed, an author may choose to imbue his work with a set of values which he specifically does not hold, for the sake of the overall effect. But it is the author who chooses these values, consciously or unconsciously, and who expresses them through the total form of the work. When we read, we 'infer [the implied author] as an ideal, literary, created version of the real man; he is the sum of his own choices' (pp.73–75). Thus, the implied author of a work of fiction is not a straightforward representation of the real author; it is an expression, possibly an unconscious expression, of certain views or values of the real author which bind the work together into a completed artistic whole. Rimmon-Kenan refers to the implied author as 'a set of implicit norms' within the text, or 'the governing consciousness of the work as a whole' (Rimmon-Kenan 1996, p.86). 'Voiceless and silent', the implied author is inferred and assembled, by the reader, as a *fictional construct* out of the components of the text (pp.87–88).

If we apply these considerations to autobiography, we could say the implied author is a *fictional construct that embodies certain norms and values of the real author at the time of writing.* These values will not necessarily be those that the author has consciously set out to express in the work, nor will they be his norms and values for all time; rather they will be a projection, or externalisation, to use Horney's term, of aspects of the author's psyche into the text – the author's prevailing *personal fiction* containing elements of his *personal truth.*

If, as Bernard Paris suggests, it should be possible, by analysing, from the Horneyan point of view, the implied author of a work of fiction, to gain insight into the inner life of the author, then it should be equally possible to analyse the implied author of our own autobiographical writings, in order to gain insight into ourselves. For this purpose we would need to produce autobiographical writings suitable for a Horneyan analysis. What sort of writings would these be? I would suggest that autobiographical writings most suitable for a Horneyan analysis would be more in the nature of autobiographical fiction than straightforward autobiography. We would use the techniques of mimetic fiction to create narrators and characters out of ourselves and other significant people in our lives. We would develop a context for these characters, construct stories around them, or simply write individual scenes[5].

---

5   One might use some of the methods suggested in Chapter 1, such as 'melody for two voices' or 'people on the page'.

For this process of fictionalising ourselves to be of value, it would be crucially important to allow our material to emerge as freely as possible, and our themes and characters based on ourselves to develop and take on a life of their own, even if we did not like what was emerging. In other words we would need to make an 'agreement' with ourselves that we would try to be as 'truthful' as possible. Such an 'agreement' would be in the nature of an 'autobiographical pact' of the kind which, according to Philippe Lejeune (1989, pp.119–137), autobiographers implicitly make with their readers: that they are engaged in a quest for truth, even though that truth may only be an approximation or what I have called 'personal truth'. The autobiographical pact with ourselves would provide us with a framework of honesty and truth-seeking, within which we would pursue our personal truth through the imagination – through primary process material, as Downing suggests – rather than through the literal facts of our lives. Having produced the writing, we would need to put it away for a period of time, in order to gain distance from it. In retrospect it is likely to be much easier to look at the writing from the more objective position of *reader* than of author, to discern the underlying philosophy of the implied author and the way it relates to the characters in the text, and to identify any conflicts within the rhetoric itself, using a Horneyan perspective[6].

As I have said above, I found the analysis from this point of view of my own unpublished novel *Stages* extremely helpful therapeutically. A Horneyan approach can also work well with non-fictional writings, as Bernard Paris discovered when using it to analyse the writing of his PhD dissertation on George Eliot. When writing the dissertation, Paris believed that he had discovered in Eliot's Religion of Humanity 'the answer to the modern quest for values' and expounded her views 'with a proselytising zeal'. After completing the dissertation, however, he suddenly lost enthusiasm for this belief and could not understand why:

> Reading Karen Horney helped me to understand what had happened.
> Horney correlates belief systems with strategies of defence and
> observes that when our defences change, so does our philosophy of
> life. I had had great difficulty writing my dissertation, for reasons that
> therapy later made clear, and had frequently felt hopeless about
> completing the PhD. Faced with the frustration of my academic

---

6   I discuss the role of the writer as reader of her own text in the next section.

ambitions, I found George Eliot's Religion of Humanity to be exactly what I needed: we give meaning to our lives by living for others rather than for ourselves. But when I finished my dissertation and was told that it ought to be published (Paris, 1965), I could once again dream of a glorious career. Since I no longer needed to live for others in order to give meaning to my life, George Eliot's philosophy lost its appeal. In Horneyan terms, my inability to write my dissertation forced me to abandon my expansive ambitions and to become self-effacing, but on triumphantly completing it, I became expansive once more, and George Eliot's ideas left me cold (Paris 1997, pp.3–4).

If Michel Leiris had reflected on *Manhood* from the Horneyan point of view, and had focused his attention on the 'philosophy of life' implicit in its pages, he might well have succeeded in increasing his self-understanding, for on close reading there is a discernible inconsistency in the rhetoric of the implied author. Whilst his stated aim is to cure himself of his obsessions, it is also clear that the 'great cause' of his writing is not cure, but self-glorification. This is strikingly demonstrated in his important 'Afterword' which reflects on the writing of the book (Leiris 1984, pp.153–164). Here, as also in the chapter on 'Lucrece' (pp.37–42), Leiris compares the autobiographer to the matador. The matador, to his mind, is a species of priest engaged in a ritual sacrifice; or he is a hero in a mythical drama who masters and kills the beast. Whilst he is the sacrificer, he is 'constantly threatened with death', which makes the sacrifice 'more valid than any strictly religious sacrifice' (p.38). Rather than being a mere 'littérateur', Leiris wants to be like the matador 'who transforms danger into an occasion to be more brilliant than ever' (p.155). Just as the matador performs his ritualised movements risking his life for the glory of the kill, so the autobiographer, or at least *this* autobiographer, risks his life by self-exposure, raising himself up in his imagination into a glorious being. When Leiris writes, he can feel like the bullfighter, courageous and virile, strutting his manhood in the public arena, to great acclaim: he becomes his idealised, expansive self. This, however, involves the sacrifice of the impotent, tortured person he actually is, the person whom his idealised self despises. 'When I go to a bullfight,' he tells us, 'I tend to identify myself with either the bull at the moment the sword is plunged into its body, or with the matador who risks being killed (perhaps emasculated?) by a thrust of the horn at the very moment when he most clearly affirms his virility' (p.42). Leiris is both matador and bull, sacrificer and victim, virile and emasculated, his glorious imaginary self and his despised actual self. His writing is simultaneously a self-sacrifice and an act of great courage which gives him the sense of identity and self-esteem he so badly needs. This self-esteem, however, only lasts as long as he goes on writing. So write he does: as Sturrock tells us, Leiris's autobiographical quest occupied him for fifty years (Sturrock 1994, p.262). For Leiris to have gained therapeutic insight into himself from his writings, he would have had to put some distance between himself and the work and to ask himself what *function* it was fulfilling. This he could not do; for as long as the writing was providing him with a means of raising himself above his self-hate, he had a vested interest in keeping his obsessions – the raw material of his writing – in place.

The Question of Transference: Writers as Readers of Their Own Texts

It could be argued that self-analysis using fictional autobiography is in principle impossible because the important transference relationship is missing. For Adam Phillips, one of the most significant differences between autobiography and psychoanalysis is that:

> psychoanalysis is self-telling to, and in the presence of, a particular other person, the analyst. The analyst's reticence invites the patient to recreate him or her from the significant figures in the patient's past. Transference – this unwitting repetition of early relationships – reveals the way one is continually inventing and reinventing the people one is talking to (Phillips 1994, p.71).

Phillips' statement implies that there is only one person present in the writing of an autobiography, the author, and this is certainly not the case. As many literary theorists have pointed out, a narrative is always addressed to someone, although there is disagreement as to the number or identity of 'persons' or 'agents' being addressed. Seymour Chatman suggests that, in the same way as there is always an implied author but only sometimes a narrator in a narrative communication, there is always an implied reader and sometimes also a narratee, as in the following schema (Chatman 1978, pp.148–151):

Real Author ↦ **Implied Author** ↦ **(Narrator)** ↦ **(Narratee)** ↦ **Implied Reader** ↦ Real Reader

---

For Rimmon-Kenan, there is always a narratee, even if only minimally, but she places the implied reader outside of the narrative proper (Rimmon-Kenan 1996, pp.88–89).

It seems to be quite difficult to differentiate clearly between the implied reader and the narratee. Seymour Chatman defines the implied reader as 'the audience presupposed by the narrative itself' (Chatman 1978, p.150) rather than a particular personification, but then goes on to imply that the narratee is also a part of that audience. Unlike the implied reader, the narratee is often a specific character present in the narrative. He or she may be named, as in Christa Wolf's autobiographical novel *A Model Childhood* (1983), where the author sometimes appears to be telling her story to her daughter Lenka, who is accompanying her on her journey. Or a narratee-character may be assumed but is not named and does not speak, such as the listeners to Marlow's stories in Conrad's *Lord Jim* or *Heart of Darkness* (Chatman 1978, p.150).

According to Chatman, there is an alliance between the implied reader and the narratee; there are novels in which the alliance is reasonably close and others in which the distance is great (p.151). But he seems to imply that it is primarily the author who determines the narratee, whilst it is primarily the reader who determines the implied reader, although taking on the role of implied reader is part of the real reader's 'fictional contract' with the text (p.150), and this suggests that the implied reader is already in place at the moment of reading. William Nelles' suggestion that one can differentiate between the implied reader and the narratee by saying that 'the narratee hears', whilst 'the implied reader interprets' (Nelles 1993, p.22), is helpful, because this makes the narratee a passive agent and the implied reader an active one. Thus, whilst the narratee is a fictional construct wholly within the narrative communication, the implied reader is both inside and outside of the narrative communication, created both by the author and by the reader, and is therefore a much more fluid entity.

Of the implied reader and the narratee, it is the former, I believe, which is most helpful in thinking about using our own writings for self-analytic purposes because, not being personified in the guise of a character, it is less under our conscious control as author and is likely therefore to contain more of our involuntary projections than the narratee.

Adam Phillips likens 'the implied ideal reader' in an autobiography to the implied listener in psychoanalysis, and suggests that it would be interesting to consider 'the catastrophic reading it is trying to avert' (Phillips 1994, p.71). There is an assumption here that all autobiographies are an attempt to hide or obscure something that the writer either does not wish to see herself or does not wish others to see; or put another way, that they are written to create a representation of self which corresponds to the way the writer wishes to see herself or to be seen by others. This would certainly fit many celebrated autobiographies, such as Rousseau's and St. Augustine's, as well as that of Michel Leiris; as I have said in my discussion of *Manhood*, the text helps the author to raise himself above the 'catastrophic reading' of himself which results from his self-hate. In the case of Jane, self-representations as the good child protect her against a recognition of other more complex aspects of her personality, such as ambitious expansiveness and its consequences. One could say that there is a collusion here, partly conscious perhaps, but more likely unconscious, between the author and the implied reader to create an identity which is acceptable to the author's dominant solution. This, of course, may have an adverse effect on the writing, as indeed Jane found, in that she had difficulties using more complex psychological material of her own in her autobiographical fictions, for fear that her self-representations might reveal material which was uncomfortable. Alternatively, the implied reader, as in the case of the implied author, may represent a subversion of the author's conscious intentions, an aspect of the personality structure manifesting itself in spite of the author's desire for it to be kept hidden.

Phillips' idea of a transference relationship between the writer and the implied reader which is similar to that between the patient and the analyst as implied listener, is an interesting one for our purposes. Phillips uses the original Freudian definition of transference as 'an unwitting repetition of early relationships', in which the patient re-creates the analyst in the guise of significant figures from the patient's past (Phillips 1994, p.71). Applying this definition to the narrative communication, a Freudian understanding of the implied reader might be that it is a parental figure, from whom the writer wishes to obtain love or retribution, as in the Oedipal scenario.

Horney was critical of Freud's view of transference and his belief '...that the patient's irrational emotional reactions [in analysis] represent a revival of infantile feelings, now attached to...the analyst...' (Horney 1939a, pp.156–157). This approach, she believed, tended to lead to misinterpretations of the significance of phenomena such as a patient's falling in love with the analyst. If this is interpreted as a reactivation of past feelings then it will be understood as a repetition of the love the patient felt for, say, his mother, which was in fact much greater than he remembers. Whilst the patient is likely to be relieved by this interpretation because it enables him to recognise 'that there is something compulsory, something not genuine, in his feelings of love', it is unlikely to resolve the dependency (pp.157–158). This is because this kind of interpretation does not sufficiently take into account the actual factors in the present configuration of the patient's personality structure which make the attachment to the analyst necessary. Horney's understanding of transference is that it is a 'special form of human relationship', and as '...neuroses are ultimately the expression of disturbances in human relationships', it stands to reason that these disturbances are likely to manifest themselves in the relationship with the analyst too (p.167). Thus, irrational love for the analyst might indicate a powerful self-effacing solution with strong masochistic trends, necessitating attachment to others as a means of allaying anxiety. Recognising this can lead to an understanding of the underlying structure that holds it in place, and its gradual dismantling (pp.158–159).

Analysing the implied reader from a Horneyan perspective might help to throw light on the writer's dominant life solutions and her customary ways of engaging with others. The implied reader of Jane's childhood stories would be someone who validates her self-effacing solution – a kind, accepting figure (whether the adult Jesus in 'The Birthday Present' or the beggar's daughter in 'How Much is that Doggy in the Window?') who smiles benignly at her, thus allaying her anxieties about being 'bad'. Again, whilst Sarah seems in the early draft of her novel to want to distract her implied reader by 'fogging up' the narrative with complex literary techniques, in 'The Circus' the implied reader is invited to celebrate with Sarah her own expansiveness, even though, for Sarah, there is an element of 'badness' about it. Rather than being 'frozen out' as she[7] was before, the implied reader here is set free to participate in the joyful feelings of Sarah's own liberation.

I would suggest that for the writer in search of insight through her writings, asking the question: 'What is the identity of the implied reader of my autobiographical fictions?' is useful, because it may help to reveal certain psychic trends in play within the text that were not obvious at the time of writing, and also to understand better why a piece of writing is not working well. But in order to do that the writer has to move from the left-hand side of

---

7   I use 'she' here, because I am thinking of Sarah as her own implied reader, but the implied reader may just as easily be 'he' or non-gendered and therefore referred to as 'it'.

the narrative communication to the right-hand side, and to become the reader or interpreter of her own text. Marilyn Chandler calls reading 'an integral part of the autobiographical act' (Chandler 1990, p.40) and quotes Janet Varner Gunn's view that 'the autobiographer is the "paradigmatic reader" of his own work – a "reader of his or her self" engaged in the act of interpretation almost simultaneously with the act of creation' (p.40; Gunn 1982, p.68). But taking on the role of readers of our self-writings for analytic purposes is far from straightforward: it places us in quite a different relationship to the text from that of writer, and this changed relationship has certain implications. When we write autobiographically, we objectify ourselves on the page. We suspend our authorial stance and engage in a transference relationship with the text, allowing our free associations to emerge. Then we 'stand back' and apply the critical faculty, crafting our free associations into a workable fiction, an object which contains fictional representations of ourselves. When we become readers of our autobiographical texts, the object is already there; we employ our critical faculty to analyse and interpret the object, to seek evidence of our own psyches. We are doubly objectified, doubly 'othered' (Rancour-Lafferiere 1994, p.30). Self-analysis here becomes other-analysis; and as in all analyses of others, we have to take into account counter-transference feelings.

Reader-response theorists have suggested many different ways in which one can think about the transference relationship between the reader and the text, using different psychoanalytic models. Norman Holland's post-Freudian approach suggests that the reader brings to his reading of a text an 'identity theme' (Holland 1980, p.120). This arises out of a 'primary identity' which is activated by the relation with the mother in early childhood and which remains invariant throughout life as 'an unchanging inner form or core of continuity' (p.121). As readers, we 'use the literary work to symbolize and…replicate ourselves', to confirm ourselves to ourselves through the recreation of the work in terms of our own identity theme (pp.124–125). Holland's research using this idea (Holland 1973, 1975) aims to show how various are individual readers' responses to the same text, but it could also provide an approach to using the text to gain self-understanding through recognition of one's own identity theme.

Bernard Paris's view is that what we see or fail to see in the text will be influenced by our own Horneyan defences. Discussing the relationship of the literary critic to the text, he says that:

> Psychoanalysts have what Horney calls a 'personal equation' that leads
> them to respond to the solutions and conflicts they encounter in
> patients in terms of their own personality structures, and the same
> thing is true for readers responding to texts. An interpretation often
> tells us as much about the critic as it does about the work under
> discussion (Paris, unpublished).

But if the text we are reading is authored by ourselves and already contains our own Horneyan defences, will we not simply reinforce them by bringing those same defences to the text as readers? Certainly this is a possibility, especially where there are deeply embedded defence mechanisms which have a vested interest in not being revealed or dislodged. How then can we, as readers, hope to gain insight from our writings into our own personality structures? I would suggest that it is a question of the attitude which the writer adopts to the self-analytic enterprise.

In his comparison of the analytic relationship to that between reader and text Peter Brooks draws attention to the essentially dialogic nature of these encounters (Brooks 1994, pp.56ff). The reader or analyst is not simply a neutral receiver of the story's meaning; nor is it the case, as is often thought of psychoanalysis, that the reader or analyst, through his interpretations, forces meaning on the text. Meaning is a consequence of the dialogue between the two sides. In listening or reading, the analyst/reader shuttles back and forth between the role of analyst and the role of patient (p.58). As readers of our own text, it is equally important to listen to the text, or read it in different ways, with free-floating attention, to enter the provisional space of the text and allow it to act on ourselves; as it is to read the text against the background of our theoretical orientation, trying out possible meanings:

> ...the work of the reader is not only to grasp the story as much as
> possible, but to *judge its relation to the narrative discourse that conveys it,*
> *seeking to understand not only what the narrative appears to say but also what it*
> *appears to intend*...our role as readers involves a finely tuned and
> skeptical hearing, a rewriting of the narrative text in collaboration and
> agonistic dialogue with the words proffered by the narrator (p.61;
> emphasis added).

This dialogic encounter with the text, which Janet Varner Gunn has aptly called the 'stereoscope of readership' (Gunn 1982, pp.90–117) is, I would argue, an important means of loosening the hold of psychic defences. It disrupts meanings which have become fixed over time and locked us into unsatisfactory ways of being. It encourages that flexible authorial stance in the relationship with ourselves which I have discussed earlier, a flexibility of self which, in Horney's view, is at the root of psychological health.

Writing Versus Speaking in Therapy

Another objection which could be made to the use of writing in a therapeutic context is that it is much less free than speaking. As noted above, Adam Phillips sees the writing of autobiography as a *non-therapeutic* undertaking, which might be engaged in only *after* analysis or therapy is satisfactorily completed. Indeed, he seems to be of the view that writing might act as a *block* to insight and self-understanding: 'It is the *continuity* of our life-stories that we use to conceal the past', he says, with the implication that writing them down, shaping and crafting them into autobiography, reinforces that continuity and hence strengthens our defences against the unspoken story which lies beneath, pressing for recognition. It is only through free-association, through the spoken word, that 'the patient's story loses its composition and becomes more like a collage in which our favourite words unwittingly find alternative contexts' (Phillips 1994, p.67).

Philippe Lejeune, one of the foremost theorists of autobiography, would agree with this view. He had great hopes for the coming together of autobiography and psychoanalysis, seeing autobiography as a powerful confessional tool in the quest for hidden knowledge of the self, primarily knowledge of a sexual nature. For him it was the act of uttering or writing down the words which potentially had a liberating effect, but this could be interfered with if the writing was structured. Hence, his championing of a kind of writing, such as that of Michel Leiris, which moved away from the traditional models of autobiography towards a free associational type of writing without form or structure. In the light of the failure of Leiris' self-analytical quest, however, he was forced to conclude that autobiography was a non-therapeutic act[8] (Eakin in Lejeune 1989, pp.xxvi–xxvii; cf. Lejeune 1971, pp.257–262).

There is an assumption underlying these views that writing is intrinsically logical and controlled, whereas the words we speak are free, spontaneous and fluid, closer to the reality of the self and therefore more likely to reveal things

8   Eakin points out that in later writings Lejeune changed his mind on this several times.

which we try to keep hidden. The view that speaking is nearer to reality than writing has, of course, been challenged by Jacques Derrida, who calls it *phonocentrism* or *logocentrism*. Writing, on the traditional view, is secondary to speech, a 'signifier of the signifier' (Derrida 1976, p.7). However, as language has progressively become dominated by writing, writing has overwhelmed speech, so much so that speech is now 'always already' inhabited by writing. What Derrida calls the 'trace' is the permanent layer of words written in our unconscious by language and society which informs our perception of the outside world and our consciousness (Sampson 1989, pp.10–11; Derrida 1978, Chap. 7). Thus, when we speak, our words are as much 'written' as writing.

Derrida is using the term 'writing' only partly in the sense of words written on the page; it also implies a process of *imprinting*, which takes place in the infant before the development of conscious awareness[9]. His discussion of the similarity between speaking and writing is therefore somewhat different from that being pursued here although, as I will show in a moment, this latter usage of the term 'writing' is also relevant. At a more easily observable level one might argue that there are certain kinds of writing which are closer to speaking, and conversely that there are certain kinds of speaking which are closer to writing. In the first category belong free associational writing techniques such as freewriting, where the demand that the writer keeps writing without reflection and does not go back to correct grammar or syntax can have the effect of undermining conscious control over her words and is therefore more likely to give rise to material which is spontaneous and more directly related to the writer's inner life than would be the case if she had applied conscious reasoning[10]. Here also belong certain forms of diary writing that may be a kind of speaking that a person does when her usual listener, whether a spouse or a therapist, is absent. Writing of this kind may not be consciously fictional or may not be crafted in any way. It may simply be the words she would speak to her customary listener if he were there, an

---

9   This idea of imprinting is made explicit in Derrida's essay on Freud where he uses the metaphor of a 'mystic writing pad' for the virgin psyche. The pad is described as consisting of an underlying wax layer into which the 'trace' is permanently inscribed, even after the upper surface is cleared by lifting it from the wax (Sampson 1989; Derrida 1978).

10   Indeed Lejeune and Leiris were on the right track in their attempts to use this type of writing as a psychotherapeutic tool, although, as I said above, their expectations that the writing on its own would have a curative effect were unrealistic.

account of her day or the difficult things she has had to deal with, or how she is feeling physically or emotionally. Writing here is the externalisation of an internal dialogue with the significant other. It is a way of making the absent person present; rather than feeling alone, she 'calls up' the other in her imagination so that he becomes the implied reader or listener. The writing may function as a safety valve, enabling her to objectify uncomfortable feelings, but it may also provide a way of 'holding' those feelings on her own or jointly with the other through imagination.

In the second category – types of speaking that are closer to writing – belong types of speaking that are 'fixed and formal' (Leader 1991, p.225), such as lectures or speeches, where the speaker may be drawing on a society's or a culture's stock forms or phrases, or where he may be speaking wholly or partly from a written text or from memorised notes. In this category too – and closer to Derrida's idea of the 'trace' that has been imprinted on the psyche – are what one might term *mechanical ways of speaking*, which derive from rigid psychic states. People who subscribe uncritically to certain religious or pseudo-philosophical views and are not open to debate and discussion could be described as speaking mechanically, as could people entrapped in Horneyan 'life solutions' who have to defend their way of being at all cost, for fear of psychic disintegration. One could also argue that the type of speaking a therapist and client do in the later stages of therapy is more akin to writing, a kind of editing or interpreting of material which has been 'written' in the early stages of the therapeutic encounter.

Whilst, then, as Derrida suggests, both writing and speaking may in a sense be secondary or mediated as a result of our immersion in language, there are situations in which either of them may be more or less fixed or rigid, more or less flexible. If the goal of speaking or writing is to access one's spontaneous thoughts and feelings, as it is in the therapeutic context, then bearing in mind what I have said about the relative fixity or flexibility of either, writing is potentially as useful as speaking. From the opposite perspective, of course, both speaking and writing may, at times, constitute a block. People who find it difficult to associate freely in psychotherapy are likely to find it equally difficult to practise freewriting. If defences are particularly rigid, writing or speaking oneself might simply reinforce entrapment within a particular life solution, in Horney's sense: it may be the means by which a writer colludes with his defensive structures in order to make him feel good about himself, as the case of Leiris shows. But there is nothing here to suggest that writing is intrinsically more blocking than speaking. Writer's block is a well known phenomenon primarily because there is an easily identifiable group of people who suffer from it; there is no comparable focus on people who suffer from 'speaker's block', although the phenomenon undoubtedly exists.

If, then, it is the case that in a therapeutic context writing is potentially as useful as speaking, it might be more important to determine *what kind of writing* is most useful at *which particular stage* in the therapeutic process. As I have already indicated, in the psychotherapeutic encounter one could say that the therapist and the client use different kinds of speaking at different stages in the process. In the early stages of therapy the client is encouraged to speak her words as freely as possible, without reflection, so that the hidden psychic material emerges. The therapist is likely to remain silent during this stage or to speak little, providing an empathetic holding environment in which the client's new words can be spoken. Certainly, interpretation is inappropriate at this stage. It is only when a sufficient amount of material has emerged that the client and the therapist work together to edit the client's material into a new and more workable story. Thus, there are two quite different kinds of speaking here which have their place at different stages in the encounter: the first is freer and closer to the reality of the client's inner world; the second is more considered, mediated by conscious thought, and therefore more akin to writing.

A similar distinction can be made between the different kinds of writing that might be used in self-therapy. Free, uncrafted writing, which is closer to speaking, may be used as a means of getting in touch with the raw material of the self. This might be done in the form of a journal or a diary and might be a person's first attempt to place herself on the page. The gradual accumulation of words on the page provides an external and solid point of reference for the self and is likely to bring about a gradual increase in confidence; instead of a chaotic and anxiety-provoking muddle of feelings 'in here', the words on the page bring a sense of order and control, a basis on which to build. Having established a degree of security in objectifying the self, the writer's logical next step is to edit and craft those words. Crafting can create an object which is both contained, in the sense that it is an aesthetic rendering of self or self-experience, which can be deeply satisfying and increase self-esteem, and containing, in the sense that it is an external repository of feelings about the self or the past, which makes them safe.

In their paper on the poet Anne Sexton, Lester and Terry stress the important role of crafting for a writer whose highly personal poems were an attempt 'to establish emotional order out of chaos' (Lester and Terry 1992, p.49). Sexton had a long history of psychiatric disturbance, breakdown and hospitalisation, and started to write at the suggestion of her first psychotherapist (p.48). Lester and Terry suggest that her way of writing, for example her use of repetition, promoted 'a sense of unity in [the] poems, [and] a sense of stability of her own confusion and fragmentation' (p.50). She devoted a great deal of time and energy to revising the poems, to finding a form that would best capture her painful experience. This concentration on form rather than on content made the creative process the controlling force rather than her illness (p.50).

Lester and Terry go on to suggest that the value of crafting lies in its enabling a writer 'to view the content [of her self-writing] from an intellectual and non-emotional perspective', and that: 'It may be that only when writers are forced to craft their expressive products into formal works of art is there a psychotherapeutic effect' (p.51). If by 'psychotherapeutic effect' the authors mean significant and lasting psychic change (they do not clarify their usage of the term), then I would agree with them. And perhaps this might be particularly useful in making the important distinction between using writing *as a process* and *as a product* in the therapeutic context: the *process* of writing, and I am thinking here of the work of White and Epston, may have a significant effect at a behavioural level or at the level of everyday insight, but using writing *as a product which one crafts and edits* might well take a person into deeper levels of the self, as do psychodynamic psychotherapy or psychoanalysis, and help to consolidate insights. Whereas the drafting stage of writing involves primarily the spontaneous, playful, chaotic part of the self, the crafting process brings into play *as well* the powers of the critical faculty, thus providing a 'cutting edge' with which a person can excavate her own material. Within a Horneyan framework, having a 'cutting edge' is particularly important in the latter stages of therapy in the final battle in which the emerging 'real self' must engage with the 'pride system', that powerful composite of idealised and despised images, neurotic claims, shoulds and self-hate (Horney 1951, pp.110ff.). If the pride system's strategy is to keep itself hidden, then forcing it repeatedly into the open (it is significant that Lester and Terry suggest that writers need to be *forced* to craft their expressive writings) through a constant refining of written material may help the writer to ally herself with the positive forces for growth and to counter her own defences.

Crafting, then, with its demand for distance and the finding of form, can enable a person to view her inner problems more clearly and can thus increase her control and management of those problems. The troublesome inner world becomes something external to be worked on, something known and malleable, rather than chaotic and threatening. By transforming aspects of the inner world into an aesthetic object, crafted writing can also enhance self-esteem. Of course it could be argued that writing did not work in the case of Anne Sexton for, like Virginia Woolf, she too committed suicide; in the longer term her writing was not sufficient to contain the pain and distress of her psychological problems. But, as Terry and Lester suggest, without the writing she may well have committed suicide a great deal earlier (Lester and Terry 1992, p.51), and perhaps the same could be said of Woolf.

In her discussion of the use of writing as a healing or transformative process Marilyn Chandler distinguishes between three different types of writing: journal or diary writing, autobiography proper and autobiographical fiction or poetry, each having a different role to play:

> They are, respectively, the results of three distinct modes of thought: introspection, retrospection, and transformation. In each mode a different kind of literary act is performed and a different stage in healing enacted. Viewed as a sequence, these modes of thought and writing successively indicate greater authorial control and more aesthetic distance from the image of the self presented in the text (Chandler 1990, p.21).

This schema makes the move to fictionalising one's autobiographical material the third and crucial stage of using writing as a therapeutic tool and implies that before a person reaches the stage of being able to fictionalise herself, she must have worked through the other two stages. I would agree that, for some people, reaching the point where they can fictionalise themselves relatively freely and at length is a fairly advanced stage in self-exploration and suggests that they already have a fairly flexible relationship with their inner world, or have already moved some way towards it. On the other hand, fictionalising, because it demands an engagement with feelings and emotions, has a potential in the earlier stages of self-exploration as well, if not in the form of extended writings, then perhaps in the form of short characterisation, or 'self as narrator' type, exercises. As I said above, one of the most important elements of good mimetic fiction is that it should be *emotionally felt*. This means that the reader is enabled not only to get into the minds of the characters portrayed, but also to experience the emotions of the characters, as if they were real people. In order to achieve this effect, writers have to be able to immerse themselves in the feelings they are trying to portray, to 'show' rather than to 'tell'. When writing autobiographical fiction, the requirement that we should 'show' rather than 'tell' means that we are forced to enter into *our own* feelings and emotions in a way that we may not be able to do simply by talking about them or by writing down the facts of our lives. The expressing of emotion in the consulting room is often very slow in coming, and fiction, with its playful and metaphorical aspects, may provide a means of circumventing or subverting a person's defences. As family therapists Peggy Penn and Marilyn Frankfurt have noticed in their clinical experience: '...writing...addresses what has been missing in a client's significant relationship – a missing body of feeling that, when included, changes the relationship' (Penn and Frankfurt 1994, p.230).

In the early stages of the therapeutic endeavour, as in the early stages of a writing apprenticeship, fictionalising ourselves may, without our being fully aware of it, shift us into a deeper mode of self-engagement, which puts us in touch with feelings and emotions that we can then explore and work on further. At a later stage of therapy or self-exploration, fiction's playful, metaphorical aspect may also help us to subvert or counter our defences. But in conjunction with crafting – the employment of literary technique and the finding of form – it enables us to engage in a different kind of process, to 'slow down our perceptions and reactions, making room for their thickening, their gradual layering' (p.229), thus providing us with a means of deepening and strengthening our understanding of ourselves. Writing extended fictions, such as novels and short stories, offers the possibility of creating a framework within which we can experiment with different versions of ourselves, give shape to parts of ourselves that may be unthought, in Bollas's sense, or felt but not yet ready to be fully enacted. They can provide us with an external point of reference to which we can come back again and again, in a process of constant self-revision. As a number of writers have pointed out (e.g. J.-B. Pontalis quoted by Phillips 1994, p.73), we should write not one but multiple autobiographies in the quest for self-understanding, and fiction offers many different forms with which to work.

Fictional Autobiography in Self-Therapy and Psychotherapy

In this chapter I have explored the possibility of using fictional auto-biography as a self-analytic or self-therapeutic tool, working on the assumption that this is a feasible undertaking. The views of psychoanalysts and psychotherapists on the viability of self-analysis are, however, mixed. Freud, for example, believed that 'genuine self-analysis is impossible; otherwise there would be no [neurotic] illness' (Freud 1914, p.21; Rancour-Laferriere 1994, pp.2–3). This is a strange view, seeing that Freud's theory grew out of his own self-analysis, and that it is largely as a result of the popularity of his theory that a method for self-analysis has become generally available. Rancour-Laferriere points out that Freud's statement '…is based on the questionable assertion that analytic insight necessarily cures' (p.3). He is of the view that self-analysis, like analysis proper, is not interminable but 'asymptotic': 'At best, analysis moves asymptotically toward a point of maximum possible insight, given the situation, and then moves on toward other points, never to actually touch any one of them' (p.2). Analysis, on this view, becomes an ongoing and infinite process rather than a 'once-for-all' undertaking.

Rancour-Laferriere suggests that in some ways self-analysis has advantages over psychoanalysis because 'one has to overcome only one set of defenses (one's own)', and that one has greater access to one's own materials and thus the potential for knowing oneself better than anyone else (p.3). On the negative side he notes the dangers of distortion of reality and of colluding with one's own defences, as well as the danger of incompleteness, the tendency when working on one's own to be satisfied with a partial explanation and thus to stop short of a proper in-depth exploration (p.3). In spite of the drawbacks, he decides in favour of self-analysis: '…the results of self-analysis are not necessarily false, even if they be partial or somewhat distorted. If practiced…for a long period of time, self-analysis can provide ever-expanding insight' (p.3).

Karen Horney, like many psychoanalysts after Freud, was essentially positive about the possibilities of self-analysis, and she was one of the few to write at length on the topic (Horney 1942). She too believed that 'we are more familiar with ourselves than any outsider can be' (pp.145–146), although before embarking on self-analysis we would be advised to acquire some knowledge of the techniques of psychoanalysis (p.146). She was very much aware of the difficulty of dealing with resistances, which she saw as the main problem of any kind of analysis (pp.146–147). However, the fact that a person is undertaking self-analysis means that there is a part of himself which seeks insight and change (p.147), and this is likely to be a strong motivating factor in the battle with his defences.

Working with an analyst has a definite advantage in that it provides 'a unique and specific opportunity for the patient to study, by observing his behaviour with the analyst, what his typical behaviour is towards other people in general' (p.147). But Horney believes that this can be replaced by close observation of a person's relationships with others (p.147). She does not underestimate the problems involved in doing this, for example the tendency to justify certain of one's own defensive behaviours as reasonable responses to the attitudes or stances of others; nevertheless she believes that working on one's own is possible, if more demanding (pp.147–150).

Horney distinguishes between 'occasional self-analysis' and 'systematic self-analysis'. The former is most useful for situational disturbances such as 'a functional headache, an acute attack of anxiety, a…fear of public performances, an acute functional stomach upset' (p.152), for which one might try to discover an underlying reason. Self-analysis here is 'comparatively easy and sometimes productive of immediate results' (p.151). Systematic self-analysis differs from occasional self-analysis in its greater frequency and continuity. It aims to delve deeper beneath surface events and to work on problems again and again (p.174). It involves exposure to 'painful uncertainties and hurts' and a willingness to take up the battle with one's own 'opposing forces' (p.175). This requires 'a spirit of ruthless honesty toward [oneself]' (p.175).

Horney does not favour the establishing of a 'rigid schedule of appointments with oneself' (p.185). There will be times when a person will be intensely engaged in working on himself, and others when self-analysis 'recedes into the background' (p.186). Horney is not as confident as Freud about dreams as 'the royal road to the unconscious'; rather, it is important for a person to try to acquire an understanding of how dreams relate to other factors operating within the psyche (p.176). Free association is, for Horney, as much the basic technique in self-analysis as in analysis proper (p.186). Through free association the self-analysand should 'try to express what he really feels and not what he is supposed to feel according to tradition or his own standards', and to 'give as free range to his feelings as he possibly can' (pp.248–249). Whilst free association is in progress, the reasoning faculty should be kept very much in abeyance (pp.250–251). Only when there is sufficient spontaneous material does the method of work change and 'reason comes into play' (p.252). Horney stresses, however, that understanding and interpretation are not done solely by reason; anticipating Peter Brooks' idea of a dialogic relationship with one's material, she suggests that there must be a flexible movement back and forth between 'deliberate thinking [and]…intuitive grasping of connections' (p.255).

Horney assumes that writing will play an important part in self-analysis, although she is not talking here about fictional autobiography. It can be helpful to note down one's free associations: 'Some people can concentrate better when they write; others find their attention distracted by writing' (p.187). Writing makes it less likely that one will 'wander off on a tangent'; also the temptation to skip thoughts or feelings as irrelevant is lessened (p.187). The most significant advantage of writing 'is that it affords the possibility of going over the notes afterward', picking up associations which were not noticed as they were written: a person '...may see the old findings in a different light. Or he may discover that he has made no noticeable headway, but is essentially still at the same point where he was several months ago' (p.187).

Horney has mixed feelings about diary writing, much of which, she says, does not attempt 'to penetrate beneath the conscious level' (p.188) and may therefore not reveal anything which is unknown to the writer. A diary is also often written with an eye to the reader, or to the writer's self-glorification (p.189). At its best, it 'is an honest recording of conscious feelings, thoughts, and motivations' (p.188). She encourages the kind of diary writing which is 'not a simple report of factual occurences' but a truthful 'recording of one's emotional experiences and motivations' (p.188)[11]. She is prepared to concede that diaries (and she adds autobiographies here) 'have their value, but they are intrinsically different from an exploration of self. No-one can produce a narrative about himself and at the same time let his mind run in free associations' (p.188). As will be clear from the foregoing, I do not believe this to be the case. By using the free associational and the editing/crafting modes of writing at different stages in the therapeutic process, the mind can be allowed both to 'run free in associations', producing information about the inner life, and then to 'step back' from this material and shape it into a narrative which can facilitate insight and deep psychic change.

Horney does not take her discussion of writing techniques further and is clearly not aware of the potential for using more structured writing such as poetry or fictional autobiography as a tool in self-analysis. But there is scope, within the framework she suggests for systematic self-analysis, for writing techniques such as those I have discussed above – freewriting, fictionalising early memories, 'melody for two voices', 'country of the mind' – to be used as

11   Horney would have found interesting the approaches to therapeutic diary writing suggested by Progoff (1975), Rainer (1978), and Milner (1952).

ways of 'recognizing [oneself]' (p.189), in addition to the other methods of self-observation she suggests[12]. Such writing techniques might also be valuable as an on-going method of self-exploration after a formal analysis or therapy is over. Horney herself points to the value of writing in the post-analysis period in her discussion of Clare (pp.190–246), a woman entrapped in an extreme form of the self-effacing solution which Horney calls morbid dependency[13]. After her analysis is over Clare continues to work on herself through writing a self-analytic diary, occasionally returning to see her therapist to discuss her progress. Again, writing fictional autobiography could have a role here, as well as during breaks in therapy, when the therapist or the client are away on holiday. A client might also be engaged on a longer piece of fictional autobiography alongside therapy. Whilst the writing might not be taken into the therapy sessions, it might well constitute a parallel process, providing an imaginative space where autobiographical material that has been evoked in the consulting room might be explored in fictional form, and insights gained fed back into the therapy sessions.

It may also be possible, within the framework of an eclectic approach to psychotherapy that puts the emphasis on the present configuration of the personality rather than on retrieving the past, or in the type of therapy which focuses on the felt nature of experience (see Hobson 1985 and Mair 1989), to suggest to patients that they engage in writing fictional autobiography between sessions. The resulting work might be used as a basis for analysis between patient and therapist or for interpretation by the therapist, although one would need to bear in mind the importance of distance in gaining a useful perspective on the writing. As I said, some of the students taking the Certificate in Creative Writing reported that they had used fictional autobiography written during the course in their therapy sessions, with positive results.

Writing of this kind would clearly not be appropriate for use with all patients or clients, as they would need to feel relatively at ease with the written word and preferably to have some familiarity with writing techniques. I would suggest that this approach might be particularly useful for

---

12   Writing exercises suggested in Bolton (1998), de Salvo (1999), Jackowska (1997), Philips, Penman and Linnington (1998), and Schneider and Killick (1998), might also be useful here.

13   Bernard Paris suggests that the case of 'Clare' is a disguised account of Horney's own self-analysis (see Paris 1994, pp.xxiii–xxiv).

writers who present with writer's block, or for people who are accustomed to keeping a diary, or are more generally interested in the literary arts. In view of the fact that it is largely women who attend creative writing courses, there are grounds to suggest that writing in therapy might be more enthusiastically taken up by women than men. Where clients are not at ease with the written word, it may be possible for the counsellor or therapist to act as scribe, taking down verbatim the client's story and working on the written text with her (see Hunt and Sampson 1998, Chapters 4, 6 and 7).

There are a number of existing therapies which already use fictional autobiography or other forms of creative writing as part of their practice in ways which bear some similarity to what I am suggesting here[14]. In Personal Construct Therapy a therapist may suggest to a client that he write a brief 'self-characterisation'. He might be asked, for example, to write a character sketch as if he were 'the principal character in a play'. This is written in the third person from the point of view of a friend who knows the client 'very intimately and very sympathetically'. These 'self-characterisations' are then used to facilitate the formulation of constructs and elements used in the therapy (Fransella and Dalton 1990, p.53).

Oral and written storytelling is advocated as a method of therapy by Alida Gersie (Gersie 1997; Gersie and King 1990). She draws on myths, folk tales and fairy stories to facilitate clients' creative story-making as a means of getting in touch with inner imagery, which leads to a deeper awareness of self. She suggests working with a number of themes such as 'Beginnings, Passages, Knots, The Tree, Trickster, Healing and Return' (Gersie and King 1990, p.25). A session (usually a group session) begins with the reading of a number of traditional myths or tales incorporating the chosen theme, then clients are asked to write (or paint) in response to an aspect of the theme. These writings are then shared and discussed, and the whole session is reflected upon. Alternatively, instead of reading out the writing, the clients might be asked to tell orally a story arising out of their associations to the theme. Dance, movement, drama, sound and sculpture can also be used as means of expressing responses to the theme.

14   Writing as part of therapeutic practice is discussed by Birren and Birren (1996), Pearson (1965), Maultsby (1971), McKinney (1976), Harber and Pennebaker (1992), and Pennebaker (1993). These papers contain many interesting and important observations on the therapeutic value of writing, but the type of writing discussed does not come under the heading of fictional autobiography as defined here.

Poetry therapy is the most developed of the therapies which uses creative writing, particularly in the States, where it has been well established for some twenty years. There is a National Association for Poetry Therapy, which has standards and procedures in place for Certified Poetry Therapists and Registered Poetry Therapists (Mazza 1993, p.51). Techniques of poetry therapy include reading poems as sparking-off points for individual, family or group discussions, the writing of poems by individuals, couples, families or groups, and the analysis of metaphors and imagery arising from this writing.

Undoubtedly, there are many individual therapists and analysts who suggest creative writing in its different guises to their clients, but much of this is undocumented[15]. One recent exception is that of Cheryl Moskowitz, who describes her use of a technique whereby the client is asked to create characters out of different aspects of the self, such as the 'good self' and the 'bad self', and then to bring them into contact with each other in a fictional story where they exchange something of value. This process is seen to encourage the recognition of different aspects of self and to promote reconciliation between them (Moskowitz 1998).

Fictional autobiography, then, can play a significant role in self-analysis or in psychoanalysis or psychotherapy, or in conjunction with them, as an additional means of acquiring information about the inner life. It facilitates what Christopher Bollas calls the 'self-analytic function', which, for him, is not by definition an activity carried on by a person in isolation, but the adopting of a stance in relation to oneself, a stance that is as important inside psychoanalysis as outside of it. It is 'a relaxed, not vigilant, state of mind' that maintains 'a receptive space for the arrival of news from within the self' and allows new internal objects to be evoked or created, objects which can then be subjected to the more rigorous process of interpretation (Bollas 1987, pp.239–241). Engaging in self-analysis involves recognition of the fact that 'being and experiencing are prior to the knowing of that which is there to be understood' (p.237). It involves the ability to objectify the self, to be a passive observer of the inner life, and understanding that interpretation, 'the more active agent...follows being and experiencing and is only part of the self-analytic element' (p.237).

This twofold process inherent in the 'self-analytic function' is precisely the mechanism of 'shelving the critical faculty' that lies at the heart of the

---

15   Bolton (1999) lists a number of papers by therapists and others who use writing in their practice (pp.204–212)

184 THERAPEUTIC DIMENSIONS OF AUTOBIOGRAPHY IN CREATIVE WRITING

creative process. Writing fictional autobiography, because it moves one away from facts that have to be *known* into fictions that need to be *felt*, encourages a state of mind in which one can 'give up the wish to know in order to experience'; it encourages a generative splitting of the ego, so that one becomes simultaneously observer and observed (p.236). As Rancour-Laferriere says, self-analysis requires the objectifying of the self, the ability to view oneself 'as an "other", who, momentarily at least, is "out there"' (Rancour-Laferriere 1994, p.18). With writing, the 'momentarily at least' becomes something more permanent, an object over which one can linger and reflect, and with fictional autobiography that object is a rich composite of fantasy and reality which, when explored and interpreted, can offer up profound insight and the prospect of deep psychic change.

Conclusion

Tensions between 'Writing as Art'
and 'Writing as Therapy'?

In this book I have moved progressively from talking about fictional autobiography as part of a writing apprenticeship that facilitates the finding of a writing voice or writing identity, through its therapeutic dimensions, to its explicit use as a tool in self-therapy or psychotherapy. In other words I have shifted the emphasis in the purpose of writing from *creating a literary end product* to *providing a mechanism for psychological insight.* These could be regarded as quite different and even conflicting aims and, to conclude, I would like to say a few words about the possible tensions between 'writing as art' and 'writing as therapy'.

There is an assumption in the minds of many people in the literary world, including some of those who teach, that producing writing which has value as art and using one's writing as a means of gaining therapeutic benefit are mutually exclusive. It is not uncommon to hear literary people and sometimes even creative writing tutors refer disparagingly to the writing done in creative writing classes as 'just therapy'. What they mean by this, I believe, is not that the writer is using the writing to gain insight into herself but that the writing is so highly personal and unformed that it is of little interest to anyone else and therefore has no value as art. This is not only a very unhelpful attitude but it is also to misunderstand the nature of therapy and of the creative process. It implies, on the one hand, that therapy is an unstructured and endless trawl through the unconscious and, on the other, that we can neatly separate our writing from the contents of our psyches. As I hope this book has demonstrated, I do not believe either of these things to be the case.

Any kind of creative art, especially in the early stages, involves a high degree of chaos, of delving down into the messiness of the unconscious and grappling with our own sometimes difficult and disturbing material. As Jenny Diski rightly observes: 'Writers who are not self-obsessed and wriggling through what they hope are their own labyrinthine psyches are very likely not writers at all' (Diski 1998, p.45). And this 'delving down' may serve different people in different ways. 'Each person who sits down to write,' says Janet Malcolm, 'faces not a blank page, but his own vastly over-filled mind' (Malcolm 1995, p.204), and many apprentice writers discover that whilst they wish to create publishable stories and poems, what they find themselves doing in the first instance is writing again and again about their own personal preoccupations. Providing space for this to happen can function, for some people, as a sort of 'housecleaning', which may be vitally necessary before the *real writing* can begin in earnest:

> The problem is to clear out most of what is in [the mind], to fill huge plastic garbage bags with the confused jumble of things that have accreted there over the days, months, years of being alive and taking things in through the eyes and ears and heart. The goal is to make a space where a few ideas and images and feelings may be so arranged that a reader will want to linger awhile among them (pp.204–205).

For others, it may not be so much a question of 'clearing the ground', as it is precisely their own preoccupations which will form the subject matter of their fiction. Drawing this material out and placing it on the page enables them to objectify it, to get some distance on it, so that they can then start shaping and honing it in such a way that it gains strength and speaks to an audience.

For some people – and my research has suggested that this is a significant number, perhaps as many as half of all those attending creative writing courses – placing their own deeply personal material on the page helps them to go some way towards clarifying or grappling with personal problems, problems which may have provided the impetus to write in the first place. They may not necessarily have come to the course with the explicit intention of using their writing for therapeutic purposes; indeed they may not even have been aware of such a possibility. The therapeutic benefit they derive from writing about themselves and their lives will come by chance rather than by design. Having gained therapeutic benefit, they may find that the desire to write disappears, or they may feel freer to engage in other activities which the preoccupation with their personal problems had previously prevented. Alternatively, they may find that the increased inner freedom the

writing brings about enables them to use their own material more imaginatively in their writing and to move beyond their own preoccupations to write
about other things.

Creative writing courses need to cater for all these different possibilities,
and tutors should try not to be prematurely judgmental of the work students
produce. They need to allow the people taking their courses to wade through
the 'murky waters' of their unconscious for a period of time, and to give them
support and encouragement in this difficult process. Within a formal educational context one hopes and expects that people will eventually move
beyond this stage to produce writing that has form and structure and that
speaks to an audience. Of course, there will always be those for whom
writing will result neither in an artistic product nor in therapeutic benefit. For
them, writing may be a refuge[1], and it will depend on the nature of the
creative writing course whether this can be accommodated.

What I am saying is that, if there is a tension between writing as art and
writing as therapy in the creative writing class, it is primarily in the mind of
the reader rather than the writer of the work produced; for in the early stages
of writing, most of us are not overly aware of the therapeutic dimension of
our writings. We may stumble across ourselves as we place ourselves on the
page, and expanding our self-knowledge may be, for many of us who write,
an ever-present but perhaps only occasionally reflected upon dimension of
our writing. Of course, when our writing threatens to reveal things about
ourselves which we do not like or prefer to keep hidden, the censor sitting on
our shoulder may well exert a stronger influence than would otherwise be the
case, which means that the free associative nature of the writing might be
compromised. But the censor may be there just as much when we are writing
for artistic purposes; the 'anxiety of influence', for example (Bloom 1975) –
the awareness of all those other writers who have written books which are,
we sometimes think, so much better than ours – can be a heavy and, for some,
a destructive burden.

Once we take the therapeutic dimension of our writing seriously and seek
to tap its potential for self-exploration, the possibility of tension between
'writing as art' and 'writing as therapy' certainly arises, but even here the distinction is blurred. As I indicated in my discussion of the autobiographical
pact with ourselves (that in producing writings that might provide us with

---

1   Again, this is not necessarily a bad thing. Many celebrated writers have used their
writing as a refuge. Joseph Conrad is a good example (see Berman 1977).

insight we need to make a pact with ourselves that we will allow the material to emerge as freely and truthfully as possible), writing for therapeutic purposes involves the same mechanism of 'shelving the critical faculty' as 'writing as art'. Thus, whether for artistic or therapeutic purposes, we need to cultivate the 'internal gesture', as Milner calls it, to loosen our customary control over our psyches, so that our material can emerge from the unconscious as freely as possible. Once our words are on the page, our intentions, whether artistic or therapeutic, will determine what we do with them, but as long as we are clear in our minds which goal we are pursuing at any one time, the tensions should be minimal.

If we are in quest of a deeper self-understanding, it may not be necessary to worry about crafting or structuring our writing into a literary end product. The words in their raw state may be sufficient; placing them on the page may already have had a considerable impact. If we have at our disposal the techniques of poetry or prose fiction, we may find that crafting our words deepens their impact on us, or provides us with a metaphor or image of ourselves that is new and surprising. Through crafting, of course, we may shift the writing into a more structured form in which it can demand the attention of an audience, so that we are simultaneously using our writing as 'art' and as 'therapy'. Alternatively, the material may need to be put away for a time, so that we gain distance from it before attempting to develop it into 'writing as art'.

As long as we as readers of our own writing can distinguish between 'writing as art' and 'writing as therapy', the tensions between these two activities are likely to be minimal. They inevitably arise if we are unable to do this. And this is where the creative writing course has an important role to play; for not only is its task to enable apprentice writers to get in touch with and place on the page their deeply personal material, but it should also help them to develop their writing, through the acquisition of writing techniques, from its deeply subjective and raw state into writing that has strength and shape and speaks to an audience.

A perfectly legitimate concern for the writer, of course, is whether the exploration, for therapeutic purposes, of the themes and preoccupations arising in our fiction, and their possible resolution, will undermine or interfere with our desire or our ability to write about them. Karen Horney was of the view that, whilst it is possible for inner conflicts and 'life solutions' to 'provide a constructive impetus to create', probably the majority 'of such conflicts and solutions has an untoward effect on the artist's work' (Horney

1951, p.331); therefore their resolution can only enhance creativity. I am not sure that the matter is as straightforward as she implies. If Franz Kafka had undergone successful psychotherapy, would he have had the impetus to transpose his painful 'feeling states' into fiction? Probably not. He may instead have developed his skills as a lawyer.

In my own case, since writing my autobiographical novels I have not felt strongly motivated to write fiction, and I have come to feel that, for the time being at least, I have 'written myself out'. It is significant also that, of the four women I have worked with, it is the two who explicitly used their writing as a therapeutic tool who have not continued with their novels. Yet I would not regard this as a negative development. In my own case, writing my novels helped to free up my psyche, so that I was able to embark on university study and then to go on to establish myself in enjoyable and fulfilling work. Similarly, whilst Jennifer and Jessica have not continued with their novels, Jennifer is now finding satisfaction in writing for her grandchildren (see Appendix) and Jessica has developed her singing to a standard where she now feels confident enough to give solo performances. Any therapeutic process has the power to change us, and that change may involve taking us off in directions other than those we had intended. It may be that when the changes brought about by the writing bring us a greater degree of freedom and allow us to do things which were not possible for us previously, we no longer need to write about ourselves. This is not to say that Jennifer, Jessica and I will never write fiction again. In fact, as I complete this book and the research which preceded it, I feel the stirrings of a desire to write fiction again, and Jessica also envisages a return to creative writing (see Appendix).

I would suggest that 'writing as art' and 'writing as therapy' are intricately bound up with each other, and trying to draw a firm dividing line between them risks compromising both. Through writing fictional autobiography I believe we have the possibility of creating, both in our fictions and in ourselves, what Iris Murdoch has called 'a house fit for free characters to live in' (Murdoch 1959, p.27)[2]. Some people will learn how to give their characters and narrators a life of their own, thus opening up the possibility of creating more spontaneous and authentic fictions; others will develop a more flexible relationship with the different parts of *themselves*, thus opening up the possibility of a greater degree of inner freedom. Some people – and, if the

2   I am indebted to Bernard Paris for drawing my attention to this quotation which he uses in *A Psychological Approach to Fiction* (1974).

results of this research are anything to go by, more than one might imagine –
will achieve both of these things.

Reflections on the Research

This book and the research project which gave rise to it have been in progress for more than five years and it is, for those of us closely involved with it, a great relief to bring the process to a conclusion. In that time we have all had occasion to change and develop our views, and ourselves, as one would hope and expect of engagement in an intensely personal project such as this. Just as there are unexpected therapeutic benefits for the writer from engaging in creative writing, there are unexpected therapeutic benefits for the researcher from engaging in research. Exploring my own practice as a creative writing teacher has taught me many lessons, as has working with Sarah, Jane, Jennifer and Jessica. Encountering myself on the page in my academic writing has been as disconcerting and enlightening as encountering myself on the page in my novels. The experience has taught me a great deal about myself and other people, and this has made me a more sensitive and capable teacher and researcher.

As the work has proceeded, I have become increasingly aware of the problems of the approach adopted, and I do now have some misgivings about it. There are considerable risks associated with applying psychodynamic theory to the written and spoken words of people one is working with, without the safeguards which would normally be built into the therapeutic relationship. In particular there is the possibility that interpretations one makes may spark off crises which one is then not there to deal with. I was fortunate in having selected for this research four women who are all fairly stable and able to cope with the increased self-awareness which the writing and the research brought about, and who had ways of locating therapeutic support when they needed it. Also, as I said in the introduction, throughout the research and the writing of this book I have repeatedly sought comments and criticisms from them, and have taken considerable pains to incorporate these into the resulting text. Thus, we were able to avoid major crises, and I believe that ultimately the project has been beneficial for all of us. However, I would wish to caution anyone proposing to adopt a similar approach to take great care in choosing suitable people to work with. This is obviously not an approach that will work with everyone, and it may well be that this kind of research is best done in a therapeutic rather than in an educational context. I do not present it here as an unproblematic model for research in continuing education.

In spite of these misgivings, I do believe that valuable material has emerged from this research. It helps to open up the field of creative writing in a number of new ways, drawing attention to a range of questions on which further work needs to be done, and highlighting in particular the scope for applying theory to practice. The therapeutic dimension of autobiography in teaching creative writing and the potential use of fictional autobiography in counselling and therapy are two areas where further research is clearly needed. Future researchers will no doubt wish to explore these topics with a constituency which, in terms of gender, class and ethnicity, is broader than the one available to me, and to consider further the advantages and disadvantages of a psychodynamic approach. Further teaching and therapeutic practice will also help to ascertain whether there is likely to be a problematical tension arising, within the creative writing itself, between 'writing as art' and 'writing as therapy', as a consequence of importing therapeutic considerations into the creative writing class, or, conversely, of relocating, within therapy or counselling, work originally done in an educational context.

Beyond the field of creative writing and personal development, the research has a potential application within the field of cultural studies, where the combination of Horneyan theory with narrative and critical theory offers a new and fruitful approach to issues around writing and identity. As this combination of theoretical approaches has proved helpful in understanding the difficulties which some people experience with creative writing, there might well be applications of this work to understanding students' problems with essay writing and with learning more generally. I look forward to further developments in these various fields and to pursuing some of these topics myself in the future.

In concluding this project, it was felt that it would be fitting to include a paragraph or two by Sarah, Jane, Jennifer and Jessica, reflecting on the work we did together. Having, as a result of the research, become much more aware of the problems of a psychodynamic approach, I was particularly concerned to know whether in retrospect they had any misgivings about the process of having their writings interpreted in this way. Their responses are mixed and there is much I could say about them, but as it my 'writing voice' which has dominated in this book, I append them here in full, without comment.

Sarah

When I first read the sections concerning me, I felt very vulnerable and exposed. It confirmed all my negative feelings about myself. I knew nothing about Karen Horney's theories, and tend to look for my explanations amongst the social rather than the psychological. But I could recognise the connections being made. Certainly, throughout that Certificate year, I'm sure my writing was influenced by the struggle I was having at work. It also seems to have been a time for looking back at the past, maybe a taking stock as I moved into my fifties.

The second reading, some eight months later – well I could see how the theory worked, however I felt it was true for the moment. My feelings at the time were influenced by the external circumstances of my work life – so, one way of seeing things was to blame myself; another way would be to say that the mistress of ceremonies knew the way things worked and could see that the ringmaster had the potential to mess up. Confusion over identity? Ringmaster or mistress of ceremonies? Well, who was really calling the shots? Anyway, the mistress of ceremonies finally left the circus (long after the ringmaster had crawled away!) and has joined a troupe of travelling players, where she's very happy.

Who knows – maybe the creative writing raised my awareness, and helped me to resolve the personal issues exposed in my writing? By chance I later found a safe place where I could explore these issues and begin to heal myself. Whatever, I'm happier and less hard on myself, and perhaps on others. I don't believe these changes would have occurred had I not articulated them in my writing so that when the opportunity came, I had already started the dialogue.

Jane

When I started the Certificate course, I had done very little autobio-graphical writing, and the exploration into my (largely suppressed) childhood, raised all sorts of anxieties. In the course of being interviewed by Celia as a case history for her essays on the therapeutic aspects of creative writing I began to reflect on my character and personality and began to see some sort of pattern there. Karen Horney's theories were very illuminating and for the first time my behaviour (past and present) began to make some sort of sense to me. I had always felt I was a terribly inconsistent person, with all sorts of contradictions in my character, which was one of the things that made it so hard to use myself as a character in my writing. The processes of self-reflection and of continuing to use my own feelings and emotions in fiction have freed me up in many ways. I used to spend a lot of energy trying to work out what was 'wrong' with me, and feeling depressed and powerless about what I felt was a lack – a kind of emptiness – in me. Now I have started to focus much more on what is outside myself – on discovering and achieving my ambitions, and on helping my students achieve this. I feel much more resilient when things go wrong, and tend to be less hard on myself (and other people). I even find myself laughing at situations which would once have seriously depressed me. Teaching and the respect and affection of my students have shown me that I am a worthwhile person and that I do have skills in working with people – especially people who need their confidence boosted – and this continues to reinforce my own self-esteem.

Jennifer

I was pleased when Celia asked me to help with her research analysing the writings of students taking creative courses. I had already commented to her and to some of my friends on the unexpected improvement in my relationship with my brothers, particularly Mark, which was a direct result of my reassessment of past memories. My discussions with Celia helped me to focus on the relationship between using one's own remembered or half remembered experiences as the basis for fiction and the 'tidying up' of problematic issues in real life. I have done little writing of this kind since the course finished, partly because I could not see any possibility of a competent novel emerging and partly because of the feeling that the past was now over and done with and that constant introspection was becoming depressing. I have even stopped keeping a diary, which I had started to do when I was taking my degree, influenced by the Mass Observation Project.

I am still writing, but for the future instead. I now have two grandsons and a granddaughter and I have opened files for all three. In these files are letters that I wrote to them on a regular basis, detailing the minutiae of their day to day experiences, including their day of birth. I am saving them until they are eighteen years old. I have not told my children about these letters. I want them to be fresh on the day that they are delivered.

My children have been pressing me to write down as much as I can remember of my own childhood and to give them as much information about my own parents and grandparents as possible. I am dragging my feet on this, I'm afraid, but I can understand why they want it done.

To conclude, I found taking part in the research rewarding. It increased my awareness of the way the creative writing course had made me rethink aspects of my past and that of my immediate family.

Jessica

It was initially quite flattering when Celia asked if she could use my work as part of her thesis. I guess some part of me thought that my selection was something to do with the quality of my writing. I have become increasingly ambivalent about the project and have now reached a stage where I feel quite a strong antipathy towards it. I am very uncomfortable with Celia's stance. She started off as my tutor on a creative writing course that was not aiming to be therapeutic. Now, in the book, she has gone beyond her role as facilitator of the writing process and has adopted the stance of a quasi therapist, in attempting to 'understand' my work through psychodynamic theory. It seems that while I have struggled to *show* rather than *say* things in my writing – and that is the nature of any 'progress' I have made – Celia has reverted to *saying* what I have *shown*.

This is not to say that I disagree with Celia's notion that writing autobiographical fiction has been, for me, an integrative process. I don't think this is necessarily the case for all writers of autobiographical fiction. Furthermore, I am aware of other domains in my life that have fulfilled a similar integrative role, such as singing. I shall return to my writing when time allows, but I shall be motivated, not simply by a desire to come to terms with my own fragmentation, but by the need to communicate with a wider audience in a way that moves them. For my writing to be moving (stimulating, interesting, exciting, enjoyable), I need to convey the fragmentation in an effective way. The writing course enabled me to experiment with style, voice and form, so that I did emerge as a more effective writer. Celia is not in a position to know whether or not the work I have done on my writing has helped me 'both to understand and to grapple with [my] inner conflicts'.

References

Abbs, P. (1974) *Autobiography in Education*. London: Heinemann.

Abbs, P. (1989) *A is for Aesthetic: Essays on Creative and Aesthetic Education*. London: Falmer Press.

Abbs, P. (1994) *The Educational Imperative*. London: Falmer Press.

Abbs, P. (1996) *The Polemics of Imagination*. London: Skoob Books.

Bakhtin, M. (1981) 'Discourse in the novel'. In Michael Holquist (ed) *The Dialogic Imagination: Four Essays by M. M. Bakhtin*. Austin, Texas: University of Texas Press, pp.259–422.

Bakhtin, M. (1984) *Problems of Dostoyevsky's Poetics*. Manchester: Manchester University Press.

Bakhtin, M. (1990) 'Author and hero in aesthetic activity'. In Michael Holquist and Vadim Liapunov (eds) *Art and Answerability: Early Philosophical Works by M. M. Bakhtin*. Austin, Texas: University of Texas Press.

Bainbridge, Beryl (1981) *A Weekend with Claude*. London: Duckworth.

Barthes, Roland (1966) 'An introduction to the structural analysis of narrative'. *New Literary History* 6, pp.237–272.

Bell, C. (1987) *Art*. Ed. J. B. Bullen. Oxford: Oxford University Press.

Berman, Jeffrey (1977) *Joseph Conrad: Writing as Rescue*. New York: Astra Books.

Berman, Jeffrey (1994) *Diaries to an English professor: Pain and Growth in the Classroom*. Amherst: University of Massachusetts Press.

Birren, J. E. and Birren, B. A. (1996) 'Autobiography: Exploring the self and encouraging development'. In J. E. Birren *et al.* (eds) *Aging and Biography: Explorations in Adult Development*. New York: Springer, pp.283–300.

Bloom, Harold (1975) *The Anxiety of Influence*. London: Oxford University Press.

Bollas, Christopher (1987) *The Shadow of the Object*. London: Free Association Books.

Bollas, Christopher (1989) *Forces of Destiny: Psychoanalysis and human idiom*. London: Free Association Books.

Bollas, Christopher (1993) *Being a Character: Psychoanalysis and self experience*. London: Routledge.

Bolton, Gillie (1998) *The Therapeutic Potential of Creative Writing: Writing myself*. London: Jessica Kingsley Publishers.

Booth, Wayne (1991) *The Rhetoric of Fiction*, 2nd ed. Harmondsworth: Penguin.

Bowie, Malcolm (1991) *Lacan*. London: Fontana.

Brande, Dorothea (1934) *Becoming a Writer*. London: Macmillan, 1992.

Brooks, Peter (1994) *Psychoanalysis and Storytelling*. London: Blackwell.

Bruner, Jerome (1986) *Actual Minds – Possible Worlds*. Cambridge, Mass. and London: Harvard University Press.

Bruner, Jerome (1990) *Acts of Meaning*. Cambridge, Mass. and London: Harvard University Press.

Campbell, Jan (1996) 'Images of the Real: Reading history and psychoanalysis in Toni Morrison's 'Beloved'. *Women: A Cultural Review* 7, 2, pp.136–149.

Carr, D. (1985) 'Life and the narrator's art'. In H. J. Silverman and D. Idhe (eds) *Hermeneutics and Deconstruction*. Albany: State University of New York Press, pp.108–121.

Chandler, Marilyn (1990) *A Healing Art: Regeneration through Autobiography*. New York and London: Garland.

Chatman, Seymour (1978) *Story and Discourse: Narrative Structure in Fiction and Film*. Ithaca and London: Cornell University Press.

Chaudhuri, Amit (1994) *Afternoon Raag*. London: Minerva.

Chodorow, Joan (1997) *Jung on Active Imagination*. London: Routledge.

Chodorow, Nancy (1978) *The Reproduction of Mothering*. Berkeley: California University Press.

Cixous, Hélène (1986) *The Newly Born Woman*. Manchester: Manchester University Press.

Cixous, Hélène (1990) 'De la scène de l'Inconscient à la scène de l'Histoire: Chemin d'une écriture'. In Françoise Van Rossum-Guyon and Myriam Díaz-Diocaretz (eds), *Hélène Cixous: Chemins d'une écriture*. Amsterdam: Rodopi and Saint Denis: Presses Universitaires de Vincennes, pp.15–34.

Cixous, Hélène (1993) *Three Steps on the Ladder of Writing*. New York: Columbia University Press.

Conley, Verena (1984) *Hélène Cixous: Writing the feminine*. Lincoln: University of Nebraska Press.

Conrad, Joseph (1899) *Heart of Darkness*. Harmondsworth: Penguin, 1995.

Conrad, Joseph (1900) *Lord Jim*. Harmondsworth: Penguin, 1974.

Conway, Martin A. (1990) *Autobiographical Memory*. Buckingham: Open University Press.

Coover, Robert (1971) 'The Sentient Lens'. In *Pricksongs and Descants*. London: Jonathan Cape.

Cox, Murray and Theilgaard, Alice (1987) *Mutative Metaphors in Psychotherapy: the Aeolian Mode*. London: Tavistock.

Day Sclater, Shelley (1998) 'Creating the Self: Stories as transitional phenomena'. *Auto/Biography* Vol VI, Nos. 1 and 2, pp.85–92.

Dentith, Simon (1995) *Bakhtinian Thought*. London and New York: Routledge.

Derrida, Jacques (1976) *Of Grammatology*. Baltimore and London: Johns Hopkins University Press.

Derrida, Jacques (1978) *Writing and Difference*. Chicago: University of Chicago Press.

de Salvo, Louise (1999) *Writing as a Way of Healing*. London: Women's Press.

de Shazer, S. (1991) *Putting Difference to Work*. New York: W.W. Norton.

Diski, Jenny (1998) *Don't*. London: Granta Books.

Downing, Christine (1977) 'Re-visioning autobiography: the bequest of Freud and Jung'. *Soundings* 60, pp. 210–228.

Dry, Helen Aristar (1995) 'Free Indirect Discourse in Doris's Lessing's "One Off the Short List": A case of designed ambiguity'. In P. Verdonk and J. J. Weber (eds) *Twentieth Century Fiction*. London: Routledge, pp.96–112.

Eakin, Paul John (1985) *Fictions in Autobiography: Studies in the Art of Self-Invention*. Princeton, New Jersey: Princeton University Press.

Elbow, Peter (1973) *Writing Without Teachers*. Oxford: Oxford University Press.

Eliot, George (1871–1872) *Middlemarch*. Harmondsworth: Penguin, 1971.

Epston, D., White, M. and Murray, K. (1992) 'A Proposal for a Re-authoring Therapy: Rose's Revisioning of her Life and a Commentary'. In S. McNamee and K. J. Gergen (eds) *Therapy as Social Construction*. London: Sage, pp.96–115.

Fairfax, J. and Moat, J. (1981) *The Way to Write*. London: Elm Tree Books.

Flaubert, Gustave (1856–1857) *Madame Bovary*. Harmondsworth: Penguin, 1987.

Flax, Jane (1990) *Thinking Fragments: Psychoanalysis, Feminism, and Postmodernism in the Contemporary West*. Berkeley: University of California Press.

Flax, Jane (1993) 'Multiples: On the contemporary politics of subjectivity'. In *Disputed Subjects*. New York: Routledge, pp.92–110.

Forster, E.M. (1979) *Aspects of the Novel*. Harmondsworth: Penguin.

Foucault, M. (1977) 'What is an author?'. In Donald Bouchard (ed) *Language, Counter-Memory, Practice: Selected Essays and Interviews*. New York: Cornell University Press, pp.113–138.

Fransella, A. and Dalton, P. (1990) *Personal Construct Counselling in Action*. London: Sage.

Fraser, R. (1979) *Blood of Spain*. London: Allen Lane.

Fraser, R. (1984) *In Search of a Past*. London: Verso.

Freud, S. (1908) 'Creative writers and day-dreaming'. In *The Standard Edition of the Complete Psychological Works of Sigmund Freud*. Trans. J. Strachey, Vol. IX, 1959, pp.141–154.

Freud, S. (1914) 'The History of the Psychoanalytic Movement'. In *The Standard Edition...*, *op.cit.*, Vol. XIV, 1957, pp.1–66.

Freud, S. (1937–1939) *Moses and Monotheism*. In *The Standard Edition...*, *op.cit.*, Vol. XXIII, pp.3–137.

Freud, S. (1938) 'Constructions in Analysis'. In J. Strachey (ed) *Collected Papers of Sigmund Freud*, Vol. V. London: Hogarth Press, 1952, pp.358–371.

Friedman, N. (1955) 'Point of View in Fiction: the development of a critical concept'. *PMLA* 70, pp.1160–1184.

Fry, R. (1909) 'An Essay in Aesthetics'. *New Quarterly* 2, pp.171-190; reprinted in R. Fry, *Vision and Design*. J. B. Bullen (ed) Oxford: Oxford University Press, 1981, pp.12–27.

Garrison, Dee (1981) 'Karen Horney and Feminism'. *Signs*, Summer, pp.672–691.

Gass, William (1979) *Fiction and the Figures of Life*. New York: Alfred A. Knopf.

Genette, Gerard (1980) *Narrative Discourse*. Ithaca, New York: Cornell University Press.

Gersie, Alida (1997) *Reflections on Therapeutic Storymaking: The use of stories in groups*. London: Jessica Kingsley Publishers.

Gersie, A. and King, N. (1990) *Storymaking in Education and Therapy*. London: Jessica Kingsley Publishers.

Goldberg, Natalie (1986) *Writing Down the Bones*. Boston and London: Shambhala Publications.

Green, D. W. and Wason, P. C. (1982) 'Notes on the psychology of writing'. *Human Relations* 35, 1, pp.47–56.

Gunn, Janet Varner (1982) *Autobiography: Toward a Poetics of Experience*. Philadelphia: University of Pennsylvania Press.

Gusdorf, Georges (1980) 'The Conditions and Limits of Autobiography'. In James Olney (ed) *Autobiography: Essays Theoretical and Critical*. Princeton: Princeton University Press, pp. 28–48.

Hanson, N. R. (1958) *Patterns of Discovery*. Cambridge: Cambridge University Press.

Harber, K. D. and Pennebaker, J. W. (1992) 'Overcoming traumatic memories'. In S. A. Christianson (ed) *The Handbook of Emotion and Memory*. Hillsdale, NJ: Lawrence Erlbaum, pp.359–387.

Heaney, Seamus (1972) *Wintering Out*. London: Faber.

Heaney, Seamus (1980a) 'Feelings into Words'. *In Preoccupations: Selected Prose 1968–1978*. London: Faber, pp.41–60.

Heaney, Seamus (1980b) 'The Sense of Place'. In *op.cit*. pp.131–149.

Hemingway (1928) 'Hills like White Elephants'. In *Men Without Women*. London: Cape, pp.44–48.

Hesse, Hermann (1924) 'A Guest at the Spa'. In Theodore Ziolkowski (ed) *Autobiographical Writings*. London: Picador, 1978, pp.76–146.

Hesse, Hermann (1927) *Steppenwolf*. Harmondsworth: Penguin, 1929.

Hillman, James (1983) *Healing Fictions*. Woodstock, CT: Spring Publications.

Hobson, Robert F. (1985) *Forms of Feeling: The Heart of Psychotherapy*. London and New York: Tavistock Publications.

Holland, Norman (1973) *Poems in Persons: An Introduction to the Psychoanalysis of Literature*. New York: Norton.

Holland, Norman (1975) *Five Readers Reading*. New Haven and London: Yale University Press.

Holland, Norman (1980) 'Unity Identity Text Self'. In Jane P. Tompkins (ed) *Reader-Response Criticism: from formalism to post-structuralism*. Baltimore and London: Johns Hopkins University Press, pp.118–133.

Holquist, Michael (1990) *Dialogism: Bakhtin and His World*. London and New York: Routledge.

Horney, Karen (1937) *The Neurotic Personality of Our Times*. New York: Norton.

Horney, Karen (1939a) *New Ways in Psychoanalysis*. New York: Norton.

Horney, Karen (1939b) 'Can You Take a Stand?'. *Journal of Adult Education 11*, pp.129–132.

Horney, Karen (1942) *Self Analysis*. New York: Norton.

Horney, Karen (1946) *Our Inner Conflicts*. New York: Norton.

Horney, Karen (1951) *Neurosis and Human Growth: The Struggle Toward Self-Realisation*. New York: Norton.

Horney, Karen (1967) *Feminine Psychology*. H. Kelman (ed) New York: Norton.

Hughes, Ted (1998) *Birthday Letters*. London: Faber.

Hunt, Celia (1998a) 'Finding a Voice – Exploring the Self: Autobiography and Imagination in a Writing Apprenticeship'. *Auto/Biography* 6, pp.93–98.

Hunt, Celia (1998b) 'Creative Writing and Problems of Identity: A Horneyan Perspective'. In J. Campbell and J. Harbord (eds) *Psycho-Politics and Cultural Desires*. London: Taylor & Francis, pp.217–233.

Hunt, Celia (2000) 'Psychological Problems of Writer Identity: A Horneyan Perspective'. In Duncan Barford (ed) *Psychoanalysis and Learning Theory*. London: Rebus Books.

Hunt, Celia and Sampson, Fiona (eds) (1998) *The Self on the Page: Theory and practice of creative writing in personal development*. London: Jessica Kingsley Publishers.

Ingram, Douglas H. and Lerner, Joyce A. (1992) 'Horney Theory: an Object Relations Theory', *American Journal of Psychoanalysis*, Vol. 52, No. 1, pp.37–49.

Ivanic, Roz (1998) *Writing and Identity: The discoursal construction of identity in academic writing*. Amsterdam and Philadelphia: John Benjamins Publishing Company.

Jackowska, Nicki (1997) *Write for Life*. Shaftesbury, Dorset: Element Books.

James, Henry (1934) *The Art of the Novel: critical prefaces*. New York: Scribner's Sons.

Jelinek, Estelle (1986) *The Tradition of Women's Autobiography*. Boston: Twayne.

Kaplan, Cora (1986) *Sea Changes: Essays on culture and feminism*. London: Verso.

Knights, Ben (1992) *From Reader to Reader: Theory, text and practice in the study group*. New York and London: Harvester Wheatsheaf.

Kris, Ernst (1952) *Psychoanalytic Explorations in Art*. New York: International Universities Press.

Lacan, Jacques (1949) 'The mirror stage as formative of the function of the I'. In *Ecrits: a selection*, Alan Sheridan (trans). London: Routledge, pp.1–7.

Lakoff, George and Johnson, Mark (1980) *Metaphors We Live By*. Chicago: University of Chicago Press.

Leader, Zachary (1991) *Writer's Block*. Baltimore and London: Johns Hopkins University Press.

Leiris, Michel (1939) *L'Age d'homme*. Paris: Éditions Gallimard. Translated as *Manhood*, R. Howard (trans). Chicago and London: University of Chicago Press, 1992.

Leiris, Michel (1948-1976) *La Règle du Jeu*. 4 vols. Paris: Éditions Gallimard.

Leitch, V.B. (1983) *Deconstructive Criticism*. New York: Columbia University Press.

Lejeune, Philippe (1971) *L'Autobiographie en France*. Paris: A. Colin.

Lejeune, Philippe (1989) *On Autobiography*. Minneapolis: University of Minnesota Press.

Lessing, Doris (1979) 'One off the Short List'. In *To Room Nineteen. Collected Stories, Vol. 1*. St. Albans, Hertfordshire: Triad/Panther Books, pp.220–247.

Lester, D. and Terry, R. (1992) 'The Use of Poetry Therapy: Lessons from the life of Anne Sexton'. *The Arts in Psychotherapy* 19, pp.47–52.

McCracken, Luann (1994) '"The synthesis of my being": autobiography and the reproduction of identity in Virginia Woolf'. In Eleanor McNees (ed) *Virginia Woolf: critical assessments*, Vol. IV. Mountfield: Helm Information, pp.290–307.

MacIntyre, Alastair (1981) *After Virtue: A Study in Moral Theory*. London: Duckworth.

McKinney, Fred (1976) 'Free writing as therapy'. *Psychotherapy* 13, 2, pp.183–187.

McLeod, John (1997) *Narrative and Psychotherapy*. London: Sage.

Mair, Miller (1989) *Between Psychology and Psychotherapy: A poetics of experience.* London: Routledge.

Malcolm, Janet (1995) *The Silent Woman: Sylvia Plath and Ted Hughes.* London: Macmillan.

Maultsby, Maxie C. (1971) 'Systematic written homework in psychotherapy'. *Psychotherapy* 8, 3, pp.195–198.

Mazza, N. (1993) 'Poetry therapy: toward a research agenda for the 1990s'. *The Arts in Psychotherapy* 20, pp.51–59.

Miller, J.W. (1982) *The Midworld of Symbols and Functioning Objects.* New York: Norton.

Milner, Marion (ps. Joanna Field) (1952) *A Life of One's Own.* Harmondsworth: Penguin.

Milner, Marion (1955) 'The Role of Illusion in Symbol Formation'. Reprinted in P. L. Rudnytsky (ed) *Transitional Objects and Potential Spaces: Literary Uses of D. W. Winnicott.* New York: Columbia University Press, 1993, pp.13–39.

Milner, Marion (1971) *On Not Being Able to Paint.* London: Heinemann.

Milner, Marion (1989) *Eternity's Sunrise: A Way of Keeping a Diary.* London: Virago.

Morrison, Blake (1994) *And When Did You Last See Your Father?* London: Granta.

Moskowitz, Cheryl (1998) 'The Self as Source: Creative writing generated from personal reflection'. In C. Hunt and F. Sampson (eds) *op.cit.,* pp.35–46.

Murdoch, Iris (1959) 'The Sublime and the Beautiful Revisited'. *Yale Review* XLIX., pp.247–271.

Nalbatian, Suzanne (1994) *Aesthetic Autobiography.* London: Macmillan.

Neisser, Ulric (1988) 'Five Modes of Self-Knowledge'. *Philosophical Psychology* 1, 1, pp.35–58.

Neisser, Ulric (1993) 'The Self Perceived'. In U. Neisser (ed) *The Perceived Self.* Cambridge: Cambridge University Press, pp.3–21.

Neisser, Ulric (1994) 'Self-narratives: True and False'. In U. Neisser and R. Fivush (eds) *The Remembering Self.* Cambridge: Cambridge University Press, pp.1–18.

Nelles, William (1993) 'Historical and Implied Authors and Readers'. *Comparative Literature* 45, pp.22–46.

Olney, James (1972) *Metaphors of Self: The meaning of autobiography.* Princeton: Princeton University Press.

Palmieri, G. (1998) '"The Author" according to Bakhtin, and Bakhtin the Author'. In D. Shepherd (ed) *The Contexts of Bakhtin.* Amsterdam: Harwood, pp.45–56.

Paris, Bernard (1965) *Experiments in Life: George Eliot's Quest for Values.* Detroit: Wayne State University Press.

Paris, Bernard (1974) *A Psychological Approach to Fiction: Studies in Thackeray, Stendhal, George Eliot, Dostoevsky, and Conrad.* Bloomington: Indiana University Press.

Paris, Bernard (1978) *Character and Conflict in Jane Austen's Novels: A Psychological Approach.* Detroit: Wayne State University Press.

Paris, Bernard (1991a) *Bargains with Fate: Psychological Crises and Conflicts in Shakespeare and His Plays.* New York: Plenum Press.

Paris, Bernard (1991b) *Character as a Subversive Force in Shakespeare: The History and Roman Plays.* Rutherford, NJ: Fairleigh Dickinson University Press.

Paris, Bernard (1994) *Karen Horney: A Psychoanalyst's Search for Self Understanding.* New Haven and London: Yale University Press.

Paris, Bernard (1997) *Imagined Human Beings: A psychological approach to character and conflict in literature.* New York: New York University Press.

Paris, Bernard (unpublished) '*Middlemarch* Revisited'.

Pascal, Roy (1977) *The Dual Voice.* Manchester: Manchester University Press.

Pateman, Trevor (1997) 'Space for the Imagination'. *Journal of Aesthetic Education* 31, 1, Spring, pp.1–8.

Pateman, Trevor (1998a) 'Writing: some thoughts on the teachable and the unteachable in creative writing'. *Journal of Aesthetic Education,* 32, 3, Fall, pp.1–8.

Pateman, Trevor (1998b) 'The Empty Word and the Full Word: The emergence of truth in writing', in C. Hunt and F. Sampson (eds) *op.cit.*, pp.153–163.

Pearson, L. (1965) *The Use of Written Communications in Psychotherapy.* Springfield, Illinois: Charles C. Thomas.

Penn, P. and Frankfurt, M. (1994) 'Creating a Participant Text: Writing, Multiple Voices, Narrative Multiplicity'. *Family Process* 33, 3, pp.217–231.

Pennebaker, James W. (1993) 'Putting Stress into Words: health, linguistic, and therapeutic implications'. *Behaviour Research and Therapy* 31, 6, pp.539–548.

Perec, Georges (1996) *W or the Memory of Childhood.* London: Harvill Press.

Philips, D., Penman, D. and Linnington, L. (1998) *Writing Well: Creative writing and mental health.* London: Jessica Kingsley Publishers.

Phillips, Adam (1988) *Winnicott.* London: Fontana.

Phillips, Adam (1993) *On Kissing, Tickling and Being Bored.* London: Faber.

Phillips, Adam (1994) 'The Telling of Selves'. In *On Flirtation.* London: Faber.

Plath, Sylvia (1963) *The Bell Jar.* London: Faber.

Plath, Sylvia (1975) *Letters Home: Correspondence 1950–63.* Edited with a commentary by Aurelia Schober Plath. London and New York: Faber.

Polkinghorne, D. E. (1991) 'Narrative and Self-Concept'. *Journal of Narrative and Life History* 1 (2 and 3), pp.135–153.

Progoff, Ira (1992) *At a Journal Workshop.* New York: G. P. Putnam's Sons.

Rainer, Tristine (1978) *The New Diary.* New York: G. P. Putnam's Sons.

Rancour-Laferriere, Daniel (ed) (1994) *Self-Analysis in Literary Study: Exploring hidden agendas.* New York: New York University Press.

Rhys, Jean (1934) *Voyage in the Dark.* In *Jean Rhys: The Early Novels,* 1991. London: Deutsch.

Rhys, Jean (1981) *Smile Please.* Harmondsworth: Penguin.

Rico, Gabriele (1983) *Writing the Natural Way.* Los Angeles: J. P. Tarcher.

Rimmon-Kenan, Shlomith (1996) *Narrative Fiction: Contemporary Poetics.* London and New York: Routledge.

Roe, Sue (1990) *Writing and Gender: Virginia Woolf's writing practice.* Hemel Hempstead: Harvester Wheatsheaf.

Rousseau, Jean-Jacques (1782) *Confessions.* New York: Alfred A. Knopf, 1992.

Salinger, J. D. (1951) *The Catcher in the Rye.* London: Hamish Hamilton.

Sampson, Edward E. (1989) 'The Deconstruction of the Self'. In J. Shotter and K. J. Gergen (eds) *Texts of Identity.* London: Sage Publications, pp. 1–19.

Sarraute, Nathalie (1984) *Childhood.* London: John Calder.

Schneider, Myra and Killick, John (1998) *Writing for Self-Discovery.* Shaftesbury, Dorset: Element Books.

Schnitzler, Arthur (1900) 'Reigen'. In *Meisterdramen.* Frankfurt-am-Main: S. Fischer Verlag, 1977, pp.57–120.

Schnitzler, Arthur (1961) 'Lieutenant Gustl'. In *Die Erzählenden Schriften.* Vol. 1. Frankfurt-am-Main: Fischer Verlag, pp.337–366.

Scholes, R. and Kellogg, R. (1966) *The Nature of Narrative.* New York: Oxford University Press.

Scott Fitzgerald, F. (1926) *The Great Gatsby.* Harmondsworth: Penguin, 1968.

Sellers, Susan (1996) *Hélène Cixous: authorship, autobiography and love.* Cambridge: Polity Press.

Spence, Donald (1982) *Narrative Truth and Historical Truth: Meaning and interpretation in psychoanalysis.* New York: Norton.

Spence, Donald (1985) 'Roy Schafer: Searching for the native tongue'. In J. Reppen (ed) *Beyond Freud: A study of modern psychoanalytic theorists.* Hillsdale, NJ: Analytic Press, pp.61–82.

Spence, J. and Holland, P. (1991) *Family Snaps: the meaning of domestic photography.* London: Virago.

Sprinker, Michael (1980) 'Fictions of the Self: The end of autobiography'. In J. Olney (ed) *Autobiography: Essays theoretical and critical.* Princeton: Princeton University Press, pp.321–342.

Stanley, Liz (1992) *The Auto/Biographical I: The theory and practice of feminist auto/biography.* Manchester: Manchester University Press.

Stelzig, E. L. (1988) *Hermann Hesse's Fictions of the Self: Autobiography and the confessional imagination.* Princeton, NJ: Princeton University Press.

Sturrock, John (1977) 'The New Model Autobiographer'. *New Literary History* 9, pp.51–63.

Sturrock, John (1993) *The Language of Autobiography: Studies in the first person singular.* Cambridge: Cambridge University Press.

Symonds, Alexandra (1978) 'The psychodynamics of expansiveness in the success-oriented woman'. *American Journal of Psychoanalysis* 38, pp.195–205.

Symonds, Alexandra (1991) 'Gender issues and Horney theory'. *American Journal of Psychoanalysis* 51, 3, pp.301–312.

Thackeray, W. M. (1848) *Vanity Fair.* Harmondsworth: Penguin, 1977.

Tucker, Robert (1973) *Stalin as Revolutionary, 1879–1929: A study in history and personality.* New York: W.W. Norton.

Tucker, Robert (1990) *Stalin in Power: The revolution from above, 1928–1941.* New York: W.W. Norton.

White, M. and Epston, D. (1990) *Narrative Means to Therapeutic Ends.* New York and London: Norton.

Wiesel, Elie (1981) *Night.* Harmondsworth: Penguin.

Williams, F. (1993) 'Thinking'. In P. Shakespeare, D. Atkinson and S. French, *Reflecting on Research Practice: Issues in health and social welfare.* Buckingham: Open University Press, pp.11–24.

Winnicott, D.W. (1958) 'The Capacity to be Alone'. In *The Maturational Processes and the Facilitating Environment.* New York: International Universities Press, 1965, pp.29–36.

Winnicott, D. W. (1960a) 'The Relationship of a Mother to her Baby at the Beginning'. In *The Family and Individual Development.* London: Tavistock, 1964, pp.15–20.

Winnicott, D. W. (1960b) 'Ego Distortions in Terms of True and False Self'. In *The Maturational Processes and the Facilitating Environment.* New York: International Universities Press, 1965, pp.140–152.

Winnicott, D.W. (1967) 'Mirror-Role of Mother and Family in Child Development'. In *Playing and Reality.* London: Tavistock Publications, 1971, pp.111–118.

Winnicott, D.W. (1971) *Playing and Reality.* London: Tavistock Publications.

Winterson, Jeanette (1985) *Oranges are not the Only Fruit.* London: Pandora.

Wolf, Christa (1983) *A Model Childhood.* London: Virago.

Woolf, Virgina (1927) *To the Lighthouse.* Harmondsworth: Penguin, 1964.

Woolf, Virginia (1928) *A Room of One's Own.* Harmondsworth: Penguin, 1972.

Woolf, Virginia (1931) *The Waves.* Harmondsworth: Penguin, 1966.

Woolf, Virginia (1941) *Between the Acts.* Harmondsworth: Penguin, 1953.

Woolf, Virginia (1976) *The Waves: The two holograph drafts.* J. W. Graham (transcribed and edited). London: Hogarth.

Woolf, Virginia (1989a) 'Reminiscences'. In *Moments of Being.* London: Grafton Books, pp.31–68.

Woolf, Virginia (1989b) 'Sketch of the Past'. In *Moments of Being.* London: Grafton Books, pp.69–173.

Worthington, Kim (1996) *Self as Narrative: Subjectivity and community in contemporary fiction.* Oxford: Oxford University Press.

Wyatt-Brown, Ann (1993) 'From the clinic to the classroom: D. W. Winnicott, James Britton, and the revolution in writing theory'. In P. D. Rudnytsky (ed) *Transitional Objects and Potential Spaces.* New York: Columbia University Press, pp.292–305.

Subject Index

Author Index